W9-ABY-281

GARLAND STUDIES IN

AMERICAN POPULAR HISTORY AND CULTURE

edited by

JEROME NADELHAFT
UNIVERSITY OF MAINE

A GARLAND SERIES

Garland Studies in American Popular History and Culture

Jerome Nadelhaft, series editor

TALES OF LIBERATION, STRATEGIES OF CONTAINMENT

DIVORCE AND THE REPRESENTATION OF
WOMANHOOD IN AMERICAN FICTION,
1880–1920

DEBRA ANN MacCOMB

GARLAND PUBLISHING, INC.
A MEMBER OF THE TAYLOR & FRANCIS GROUP
NEW YORK & LONDON / 2000

Published in 2000 by
Garland Publishing Inc.
A Member of the Taylor & Francis Group
19 Union Square West
New York, NY 10003

10 9 8 7 6 5 4 3 2

Library of Congress Cataloging-in-Publication Data
MacComb, Debra Ann.
     Tales of liberation, strategies of containment : divorce and the representation of womanhood in American fiction, 1880–1920 / Debra Ann MacComb.
        p. cm. — (Garland studies in American popular history and culture)
     Revision of the author's thesis.
     Includes bibliographical references and index.
     ISBN 0-8153-3804-X (alk. paper)
     1. American fiction—20th century—History and criticism. 2. Divorce in literature. 3. American fiction—19th century—History and criticism.
4. Married women in literature. 5. Marriage in literature. 6. Women in literature. I. Title. II. Series.
PS374.D55 M33 2000
813'.409355—dc21   00-026133

Printed on acid-free, 250-year-life paper
Manufactured in the United States of America

To Arthur

Contents

Illustrations

Following Page 182

Preface

Divorce has been something of an American tradition ever since its introduction into Puritan New England, yet no substantial study of the role divorce plays in American fiction has been undertaken since the 1940s, nor has any connection been traced between divorce plots and novels of manners, domesticity or adultery. This project begins to address that absence and to respond to the common misperception that divorce as a thematic concern is a relatively recent phenomenon. As a legal remedy for failed marriages and a metaphor for cultural upheaval, divorce has in fact been a feature of American life and letters since the "split" between England and America provided a model for a surge in divorce petitions. Of particular interest is the way in which women—as inheritors of a national tradition sanctioning an individual's pursuit of happiness and as guardians of a domestic sphere upholding communal value—are represented negotiating feminine roles and values around faltering marriages. Such negotiations invariably test whether divorce functions in a text as a strategy for containment and preservation of old hegemonies, or as a legitimate mode of liberation and expansion of female roles. In pursuing these issues, a range of "divorce" narratives—including novels by Fanny Fern, Harriet Beecher Stowe, Henry James, Edith Wharton, Edna Ferber and Sinclair Lewis—come under scrutiny. In addition to canonical (or nearly so) works by these authors, this project incorporates an array of nineteenth and early twentieth-century texts—fiction of the popular culture, conduct books and self-improvement manuals, women's mass-circulation journals, newspaper and magazine articles, society columns, advertising, *Life* cartoons, and contemporary theories of economic and social development—in order to provide an historicized context in which to probe the range of emerging identities implicated in divorce: the New Woman, the social climber, and the extra-domestic worker. By thus raising questions about the influence that fictional representations of divorce might exert in defining, modifying or subverting women's social role and economic function, *Tales of Liberation* adds a necessary dimension to recent studies focused upon tales of courtship, marriage and motherhood.

Acknowledgments

I have been particularly fortunate in the support and encouragement I have received from institutions, colleagues and friends in completing this project. I am very grateful to the UCLA Center for the Study of Women whose travel grant allowed me to do research in Sioux Falls, South Dakota, during the summer of 1993. Its support has not been financial only, for the Center's programs and lectures—indeed, its very presence on campus—provides invaluable moral and intellectual support for women students and faculty alike, and for all of those whose research focuses upon women. The Lee F. Payne Research Fellowship (1993–1994) for the use of journalistic sources in research and writing provided a year long stipend in support of my dissertation studies. UCLA's Department of English also has been most generous, awarding me the Irving and Jean Stone Dissertation Year Fellowship (1994–1995) as well as discretionary funds to photographically reproduce some of the old and faded illustrations included in this project. The Department of English and Philosophy at the State University of West Georgia has also generously granted release time so that I could at last turn my dissertation into a book.

The personal debts are more difficult to articulate, and I hope that everyone to whom I owe these thanks will know that I am profoundly grateful for their support. While I was at UCLA, Deborah M. Garfield, William A. Gleason, Danielle Price, Marge Kingsley, Karen Rowe, Emily Schiller and Eric Sundquist (unflinchingly) read large portions of this manuscript and offered much insightful criticism and encouragement. My colleagues at the State University of West Georgia—most particularly Lisa Plummer Crafton, Jane Bower Hill, Alice Kinman, Peter Morgan and David Newton—have provided a model of professionalism and collegiality that makes work a genuine pleasure. Stacey Carter, Graduate Research Assistamt *par excellance,* tirelessly assisted me in the manuscript's final preparation. And Martha Banta—who directed this project from its seminar origins—continues to be, by the example of her own scholarship, her love of literature, and her delight in discovering "the good stuff," a joy and an inspiration. Thank you for believing that I might do justice to the things you love so much.

But it is to Arthur that I owe the most: you have read endless drafts of all my work, you have comforted and cajoled. Thank you.

Tales of Liberation,
Strategies of Containment

CHAPTER ONE

Plotting Marriage and Divorce: the Nineteenth-Century Cultural Background

I

Although we tend to regard divorce as a modern phenomenon which, precipitated by the tensions unique to the urban-industrial world, disrupted a golden age of marital stability and accord, it has in fact been something of "an American tradition" since Puritan colonists introduced the practice to New England in the seventeenth century.[1] Petitions for absolute divorce (divorce *a vinculo matrimonii*) and for separation from bed and board (divorce *a mensa et thoro*) were granted by colonial legislatures throughout the eighteenth century and, when the break between England and the American colonies came, the political ideals and rhetoric of the revolution, grounded as they were in contractual terms which highlighted voluntary consent, reciprocal duties and the possibility of dissolution, supplied an example of national independence on which married Americans would ever after model their own claims for independent selfhood.[2] Perhaps because the architects of the revolution tended to describe the crisis with England in terms of a domestic dispute, republican ideals found almost simultaneous expression in petitions for and legal writings about divorce. The terms and conditions which validated the social contract were extrapolated to cover the marriage contract as well, and petitioners thus maintained that an individual was morally justified in breaking away from his marriage partner if the union lacked mutual fulfillment and happiness.[3]

Yet even as divorce seemed to find justification when it was construed as a means of preserving individual "natural" rights, the stable family was still envisioned as the primary institution of American society. The home and the community, both encoding hierarchical relations and manifesting centralized authority/power, were held to constitute "a lively representation" of each other. Noting this congruence, revolutionary lawyer and future President John Adams declared in 1778 that "the foundation of national morality must be laid in private families."[4] Because of their perceived importance to the national enterprise, the tenets of the ideal family were soon transformed into a series of strict injunctions which asserted the permanence of the marriage tie, the sanctity of the domestic sphere, and the dependence of civilization upon the firmly united family.[5]

The domestic ideal of sound marriages and stable families provided a potent symbol of hierarchical order and authority that extended into nineteenth-century fiction as well; insofar as it reflected the social hegemony, the novel in particular adopted marriage as its central thematic concern and organizing device.[6] As Tony Tanner has observed, "marriage is the all-subsuming, the all-containing contract. It is the structure which maintains the Structure" of society as well as of the novel.[7] Indeed, Evelyn J. Hinz asserts that the concept of wedlock, depending upon which syllable of the compound word receives the emphasis, structures two basic novelistic plots, one comic and one tragic. If the emphasis is upon "wed," the comic resolution of the plot resides in the union of a young couple who have overcome a series of obstacles to their final social integration in marriage; if the emphasis is upon "lock," the tragic version of the marriage plot, "entrapment leads to suffering and concomitant moral development" in which a conversion from an idiosyncratic to a social perspective is wrought in at least one half of the unhappy pair.[8] While Joseph Allen Boone distinguishes three main plots (as well as their comic/tragic variations) structured upon marriage,[9] he concurs with Hinz that despite their difference in tone and outcome, the thematic import of these marriage plots is the same:

. . . both the "happy ending" concluding the trajectory of courtship, in which converging lovers are rewarded with the bliss of matrimony and countless progeny, and its inverse, the tragically closed outcome befalling those who abuse the ideal, equally conspired to uphold a belief in romantic marriage as the most desirable end of existence and, hence, as a virtually unassailable, closed truth.[10]

Thus the novelistic representation of romantic marriage as "*the* ultimate signifier of personal and social well-being"[11] and the stabilizing formal structures of linearity and closure which characterize these plots encode and reinforce a cultural ideal.

Not surprisingly, perhaps, neither Boone nor Hinz detect in divorce an element disruptive to either narrative representation or formal trajectory of the marriage ideal. Indeed, they argue that divorce most often operates within a text as the ultimate punishment society metes out for violating that ideal, expelling the sinning individual from the paradise of conjugal bliss and, thereby, from the community for which it serves a metonymic function. As Hinz observes, marriage plots which include divorce as an element essentially take the position that society, having the power to ratify marriage, "can also annul it; and if two people are incompatible, it is unrealistic, impracticable and of no benefit to the social order to keep them together."[12] Certainly, the possible conclusions to a divorce narrative would seem to bear out this logic: after separating, one or both former spouses remarry happily (divorce's "comic" outcome); or, disillusioned by the experience of marriage and divorce, one or both partners to the failed union remain withdrawn and socially isolated; or, finally, a bitterly divided couple reach an impasse in their disputations and, although technically wed, are in figurative terms "divorced." Each of these endings ratifies the ideal of conjugal love and companionate marriage on the level of plot even as they lead to a formal stasis that, as Boone asserts, "cuts short serious questioning of the social ethos, the ideological grounds, underlying the fictional construct."[13] The fault for the marital failure resides with the individuals who were party to the marriage, for as Robert Kiely notes, a bad union "is never to be blamed on the institution itself."[14]

The manner in which divorce operates in concert with the novelistic marriage plot provides an important insight into the way

American divorce law, considered the most liberal codes governing domestic relations in the western world during the nineteenth and early twentieth centuries, itself "plots" an essentially conservative social course—conservative, that is, not of individual unions but of marriage as an institution, particularly as it emerged as a companionate ideal. In that the legal grounds for an absolute decree of divorce multiplied from the single, biblically sanctioned cause of adultery to include a variety of physical, mental and social infirmities as justification for parting spouses, the divorce laws did seem increasingly liberal. Yet with the proliferation of these laws (and it is in the sheer number of grounds that the perceived liberality resides), the ideal of marriage—and especially the expectations governing the feminine domestic role—was ever more strictly encoded. Thus while divorce law seemed a liberating mechanism that was disruptive of marriage and, thereby, of society, it in fact maintained the domestic sphere as the repository of communal value, order and authority. Indeed, the very fact of the multiplying "escape clauses" seemed to guarantee that the institution of marriage would remain unquestioned and unreformed.[15]

The conservative tendencies of American divorce law can be traced to seventeenth-century New England and, in particular, to two features of Puritan matrimonial practice. First, rather than a sacrament, marriage was considered a civil contract over which civil magistrates rather than church ministers officiated. The secular administration of family policy and law thus symbolically asserted the temporal significance of marriage as an institution constituted *by* and constitutive *of* the local community. While the Puritan treatment of marriage as a secular contractual concern did not automatically license divorce, it was, as Roderick Philips observes, "an indispensable precondition" for it.[16] Second, Puritan ideology held that family was the basis of social organization and stability; solitary living was not tolerated in the New England colonies, for single men or women outside of the family unit escaped both its positive moral influence and its paradigmatic hierarchical structure. Laws were passed against living alone, and those who resisted community integration were tried, convicted and, as in one case, sentenced to "settle in some orderly family in the town, and be subject to the orderly rules of family government."[17] In short, anything that promoted the family and its attendant benefits to the governance of individuals within the community won approval; anything that detracted from its structure or authority was severely condemned. It is in this context that divorce was perceived as a remedy for marital disruption and family disintegration.

In the New England colonies, a decree of absolute divorce was generally permitted for the causes of adultery or desertion; additional limited relief in the form of legal separation from bed and board was allowed when a marriage lacked harmony and tranquillity, fundamental tenets of the Puritan ideal of matrimony. In these cases, secular authority attempted to reconcile rather than separate spouses; when such efforts failed, a decree of divorce *a mensa et thoro* was granted. Because adultery and desertion were construed as particularly grievous offenses against marriage and the family, absolute divorces were granted with the purpose of allowing the innocent spouse to contract another marriage, much as if death (rather than sin) had claimed the offending spouse. Indeed, the guilty party was as if "dead" to the community as well, for his (or her) remarriage was prohibited and, as we have seen, so was solitary living.[18] In Massachusetts in the 1690s, further liberalization of divorce was urged for the purpose of promoting a strict definition of marriage. Bigamy—insofar as it "rendered [the offending party] one flesh with another object than that unto which their marriage has united them"—and impotence—because it "utterly disappoint[s] the confessed ends of marriage"—were proposed as additional grounds for absolute divorce.[19] Although Massachusetts law did not recognize these grounds until decades later, the import is clear: divorce was a tool wielded in defending the marriage ideal, not in liberating frustrated or oppressed individuals from their matrimonial vows.[20]

A second feature of American divorce history also helped to plot the essentially conservative impact of the law. During the eighteenth century and in accordance with British parliamentary procedure, divorce cases were heard and acted upon as individual bills before the colonial legislatures. After independence from Britain was won, legislative divorces continued to be granted until it became apparent that the courts could assume at least some of the load and relieve the increasingly burdened law makers. With the advent of judicial divorce, detailed statutes outlining the grounds for marital dissolution were forged; in codifying the offenses to matrimony, these laws also defined a marriage ideal that was increasingly companionate in nature. In the eighteenth century, judicial divorce was granted in New Hampshire on the grounds of impotence, adultery, extreme cruelty, or absence of three years. Wives could sue on the additional grounds of abandonment or failure to provide for three years. In Vermont, the statutes outlined impotence, adultery, intolerable severity, three years willful desertion, or long absence with death presumed as grounds for divorce; Rhode Island allowed divorce on the same general grounds, but it also granted its courts broad authority to provide legal relief in cases of "gross misbehavior and wickedness in either of the parties, repugnant to and in violation of the marriage covenant."[21] The transfer of authority in divorce cases from the legislature to the courts continued through the nineteenth century but, even in states with judicial divorce, private divorce bills continued to be brought before legislative assemblies. The trend, however, was to exclusive judicial authority, a trend that led to the delineation of an increasing number of general statutes[22]—statutes which clearly implied what marriage *ought* to be and how spouses *ought* to behave.

Many states included among their general statutes provisions for divorce (either absolute or separation from bed and board) in cases of cruelty. In the early nineteenth century, cruelty referred specifically to physical abuse suffered repeatedly at the hand of one's spouse; by mid-century, under the pressure of emerging ideas about companionate marriage, gender roles, class relationships and mental health, a new doctrine of cruelty began to take shape.[23] Based on essentialized models of feminine moral superiority and physical fragility, jurists began to argue that harsh behavior by a husband, whatever its nature, that contributed to a decline in his wife's health constituted cruelty. The gender of the victim was not the only consideration, however; class, too, played a vital role, and in adjudicating divorce cases in which cruelty was alleged the courts tended "to take into consideration the station in life, habits, training and refinement of the parties, as what might be cruelty to a person of refinement would not be to one of grosser sensibilities."[24] By 1860, several states had "indignities" statutes, so called because they made rudeness, vulgarity, reproach, neglect and ridicule sufficient cause for divorce if such behavior threatened a spouse's life or health or, more vaguely, made the "discharge of marital duties burdensome and intolerable" or made "life too humiliating to bear."[25] The link between mental and physical cruelty was made plain in a 1859 California Supreme Court decision regarding verbal attacks upon a woman's purity and reputation: "[a] woman prizes virtue dearer than life itself, and he who attempts deliberately to rob her of her good name, saps the foundation of her happiness and inflicts a deeper wound than the ruffian does by his repeated blows."[26]

By the dawn of the Progressive Age, mental cruelty might be as broadly construed as denying one's spouse "personal happiness," and did not need to result in observable damage to the health of the victim to warrant divorce. The popular press frequently pilloried such legal practice, running stories about the latest act of cruelty to be brought before the court for judicial relief:

> To the list of divorces for seemingly trivial causes—such as "cruelty in not taking me out riding," "cruelty in requiring me to sew on buttons," etc., has now been added a divorce granted to a man who charged his wife with "cruelty in keeping cats in the house," thereby preventing him from occupying his favorite chair. On the judge's inquiring, "Why didn't you put the cats out of the house?" the man answered, "My wife is a member of the Society for the Prevention of Cruelty to Animals, and I was afraid she would have me arrested."[27]

Although this piece scoffs at the supposed severity of the offense, it too encodes the male and female roles proper to the domestic ideal by ridiculing the inverted gender relationships. While for the most part mental cruelty statutes responded to an ideology which held that women, as moral and spiritual guardians of the home and family, possessed delicate, easily offended sensibilities that required protection, these codes "also offered males some leverage" when wives's behavior deviated from the ideal.[28] Ironically, the ideal of the companionate marriage, because it increased expectations of marital happiness and fulfillment, undermined marital stability; the codified pattern seemed out of reach for most real spouses.

In evaluating the significance of divorce as a trope in the marriage plot, it is appropriate to recall that divorce has had a broader function in American socio-political history (and potentially, therefore, in American literature) than simply a legal remedy for failed marriages. As a metaphor for the cultural upheaval which marked America's "split" from England, "divorce" has operated to suggest an open, indeterminate plot which frees the individual from the closed political narrative inscribed by "tyranny," "misrule," and "injustice," liberating him to chart his own course in the "pursuit of happiness." The use of the masculine pronoun is both deliberate and significant, for this indeed seems a gendered scenario. For the American man, the competing claims of republican and domestic ideologies posed little problem in the decision to divorce. Although he moved freely between public and private spheres, his masculine identity was a product of individual exploit and accomplishment in the public realm; the private world, functioning at least partially as a retreat from the vicissitudes of the public, was constructed *for* rather than *by* him. The integrity of the private domestic sphere was, however, woman's special—indeed, essential—prerogative and was in direct conflict with her political inheritance which asserted a "natural right of equality" in the pursuit of individual happiness.[29] Thus the way in which women—as inheritors of a national tradition sanctioning an individual's pursuit of happiness and as guardians of a domestic sphere upholding communal value—negotiate feminine roles and values in and around faltering marriages will invariably test whether divorce functions in a text as a strategy for containment and preservation of old hegemonies, or as a legitimate mode of liberation which provides an expanded definition of what might constitute marriage.

However, given the tenor of and the rationales for the laws governing marriage and divorce, it is not surprising to discover that the several mid-nineteenth century novels that do deal with marital disruption follow the plot trajectories already described as encoding the ideal of conjugal partnership. Whether pro- or anti-divorce in sentiment, these novels have as their primary concern the preservation of a well-ordered domestic sphere with feminine virtue as its centerpiece and guarantor. Although each details a marital breakdown that ends in divorce, it is the partners in the union who, because of their deviation from the feminine or masculine ideal, bear the blame for the failure and not the institution itself. T. S. Arthur's work focuses on the tendency of "love-struck" individuals to make uninformed, unrealistic choices of matrimonial partners and their unwillingness, when faced with the inevitable disappointments and strife engendered by those poor decisions, to subordinate—and this is represented as a particularly feminine failing—their personal feelings for the sake of union. In *The Hand But not the Heart* (1858), Jessie Loring, under pressure from her socially ambitious aunt, agrees to marry a wealthy man who flatters her vanity but who fails to win her heart. Although she attempts to withdraw her promise to wed when she realizes that she loves another, Jessie is reminded of the power of the word: the marriage contract is sealed by her voluntary consent, symbolized by a handshake, even if it isn't consecrated by her heart's assent. Having promised, albeit mistakenly, "to become the wife of Leon Dexter, she saw but one right course, and that was to perform, the best she could, her part of the contract."[30]

Dexter, no match for Jessie's "enlarged intelligence" nor her "highly cultivated tastes," nevertheless recognizes the value of those qualities. He demonstrates his pride in his wife's accomplishments by placing her "on exhibition" at a series of fashionable resorts (*HBH* 130). The obvious discrepancy in quality and refinement between them compounded by the recollection that Jessie had tried to break their engagement sends Dexter into frequent tirades against his wife, which at first she bears "with a wonderful power of endurance and self-control" (*HBH* 128). For over a year, she seems by all outward appearance to be the embodiment of the happy wife, while inwardly she chafes at "the hard, icy, galling links of the chain" which bound her to Dexter "in a union only death could dissolve" (*HBH* 129).

At Newport, Jessie becomes acquainted with two women who, detecting signs of her distress, seek to comfort and advise her. Mrs. DeLisle, although she expresses the opinion that Jessie's consent to marry was wrongly "extorted" from her, nevertheless counsels fidelity to her marriage vow and duty to her husband:

> In consenting to enter the most solemn human compact that is ever made, you assumed a position that gave you power over the happiness of another. If . . . you went to the altar under constraint, an unloving bride, so much more the binding on you are the promises then made to seek your husband's happiness—even at the sacrifice of your own. In that act you wronged him—wronged him as no woman has the right to wrong any man, and you can never do enough by way of reparation. (*HBH* 152)

Mrs. Anthony, Jessie's other friend at Newport, has quite a different view of the Dexter marriage. Modeled after such period feminists as Elizabeth Cady Stanton and Mary Dodge, she embodies the shrill voice of protest against the wrongs suffered by women at the hands of men. An hour spent in this woman's company always leaves Jessie "in a state of disquietude, and suffering from a sense of restriction and wrong" (*HBH* 143). Although she tries the path prescribed by Mrs. DeLisle, when Dexter breaks into another of his jealous rages she reacts as we imagine Mrs. Anthony would, angrily recounting the ways she has suffered "irreparable outrage" as a result of his baseless attacks on her honor (*HBH* 179).

Jessie leaves Dexter and seeks the protection of her aunt, vowing never to return to her husband unless he demonstrates the proper regard for her feelings. Neither spouse will move an inch from their deadlocked opposition, even when Mrs. DeLisle reminds Jessie of the moral as well as social power of her marriage vow: "The want of harmony, interest, feeling and character is no reason for disseverance. You cannot leave him, and be faultless in the eyes of God or man" (*HBH* 212). Jessie refuses to be reunited with her husband and, therefore, is guilty of desertion—on which ground Dexter secures a divorce and remarries. And although the law "cancels" her marriage and re-establishes her as a single woman in her "old relation to the world," Jessie cannot but feel that "she did not stand in her old relation to herself" (*HBH* 273). She withdraws from the world, never once "stepp[ing] beyond the threshold of her aunt's dwelling" and only rarely receiving visitors (*HBH* 273). After six years of seclusion, she hears of Dexter's death, and only then does she consider herself free— free to resume her place in the world and to marry the man she had loved from the beginning. Rewarded at last for honoring the full magnitude of her vow, Jessie is united with "the companion of her soul."

Arthur's 1864 novel *Out in the World* reprises essentially the same sentiments about the permanence of the marriage tie, although it issues a far stronger caution to wives about the need to submit to its "natural" hierarchy. In brief, Madeline Spencer and Carl Jansen, knowing little about their own or each other's true nature, marry; while both are honorable people, their new relation reveals that both are stubborn to a fault. Thus when Carl's persistent and ill-concealed jealousy at his wife's innocent friendship with a Mr. Guyton causes her embarrassment and illness, she delivers an ultimatum that he regard her as an equal in their marriage relation. He refuses and she leaves him. "Out in the world" without a male protector, Madeline endures a series of misadventures which cast her down the social ladder and bring her ever closer to the "real" discomforts of hunger and exposure on the streets. Although she falls prey to the machinations of others, Madeline manages to remain pure and true. Believing the worst of her, however, Carl divorces Madeline for desertion after a year's absence, and eventually remarries a coarse woman who teaches him how foolish he has been in his treatment of his first wife. After some fifteen years, his health broken by his second wife's selfishness, he determines to find Madeline and make some reparation to her. However, after years of hard work and deprivation, Madeline, too, is desperately ill. They manage a brief re-union during which they confess their mutual mistakes; thus unburdened, both die.

Madeline's melodramatic fall illustrates even more clearly than did Jessie's self-inflicted confinement the pitfalls of asserting unwomanly claims for equality and independence. *Out in the World* launches a particularly vitriolic attack upon feminists who agitate for women's rights, portraying them as mesmerizing serpents more concerned with general principles than with individual instances of feminine distress. Like Jessie's (less extreme) misstep, Madeline's downward trajectory into desperation, suffering and death is precipitated by contact with such "unnatural" women who "warped her views touching her relation to her husband."[31] Mrs. Woodbine, whose invective against the "brutes" and "domestic tyrants" (*OW* 43) who destroy their wives' happiness finds a responsive chord in Madeline's breast, is portrayed as an "enchantress" who seduces women from their rightful duty as wives by throwing "deeper and deeper spells around [them]. For hours she talked on the absorbing themes to which she had given so much thought.—On the social disabilities of her sex—on man's wrongs to woman—on the false ideas that prevailed touching equality in the marriage bond—on the wife's duty to herself—and topics of a kindred nature" (*OW* 49). However, when Madeline appears on her doorstep after leaving her husband, Mrs. Woodbine chides her for taking so foolish a step:

In the first place, you have given up an elegant home, and money to any fair extent that you may see fit to demand. Have you rich relatives, who will, in turn, supply these? Your name is today unsullied before the world. Abandon your husband, on almost any pretext, and though your life be pure as an angel's, the soil óf slander will be cast over your garments. . . . Hold to your legal position as Mr. Jansen's wife, but maintain your independence. If he seeks to put on the tyrant, set him at naught, but hold to the material rights acquired in wedlock. If you abandon him, you abandon everything; but if he abandons you, the law will give you alimony, and so leave you independent. You see, child, that I take a sober, common sense view of things. I look to the main chance. Understand me, I counsel no submission. (*OW* 73–74)

Mrs. Woodbine's inconsistencies betray the fact that feminists are not at all concerned about individuals, but are rather opportunists preying upon helpless, hopeless wives who might advance their political agenda. Indeed, Arthur's representation of these women's actions suggests a version of the seduced and abandoned plot: feminist-seducers mislead wives into believing false notions about female equality and independence, drawing them away from the path of feminine submission that would otherwise stabilize their faltering marriages, leaving them to their own devices when they no longer serve the feminist cause.

Out in the World attempts to curb the feminine desire for independence in part by representing the talk, "the soil of slander," that inevitably besmirches the reputation of any woman who leaves her husband, even when "innocent" of wrong. Every minor indiscretion of Madeline's past, every incident in which her husband manifested some displeasure or jealousy at her conduct is revived and discussed among her friends as evidence proving her guilty of immorality. The public exposure risked by a woman in her position is emphasized when Madeline, craving allies, takes up with a feminist crusader who launches her as a public speaker. Before a large crowd, Madeline exposes the "wrongs" she endured as a wife and, per script, advocates female equality and independence. After only one such performance, however, she breaks down and refuses to continue; again she is abandoned by the "friend" who claims to have a woman's best interests at heart. In close conjunction with this episode, Madeline—desperate for shelter—mistakes a kindly, well-dressed madam for a respectable, sympathetic friend. That Madeline nearly falls into prostitution at the hands of another female opportunist provides a neat literalization of the "use" she has been put to by the forces of feminism and serves as the ultimate warning to women contemplating freedom from their place in the domestic hierarchy.

Mary Lyndon (1855), by Mary Sargeant Nichols, and *Rose Clark* (1856), by Fanny Fern, assert positions about female independence and divorce quite different from those put forward by T. S. Arthur, yet they do so in order to validate the sanctity of marriage and the domestic sphere. By exploring the reasons that some women contract bad marriages, both Nichols and Fern implicitly argue that until women achieve some measure of social and economic freedom, unhappy unions and compromised homes will result. Mary Lyndon, a learned and deeply spiritual young woman, gains a teaching position some distance from her home, requiring her to take up residence with an uncle who happens to live in the village where the school is located. The uncle, none too pleased with the burden his niece represents, urges her to marry a Mr. Hervey, a Quaker well respected in the local community. Mary, believing the Quakers to be the least hypocritical in their Christian practices among the organized religions, bends to her uncle's pressure and to Hervey's ardent proposals and promises to wed. Realizing that she neither loves nor esteems Hervey, she attempts to withdraw her consent but, like Jessie Loring, is reminded of the power of her word and the humiliation "a good man" would suffer should she retract it. Feeling "cheated into marriage," Mary nevertheless determines "to be sacrificed" into a union which promises nothing but misery, for Hervey is neither educated nor ambitious.[32] Indeed, it is apparent that Hervey has secured in Mary a wife who will slave to support them rather than endure humiliating poverty; she makes a meager wage while he exerts control over her earnings and her labor: "My husband was miserably inefficient, and on the proceeds of his labor we must have starved or asked for charity. I worked night and day with my needle, often sitting up till two or three at night to finish a piece of work. His idleness, a sort of deathly powerlessness to plan or accomplish any worthful work, compelled me to this cruel and severe labor" (*ML* 127).

Not only does Hervey violate that masculine ideal which holds that the husband shall be the provider, but he also proves to be a brute, subjecting Mary to any number of indignities in the name of his rightful authority over her. She longs that her marital "chains" be "loosened and lengthened," but "dare[s] not break them" (*ML* 134). Mary's desire for relief does not constitute a critique of the ideal of wifely obedience and submission, but rather of the concrete example her own marriage provides of an obviously inferior man exacting from her a "wifely" standard of conduct. She comes to realize that any matrimonial union "without love was but legalized adultery" (*ML* 135), and elects to break the chains binding her to Hervey. Under her father's protection, she separates from her husband, whose several desperate attempts to force her back into the home fail.

Mary's conviction that marriage, unsanctified by mutual love and respect, exists only as "a legal fiction" (*ML* 266) is borne out when her heart chooses other men, first an angelic philosopher (who dies) and then a spiritualist/philanthropist, with whom to unite. Free of the "superstition" that the law has power over such unions, she nevertheless worries that, if known, her devotion to Vincent while still legally wed would irrevocably blacken her name. Thus, despite her own sense of what truly validates a marriage, she resolves "to wait for the legislature to grant me leave to love" and to "pay largely for the liberty, the bill of divorce" (*ML* 344). "Fortunately," Hervey himself secures the decree on the grounds of Mary's willful desertion, and she and Vincent are married with vows that reaffirm the familiar tenets of companionate marriage.

As Joyce Warren has argued, Fanny Fern undercuts the sentimental ethos of the period's "woman" novel in *Rose Clark* by juxtaposing the history of the innocent and helpless Rose with that of the independent and resourceful Gertrude Dean, thereby asserting an alternative model of female conduct. With Gertrude's story, Fern also achieves the more personal goal of recounting the circumstances of her own disastrous second marriage and divorce.[33] Gertrude, widowed from a husband who possessed "the true[st] heart" ever to "bless" a marriage, endures "years of privation and suffering" because she is unable to find employment that will support her and her child.[34] In this extremity, she reluctantly agrees to marry a widower with two young sons for her own child's sake, believing the best when Mr. Stahle vows to treat him like one of his own. Finding in him no resemblance to her ideal, she argues that her role as wife must be limited to that of caretaker to the children because her "heart was in [her] husband's grave" (*RC* 232). Once they are wed, however, Gertrude discovers that the man respected by the community as deeply religious and honorable is but "a hypocrite, and a gross sensualist" (*RC* 235) who not only intends to use her sexually, but plans to send her son away to a boarding school along with his own neglected boys. Although she feels that her situation metes out a justified "penance, for a sin against God, of which every woman who goes from the altar with perjured lips" (*RC* 236) must expect to pay, Gertrude nevertheless resists her husband's conjugal advances and refuses to go into public with him.

To the list of Stahle's offenses against marriage and the honor of women, Fern adds a portrait of him as distinctly feminized, a "man" constitutionally unfit to be a husband:

> He was under-sized, with a pale complexion, and a light brown beard.
> He wore his hair long, and parted it on the left temple, its sleek,
> shining look, giving him a meek appearance; his lips were thin, and,
> in a woman, would have been called shrewish; this tell-tale feature he
> dexterously concealed with his beard . . . his eyes were a pale gray,
> and were always averted in talking, as if he feared his secret thoughts
> might shine through them. He appeared to great disadvantage in
> company, both from his inferior personal appearance and his total
> inability to sustain a conversation on any subject. (*RC* 242)

Given this unmanly construct, it isn't surprising to find Stahle attempting by a variety of ruses to drive Gertrude into some breech of conduct that might win sympathy to his side. However, whether he removes them to a tawdry boarding house, denies her money, or spreads slander against her good name, Gertrude retains a remarkable self-control. At last he contrives a situation that makes Gertrude appear the deserter in their marriage and secures thereby the grounds to win an unopposed divorce.

In Gertrude's opinion, the divorce both frees her from a union that sullies the institution of marriage and purifies her home from such contamination. To her brother, who worries that "the world . . . will not understand" nor forgive her position as a divorced woman, Gertrude explains that "a woman can never be injured *essentially*, save by her own acts" (*RC* 281). She resolves never again to marry—not because the ideal is suspect, but because so few men are capable of making the grade: "Men are so gross and unspiritual . . . so wedded to making money and promiscuous love, so selfish and unchivalric . . . who would be foolish enough to wade through leagues of brambles and briars to find perchance one flower?" (*RC* 283).

Significantly, in each of these four novels the female character, believing that some element of the sanctioned/sanctified domestic situation has been violated, separates (actively in three of the novels) from her husband and refuses to be reconciled to him. Yet none of these wronged wives—even in the novels which approve divorce as a means of purifying the violated domestic sphere—seek to end their own marriages by direct appeal to law although each has recognized grounds for divorce (non-support, cruelty, indignities) which exist prior to the desertion allegations lodged against them. In the instances authored by Nichols and Fern, the heroine's passivity in seeking legal redress may signal an implicit critique of the patriarchal system of law which excludes them: foreclosed from participating in political policy decisions, their domestic concerns are not addressed by the laws as they stand. Or, along similar lines, their inaction serves to reveal the manner in which "impartial" law favors men and may be manipulated to undermine the very institution it pretends to protect. On the other hand, reader expectation and desire may account for these female characters' passivity: having taken steps to preserve domestic integrity by vacating the site of their violation, these women prove their essential conformity to the feminine ideal by refusing to expose themselves or their private grievances in public forum. Whatever the source of their resistance to the law, these women's narratives validate the feminine role as guardian of the domestic sphere and plot familiar ground in upholding the marriage ideal.

II

American literary history traditionally has pointed to William Dean Howells' *A Modern Instance* (1882) as "the first full length divorce novel of merit,"[35] yet it is with the publication in 1841 of Emma Embury's cautionary tale "The Mistaken Choice; or, Three Years of

Married Life"[36] that divorce—and particularly women's complicity in generating the domestic disharmony which ends in marital dissolution—enters American fiction as a social, moral and economic issue. The story follows the progress of businessman Charles Waterton who, "seduced by the ambition of equaling his richer neighbors," lets "motives of interest" rather than affection guide his wedded life. He chooses as his bride not the "young, fair, and gifted girl whom he had loved with all the fervor of sincere attachment" but rather a fashionable heiress whose ample fortune seems to compensate for her lack of formal or practical education and over-indulged character. Although his bachelor uncle warns against the liaison with the axiomatic wisdom that "a prudent wife without money is a better companion in misfortune than an extravagant one [with] a rich dowry," Waterton marries Laura Tarleton, finding "the idea of what you call a *prudent woman* . . . shocking to my notions of feminine character." Indeed, in its opposition to "the foible most natural to the sex—extravagance," the domestic economy suggested by the model of prudence conveys a generalized parsimony of circumstance and spirit that, to Waterton's mind, "unsexes" a woman ("MC" 13).

By this standard, then, Laura is nothing if not "feminine": although her personal fortune proves in fact to be but a third of what rumor had claimed for it, she nonetheless dedicates her days to shopping and "fashionable" visits, her nights to "brilliant parties" and "the pleasures of some public amusement." Having secured his "glittering prize," Waterton feels bound to pursue his original course even though providing the resources and a setting commensurate with their shared social ambitions keeps him ever more "closely chained to the galley of commerce." Their newly purchased stately house is soon filled with ornate Parisian furniture, plush fittings, and "all the thousand expensive toys which seem to minister to the tastes of fashion." However, this proves mere window dressing: the upper rooms—unfurnished and uncarpeted—"would have been found to afford a striking contrast to the splendors of those parts of the mansion which were intended for display" ("MC" 15). The display afforded by these public rooms after an evening's entertainment stands at even greater odds with the order and economy of the domestic ideal; the "sad disorder" and "desolation" of the rooms instead bespeak tremendous waste and indulgence: broken champagne bottles litter the floor, their contents soaking into the rich carpets; plum cake besmears the snow-white hearth rug; and draperies drip with melted ice-cream as servants—following the example of their privileged employers—sleep it off amid the mess.

Laura's increasingly lavish schemes for balls, parties, soirees, musicals and other such social extravaganzas fill Waterton with an ill-concealed anxiety, yet he is determined to support the spectacle which betokens their rising social credit. To do so, he resolves to extend his business beyond "the regular cash trade" and "follow the example of his neighbors and engage in speculation." By extending credit to his clients and investing in out-of-state land development schemes on credit, Waterton's paper fortune grows from "a paltry two thousand a year" to ten times that amount, "while at the same time, the fashionable society of New York were in raptures with Mrs. Waterton's splendid parties, her costly equipage, and her magnificent style of dress" ("MC" 16). However, like their synecdochic reception rooms and inflated social standing, the Watertons' new fortune is of deceptive solidity. Not surprisingly, the widespread *"speculative mania"* of 1836 brings on the economic panic and collapse of 1837:[37]

> The following year began to afford tokens of trouble. Credit was still good, but money had entirely disappeared from the community, and men who had learned to make notes in order to *acquire fortunes*, were now obliged to continue their manufacture in order to *avoid ruin*. Rumors of approaching distress arose in the money market; men began to look with distrust upon their fellows, and as unlimited confidence in each other had been the foundation of the towering edifice of unstable prosperity, the moment that was shaken, the whole structure fell crumbling to the earth. As soon as doubt arose, destruction was at hand, and at length one wild crash of almost universal bankruptcy startled the dreamers from their golden visions. ("MC" 17)

The money-currency that insures exchange value is like the social currency that maintains the community interest: both must be based on standards more substantial than ephemeral and selfish desire.

Waterton is doomed to know the truth of his uncle's pre-nuptial advice, for he loses not only his paper fortune, but his fashionable wife as well. Raving "like a mad woman," she reproaches her husband "in the vilest terms" for bringing on her ruin, accuses him of base deception in contracting their marriage, and then deserts him, ostensibly to seek her sister's protection in France. However, her entourage is rumored to include "a certain black-whiskered foreigner . . . [as] the companion of her voyage" ("MC" 17). Not long after this stormy split, "the doors of one of the most stately homes in ___ Street were opened to the public" and the auctioneer's "ominous red flag" waved a "general invitation to every passer-by" to gaze upon the "abode of wealth, and luxury, and taste" in ruins. "Desecrated," "disfigured," and dirtied by the "impress of many a soiling touch," the "delicate and costly toys which had once been the admiration of the fashionable visitants to the family" are brought before the eyes of the curious to be sold, and the domestic scene is exposed in an unforeseen and humiliating kind of display. It is whispered that Waterton, unbalanced by his misfortune, would enter a lunatic asylum; however, he "recovered his senses so fully that he obtained a divorce from his wife." Marital dissolution ironically proves the index of his restored equilibrium, and Waterton settles down—as a bachelor—to enjoy "as much tranquillity as a remembrance of his former follies, his imprudent choice, and three years of wedded life will allow" ("MC" 17).

This short story's significance transcends the status conferred upon it by being merely "the first" to raise the topic of divorce, for in addition to achieving its narrative resolution with the ironically flat announcement of a divorce and the literalized domestic dissolution such legal remedy suggests, "The Mistaken Choice" provides a sketch of the contributive elements in a marital breakdown that proves remarkably prescient in focus: the representation of marriage as a business venture between contracting spouses; the ascendancy of individual desire over community well-being; the link between extravagant expenditure and the feminine; the infiltration of fashion— and thus the influence and pressure of the public gaze—into the private domestic sphere; and the literal as well as figurative connection of the "inflation-credit system" ("MC" 16) of speculative purchase with the notion of social credit/creditability based on ostentatious display. Certainly Embury's brief tale has much in common with the mid nineteenth-century divorce novels which followed its lead in broaching the topic of divorce, particularly in their shared emphasis upon ill-chosen and mismatched spouses as the source of conjugal disruption.

However, its true thematic affinities are with the much later and better known Progressive Age novels of marital upheaval (Howell's *A Modern Instance* among them) in which the private domestic sphere— once considered a stable, well-ordered refuge from the chaotic market world of fluctuating desire, value and commodity—can no longer withstand its capitalist imperatives. Indeed, in these later works the market economy's threat to the domestic no longer comes exclusively from without: women, once imaged as the virtuous defenders of the hearth, become its most potent threat as they "go public" as consumers and as objects of consumption.

In the early 1870s both T.S. Arthur and Harriet Beecher Stowe adopted Embury's tack, attempting to counter the perceived threat to home and family—and thus to community stability and morality—by portraying the devastating effects wrought by the woman of fashion who eschews the domestic ideal. While these authors have as their primary purpose the recovery and preservation of a sanctified domestic sphere, both link consumer extravagance with representations of denatured femininity and employ the scandal of divorce as the calamity certain to befall wives who, careless of their true vocation, pursue their rewards in society rather than in the home. Divorce, whatever its ultimate cause, spelt certain social ostracism in the decades immediately following the Civil War,[38] and thus functions in these texts as a means of containing the threat to domestic as well as communal order posed by the fashionable woman.

T. S. Arthur's short story collection *Orange Blossoms Fresh and Faded* (1871) examines a range of marital situations which culminate, depending upon the attitudes and actions of spouses, in success or failure; "Marrying a Beauty" most assuredly falls into the latter category. Based on the maxim that beauty is indeed only skin deep, the story details the costs borne by a husband who mistakenly equates his wife's "enchanting"—if novelistically conventional—loveliness with moral rectitude. Although Marion bears "his prize . . . away to the sanctuary of the home,"[39] he soon discovers that his private love and admiration cannot suffice for one whose "life was in the world" (*OB* 279), constructed by the gaze of many and successive admirers. Before long, he finds that while he is at the office his wife meets her admirers on the sly in order to indulge in public amusement. Although Marion forbids Julia to further compromise herself in such display, she willfully persists until one day, while out riding with one of her special friends, she falls, injures herself and requests that she be taken to her aunt's rather than her husband's home. The open and unresolved breach between husband and wife becomes grist in the mill of scandal; Julia's friends and admirers "presently dropped [her] company when separation from her husband made her notorious" (*OB* 324), and thus she "fell more exclusively into the company of a class of men and women who represent a low standard of honor" (*OB* 323). His hopes and ideals shattered, Marion is transformed from "a kind-feeling, gently-deferring man . . . [into an] inflexible one," realizing at last that "feminine" beauty had in fact hidden from him "a mean deformity"(*OB* 310) of a woman, a being not authentically a woman at all.

The disappointment of marriage is followed by the bitterness of a divorce in which Marion, who does not contest his wife's suit, is portrayed as the perpetrator of domestic discord and ordered to pay alimony. Divorce in this case proves particularly blighting, for not only does it damage Marion's character and ruin Julia's already jeopardized social reputation, it also frees her to recirculate on the marriage market and thus repeat her wrongs. She quickly moves on to a new husband, an ardent Southerner, who "in the first warmth of affection laid his heart and his fortune at her feet" (*OB* 325). Two years later, this husband is killed in a duel with a man charged with being unduly familiar with Julia; before her mourning is decently at an end, she "married the murderer of her husband"(*OB* 326) and begins her destructive work anew. Sometime thereafter, Marion accidentally catches sight of his former wife and her latest husband at a fashionable watering-hole; she is now a "showily-dressed woman" with a "thin, sallow face," "sunken orbits," and a "dullness of expression," her beauty exhausted by her scandalous career (*OB* 328). The husband, too, bears the imprint of her conduct on his face and in his bearing. Had Marion and his successors been privy to the advice given the prospective young groom in "Can You Afford It?" the companion piece to "Marrying a Beauty," they might have discovered that they could not, in fact, "afford the possession of so costly an ornament" as a fashionable beauty. As this would-be husband learns, the "original cost" of a society wife is modest, "for the article is cheap in our market." Rather, "it is the expense of maintenance" after marriage that makes investment in such a wife a foolish venture (*OB* 239). Once again, the creature who inhabits the world of society and fashion proves but a counterfeit woman who should be rejected as a mate and thus taken from circulation.

Harriet Beecher Stowe's enduring conviction that "there is no one fact of our human existence that has a stronger influence than the house [in which] we live" informed not only her most famous work, *Uncle Tom's Cabin* (1852), but her later "New York" novels as well.[40] Indeed, *My Wife and I* (1871) and *Pink and White Tyranny* (1871) extend into the post-slavery era the importance of domesticity of the type enacted by Rachel Halliday and Little Eva in which women imitate God's "parental economy" of abundant love and thereby "approximate heaven in their homes."[41] Certainly the New York novels share the logic of radicalized domesticity outlined in *Uncle Tom's Cabin:* womanly power is elevated as "mothers," raised to the status of sacred beings, serve as the indices and arbiters of universal value. Contrary to conventional understandings of domestic functioning in which the well-ordered home acts both as a mirror of and a refuge from the chaotic market world, Stowe's matriarchal "heavenly home" stands completely outside that world as an alternative mode of social organization and thus supplants rather than supplements the market economy of desire, demand, fluctuation and fashionable commodity. The fact that *My Wife and I* and *Pink and White Tyranny* were published in the same year and that both take up the subject of a young couple's domestic arrangements suggests that Stowe may have intended them as complementary pieces to instruct her female readership, first by positive and then by negative example, in the lessons of proper household economy, for these two tales illustrate the tremendous power for good or ill exerted by a woman's management of the domestic sphere.

Although once a pretty society flirt seemingly destined for a moneyed but loveless marriage, Eva Van Arsdale consents to be poor-but-honest Harry Henderson's bride, and is thus on her way to becoming Stowe's model domestic goddess in *My Wife and I.* Upon her betrothal, Eva determines to properly cultivate her natural housekeeping tendencies by learning the lessons of "ornamental housewifery" from the "elderly priestess in the temple of experience," Mrs. Henderson.[42] Eva's mission is to replicate the economy of abundance characteristic of her mother-in-law's home, to "make life beautiful, to keep down the hard, dry, prosaic side and keep up the poetry" and thus transform the hearth's warmth into an "altar flame" (*MWI* 448).

The sanctified nature of the hearth over which Eva presides derives in large part from what Gillian Brown terms "sentimental possession," a "Christian purification of [the] market economy in which commodities are transubstantiated into possessions."[43] In an essay collected in *Household Papers,* Stowe stresses that creating the proper domestic environment requires a special mode of consumerism which distinguishes objects for their potential utility, comfort and endurance as well as their independence from ephemeral fashion.[44] The use provided by such household items bespeaks an intimacy, a congruence, between objects and their possessors that transforms them into mediums of their possessors' essence. As Brown notes, these transformed (and transforming) possessions "so closely correspond to the wills and feelings of their owners that they appear to be them rather than to be serving them."[45] Thus to be in the "mother's" home, surrounded by objects possessed of her abundant love, is to exist in sacred precincts. The Henderson home, in which Eva works her generative womanly "talent for creating out of nothing," contains none "of the stereotyped sets of articles expected as a matter of course in good families" (*MWI* 479), but instead is comprised of cast-off articles and inexpensive materials that are, through Eva's "ministry," invested with her charms:

> The house was as much an expression of my wife's personality, a thing wrought out of her being, as any picture painted by an artist. . . [it] formed itself around my wife like the pearly shell around the nautilus. My home was Eva—she the scheming, the busy, the creative, was the life, the soul and the spirit of all that was there. (*MWI* 478)

Because the standard of value which marks the Henderson household inventory as precious is inherently stable, resting as it does on Eva's feeling, it evades the dangerous fluctuations of the desire-driven market which threatens to overthrow any domestic setting which obeys its imperatives. Rather than investing in the fashionable but finally impersonal furnishings "expected . . . in all good families," the

Hendersons occupy a home furnished with Eva's spirit and thus tender another meaning for "good family."

If Eva Henderson is the character Stowe created to express her anti-market domestic economy, then Lillie Endicott stands as the character created to demonstrate the havoc wrought within the home, the family and the community when a woman neglects her sacred duty as a mother-wife and pursues a fashionable course. *Pink and White Tyranny* thus serves as a cautionary tale for the instruction of potential wives and husbands: for both, Lillie's ruinous self-absorption provides a powerful negative image of corrupted femininity that must be avoided, while John Endicott's disillusionment demonstrates the folly of being satisfied with appearances, the trap inherent in a market economy. Like Harry Henderson, John had sought a wife who was "the embodiment of all his mother's virtues," but had chosen instead a woman who merely "look[ed] like his mother's picture."[46] Indeed, Lillie is all insubstantial appearances; "a belle by profession" (*PWT* 8), she is most concerned with attracting a suitor wealthy enough to provide the means for her endlessly renewed self-decoration. Her personal/domestic economy seems the very antithesis of Eva Henderson's: rather than the loving, all-bountiful, giving "mother" presiding over a hearth at which "not even a dog shall have an ungratified desire" (*MWI* 498), Lillie is "a perpetual child" (*PWT* 49) selfishly appropriating everything to her own use and adornment. Instead of the domestic goddess who short-circuits the effect of market forces in the home, Lillie, having "early acquired the idea that her charms were capital to be employed in trading for the good things in life" (*PWT* 46), allows the idiom and mode of market exchange to govern her most intimate relations.

A central episode delineating Lillie's deviation from Stowe's ideal occurs when she decides that the Endicott home "has sort of an old look" that exerts a "depressing effect on [her] spirits" (*PWT* 105). Crying and cajoling, she convinces John that the parlor must be redecorated if there is to be any domestic peace. Soon, the traditional New England interior is done over "*a la* Pompadour," and solidity, function and familial association are sacrificed to the gilded effect of "everything Frenchy and pretty, and gay and glistening" (*PWT* 126). But as Stowe forecasts in her parable "The Ravages of a Carpet," when fashion rather than function and attention to established household ambiance dictates decorating decisions, waste inevitably results.[47] Once the Endicott parlor was "furbished and resplendent," it

> . . . cast such invidious reflections on the [other] chambers that the chambers felt themselves old and rubbishy, and prayed and stretched out hands of imploration to have something done for them!
>
> So the spare chamber was first included in the glorification program; but when the spare chamber was once made into a Pompadour pavilion, it so flouted and despised the other old-fashioned Yankee chambers that they were ready to die with envy; and, in short, there was no way to produce a sense of artistic unity, peace and quietness, but to do the whole thing over. . . . (PWT 126–7)

The result is a showcase rather than a home, and John finds "there was not, in fact, in all the reorganized house, a place where he felt *himself* to be at all the proper thing." To find comfort and a sense of belonging, he periodically leaves his own house to seek refuge in his sister's modest domicile, where he "stretched himself on the sofa and sat in his mother's old armchair" (*PWT* 139). John must finally admit that "where divinity ought to be in his household," there is "nothing . . . where [Lillie] is" (*PWT* 314). And John is not the only one so oppressed. Lillie's inability to create a homey environment generates an effect which ripples outward from the cold Endicott hearth and into the community, "demoralizing the public conscience . . . [and] bringing luxury and extravagance" to a hard-working New England community. The paralyzing influence of Lillie's excess ultimately is literalized in John's financial failure that, in turn, imperils the local industry and its dependent townspeople. Confronted with the need to trim her ruinous expenditure, Lillie cries "I'd rather die" than do without (*PWT* 309), reinforcing the notion that things become dangerously equated with the self in a market economy. In the modest life that follows Endicott's financial embarrassment, she indeed withdraws and diminishes, dying a figurative death to the fashionable world she once inhabited.

Although Lillie eventually retires into the private precincts of the home, her fate at the moment of her husband's crisis is by no means secure. Her resistance to the necessary economizing causes her to insist that John act as "smart men" do when "caught in such scrapes" (*PWT*

316) and renege on the contracts which have brought him to the brink of financial ruin. Disgusted with her selfishness, he recognizes that his wife, "in whom he had been daily and hourly disappointed since he was married" but for whom he had always held out hope for moral regeneration, was in fact "of a nature not only unlike, but opposed to his own" (*PWT* 311). Failing to find in his wife a womanly complement to his own nature, he turns to his sister Grace and reveals his shame at Lillie's scheme "to put my property out of my hands dishonestly, to keep her in luxury" (*PWT* 316). Divorce seems to offer his only hope of relief:

> I have nothing to live for,—nobody and nothing. My wife, Gracie! she is worse than nothing,—worse than nothing,—worse, oh! infinitely worse than nothing! She is a chain and a shackle. She is my obstacle. She tortures me and hinders me every way and everywhere. There will never be a home for me where she is; and, because she is there, no other woman can make a home for me. (*PWT* 314)

While acknowledging that Lillie is indeed a "moral invalid," Grace nevertheless reminds John that he freely chose to set up housekeeping with this worldly creature. As the only approximation of Stowe's domestic goddess in *Pink and White Tyranny*, she counsels against breaking up even so desolate a home as the Endicott's. Yet it is the world of business that supplies the model of contractual fidelity that she uses to illustrate the nature of the marriage relation, arguing that "if you stand by a business engagement with such faithfulness, how much more should you stand by that great engagement which concerns all other families and the stability of all society" (*PWT* 316). Recognizing the aptness of the comparison, John returns to Lillie to carry on the best he can. His determination to honor both his business and marital contracts yields eventual rewards. Not only does he recoup his losses and regain his position in the community—as befitting one who has "endured for the public good"—he also witnesses his wife's redemption. Long "dead" to the world of fashion and society, Lillie finally recognizes that she, "like Undine before her soul came into her," had been unwomanly in her conduct. With this realization, "a better spirit seemed to enter" her and she dies, leaving John to reflect on the wisdom of honoring one's contracts.

Stowe's own voice concludes the tale in order "to put conspicuously into our story exactly what the moral of it is." While this moral might logically be expected to warn against Lillie's profligate household economy, Stowe instead takes aim at women's rights advocates who "clamor for easy dissolution of the marriage contract, as a means of righting their wrongs." She comes down against divorce for any cause, based on the reasoning that equal rights and thus equal access to legal remedies to end bad marriages would in fact "always tell against the weaker sex," especially those who barter their feminine charms in order to secure a husband:

> [I]f the woman who finds that she has made a mistake, and married a man unkind or uncongenial, may, on the discovery of it, leave him and seek her fortune with another, *so may a man.* And what will become of women like Lillie, when the first gilding begins to wear off, if the man who has taken one of them shall be at liberty to cast her off and seek another? . . . once marriage is made and consummated, it should be as fixed a fact as the laws of nature. (*PWT* 319–20; emphasis added)

Thus Stowe argues against divorce as a component of a wasteful market logic that would jettison women who are perceived to be mere products for consumption and disposal.

Although Mary E. Walker was exactly the sort of women's rights advocate against whom Stowe would seem to be writing, she, too, in her feminist treatise *H.I.T.* (1871) seizes upon the danger for women inherent in the prevalent conception of wives as items for display. Arguing for reform in marriage rather than against divorce, Walker notes that the sanctioned courtship relation in which men actively pursue and then provide for the "beautifully feminine" charmer who passively waits for masculine notice may lead to women being discarded when they lose their most significant asset, the "gilding" of youthful beauty:

> Some men love women just as children love dolls, and, as a natural result, treat them just as dolls are cared for. They dress them in all the finery they are able to procure, pet and exhibit them until the clothes become old, and the beautiful color of the face is gone, and the eyes

are contracted and dim, and then, like worn out dolls, they are thrown aside for neighbors' dolls, or for some beautiful images in the show windows of false society's market.[48]

Such representations of women as commodities to be purchased and exchanged on "society's market" and whose value as display items ("trophies,"[49] as Thorstein Veblen would characterize them in his 1899 *Theory of the Leisure Class*) is determined by their congruence with the fashionable images found in ever shifting "show windows" became a staple in a range of social documents during the Progressive Age. Yet if "marriage ha[d] become a money market [and] a stock exchange,"[50] as the authors of *The American Code of Manners* exclaimed, it was a market in and on which women exercised some limited agency for their own advancement. Indeed, women's association with ornamentation and consumerism was no longer perceived as a simple manifestation of "natural" feminine extravagance, but rather as a finely-honed survival skill which fitted them for the *occupation* of marriage. According to Veblen's satiric ethnography of the American culture of consumption, men's vestigial barbaric desire to demonstrate their prowess by means of physical exploit is sublimated into economic activity in which "conspicuous consumption" of goods and services beyond mere need testifies to their "pecuniary prowess." Employed, so to speak, by husbands seeking community status, wives function as consumer-ornaments and thereby provide just such an index of power. In this paradigm of social organization it becomes "the office of women to consume vicariously for the head of the household" and prove by her "consumption of food, clothing and . . . furniture" her husband's "ability to pay." The more expensive wives are in their habit of personal and domestic consumption, "the more creditable and more effective for the purpose of the reputability of the household or its head their life will be."[51] Ward McAllister, in his conduct-cum-gossip book *Society as I Have Found It* (1890), proves Veblen's theory to be firmly grounded in general practice and popular understanding in his advice to wives "not to neglect their toilet, but rather improve it" after marriage since the admiration thereby garnered by a well turned-out woman "advances and strengthens her husband."[52] Thirty years later, this social wisdom had lost none of its force, and Dorothy Dix reminded her female readers that "woman makes the family's status" by means of liberal display rather than conservative economy: "the woman who makes herself nothing but a domestic drudge . . . is not a help to her husband. She is a hindrance . . . a man's wife is the show window where he exhibits the measure of his achievement."[53]

If in *Women and Economics* (1898) Charlotte Perkins Gilman puts a different spin on exactly what was traded between spouses, she concurred with Veblen that marriage was indeed a contractual exchange that constituted a woman's sole "livelihood": "all that [a woman] may wish to have, all she may wish to do, must come through a single channel and a single choice. Wealth, power, social distinction, fame— not only these, but home and happiness, reputation, ease and pleasure, her bread and butter,—all must come to her through a small gold ring."[54] With the passing of the home as a site of production and with the extra-domestic job market for the most part closed to them, wives fulfill their role as domestic "provider" by consuming "goods and labor to an extent limited only by the purchasing power of their male relatives."[55] Unlike Veblen, Gilman does not count women's "labor" as consumers as a value contributed to the household welfare of reputation, but she does agree that as an economic dependent deprived of functions productive of goods or economic value, a wife becomes a "priestess in the temple of consumption."[56]

Given either Gilman's or Veblen's account of woman's function within the home, "the mercenary marriage" that affords a wife the greatest opportunity for consumption becomes "the perfectly natural consequence of [her] economic dependence."[57] While it might be "degrading to behold a woman willing to sacrifice all that a woman should hold most dear to obtain what money can buy," the spectacle of "a woman . . . dragging around a rich, vulgar husband who is merely an appendage to her diamonds" is nevertheless everywhere in view.[58] As Gilman describes it, "the girl who marries the rich old man or the titled profligate is condemned by the popular voice; . . . yet why should we blame the woman for pursuing her vocation? Since marriage is the only way to get money, why should she not try to get money in that way?"[59] Indeed, since "the good name of the household" is sustained, according to Veblen, by a wife's "honorific expenditure and conspicuous consumption," it behooves her to marry well; the woman whose capacity for consumption outstrips her husband's ability to provide not only threatens his social creditability, but risks devaluation herself.[60]

This image of the American female as a creature driven by economic imperatives is nowhere better illustrated than in the pages of *Life* magazine which, from its inception in 1883 and throughout the Progressive era, proved a sure delineator "of developments in morals and manners" in American society.[61] Although the magazine delivered its comic "thrusts at Society with a capital S" (Ward McAllister and his "four-hundred" were among those satirized "mercilessly"), it nevertheless exercised such tremendous general appeal that its circulation reached 50,000 by 1890.[62] The pecuniary nature of the relation between the sexes was frequently lampooned in *Life's* pages so that it became both an instantly recognizable and easily understood subject. "The Education of the American Girl" (Fig. 1.1) is a study in social causation, seeking answers to the problematic question of why she is so completely entangled in the web of monetary gain. From the Fifth Avenue finishing school where her attention is fixed upon attracting the approving gaze of young admirers, to the private moments caught up in the latest romance; from the theater's presentation of the supplicant male suing for a woman's favor, to luncheon table talk in which debutantes boast of their latest conquests, the whole force of the American Girl's education is bent on securing masculine "tribute," whether in the adoring eyes of the one or the many. Such tribute is soon literalized into the gold ring that tempts her down the aisle with the man who can best gratify her need for "social" distinction. Money is the standard by which tribute is measured, and so it fuels the engine of courtship; love proves a poor motivator if one desires a "successful" marriage. Thus it comes as no surprise when, in another *Life* cartoon, a disappointed suitor begs to set the record straight on his rejection and receives a lesson in gendered economics: He: "And you say we are too poor to marry? —would you marry me if you were rich?" She: "No, but I would marry you if *you* were rich."[63] A verse entitled "A Bargain"[64] abides by this arrangement, and further encodes its business aspect:

> She loved me not, and yet she wed me,
> For I was rich, had wealth untold;
> Her heart and hand she gladly gave me—
> A fair exchange for all my gold.
> Fair and sweet, at first I loved her,

But found her heartless, cruel, cold;
And yet our bargain's fairly equal,
For she was bought, and I was sold.

Indeed, the language of business, contract and exchange proved a particularly fruitful source for captioning the "amatory" exploits of American society. Cartoons bearing the inscriptions "Let the Buyer Beware," "The Supply and the Demand," and "Compound Interest," punning on various courtship concerns, proliferated in the pages of *Life*. One well-heeled gentleman sought to explain "The Business Principle" determining the success or failure on the marriage market to two young things who comprise his rapt audience. In other illustrations, onlookers at society weddings discussed the terms of the marital bargain: "The bride's father gives her away, I suppose?" "No, he sold her privately"; or, as a decrepit but wealthy old geezer is propelled down the aisle by his young bride, a friend exclaims, "Poor Clara! What a pity she should sell herself to that wheezy old skeleton," and receives the astute reply, "My dear, it is not a sale; only a lease." One suitor, having dedicated considerable capital to the amusement of a young lady who nevertheless has rejected him, reveals that he has a right to expect a better return on his investment: "You will be a sister to me! A ten dollar sleigh ride this afternoon, a box at the opera tonight, supper at Delmonico's and a car home! A sister to me? Great Scott! What kind of fool human do you take your brother to be?" The American Girl's tendency to hold out for the highest bidder is represented in "The End of the Season" (Fig. 1.2) in which the modern Cupid—whose signal heart is emblazoned with a dollar sign—auctions off "surplus" debutantes. It seems particularly appropriate that the season, which began with the Madison Square Garden Horse Show, should culminate in the sale of "a fine lot of Thoroughbreds" to an equally resplendent lot of prospective grooms. More than twenty years later, the young woman portrayed in the cartoon "Advertising Pays" still looks for the best offer from the highest bidder before committing herself to matrimony. Although she, unlike the society "high-steppers" of by-gone years, exercises the agency to select her own offer, the relation continues to be constructed as a market exchange.[65]

Once wed, the wives represented in the pages of *Life* prove faithful to both Veblen's and Gilman's analyses of their socio-economic role within marriage; the "success" of a union, whether viewed in individual or community terms, is determined by the husband's ability "to pay." The conversation between two women as they stroll down a fashionable avenue bears this out: "In your case, marriage doesn't seem to be much of a failure." "Failure! Why I've not stopped shopping more than long enough for luncheon in ten days!"[66] Certainly, the financial resources of the husband-provider allow the "highly cultivated flower" of society to bloom (Fig. 1.3), and supply "The Power" (Fig. 1.4) propelling her in style toward the social position to which she aspires. Tellingly, both of these illustrations reveal the separate and gendered spheres inhabited by spouses—a phenomenon Henry James would term a figurative "divorce" between them[67]—in which the husband, rendered invisible by his Wall Street occupation/preoccupations, pushes his wife upward on the scale of Fifth Avenue success.

The contract which grounds marriage dictates that the husband provide his wife support sufficient not only for maintenance but also for display, thereby meeting standards of social and pecuniary "decency" in the community; failing adequately to provide such support, the basis of the contract would be violated and, thus, lead quite logically to divorce. As the authors of *The American Code of Manners* noted, the leisure class wife is predisposed to cut short her marriage if it disappoints: "The worldly woman who determines to marry for money is often sort of a robber baroness sallying forth from her castle armed to destroy. The world is her oyster. If her husband proves generous, she may live with him; if he is not, she soon finds an excuse to leave him."[68] Similarly, Gilman hints at just such an end should society wives be frustrated in their vocation: "to consume food, to consume clothes, to consume houses and furniture and decorations and ornaments and amusements, to take and take and take forever—from one man if they are virtuous, from many if they are vicious, but always to take. . . ."[69] And since marriage provides a woman with her economic livelihood, she naturally moves on to her next husband, one of the "many," to secure her position in the world. This pattern of marriage and divorce for which leisure class wives serve as the template trickled down into the habits of middle class American as well. As the authors of *Middletown* (1929) indicate, in the years between 1890 and 1920 the population of "Middletown" (Muncie, Indiana) increased by 87%, while the divorce rate grew at six times that rate.[70] According to a

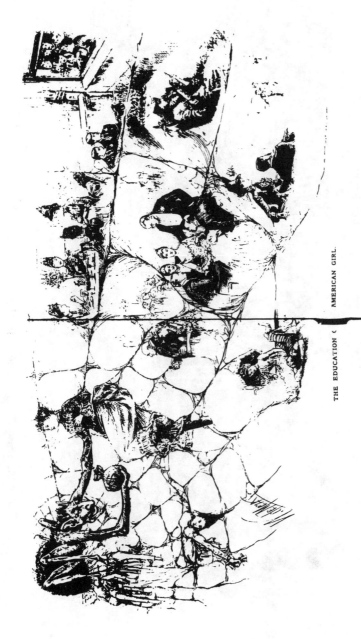

THE EDUCATION OF THE AMERICAN GIRL.

Fig. 1.1 "The Education of the American Girl" [*Life* 10, no. 260 (Dec. 22, 1887)]

Fig. 1.2 "The End of the Season" [*Life* 9, no. 230 (May 26, 1887)]

HIGHLY CULTIVATED FLOWER—FLOURISHES BEST IN
RICH SOIL

Fig. 1.3 "Highly Cultivated Flower" [*Life* 63, no.1649 (June 14, 1914)]

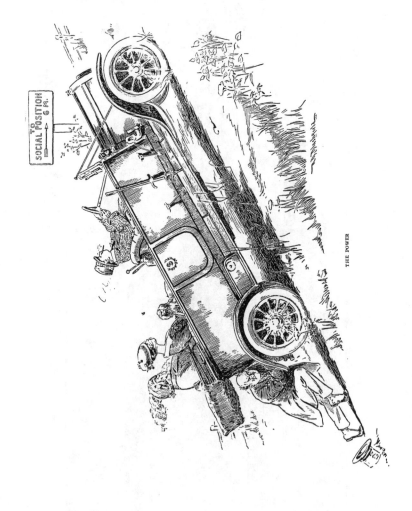

Fig. 1.4 "The Power" [*Life* 64, no. 1653 (July 2, 1914)]

APROPOS OF PASSING EVENTS.

Fig. 1.5 "Apropos of Passing Events" [*Life* 2, no. 49 (Dec. 6, 1883)]

Fig. 1.6 "Knots" [*Life* 54, no. 1397 (Aug. 12, 1909)]

"Middletown" lawyer, "seventy-five per cent. of the people seeking divorce are women, and two-thirds of [these] women ask divorce for non-support,"[71] a legal cause which, as Elaine Tyler May has shown, became an increasingly ambiguous phrase during the Progressive era. This period, marked by prosperity and the abundance of consumer goods, saw a rise in the standard of living across a broad segment of the American population. Rather than improving relations between spouses, however, the new affluence made the notion of adequate support unclear. No longer confined to what was necessary to support life—food, clothing and shelter, the concept of support expanded to include what was necessary to support a "decent" and "reputable" life in the community. Thus "the 'provider' was often expected to fulfill the increased demands sparked by widespread prosperity," an expectation that led to divorce disputes over status and social mobility, broadly construed as issues of "non-support," in the years from 1880–1920.[72]

Life's illustrations chronicled America's divorce phenomenon as assiduously as it had documented the foibles of society courtship and marriage. Appearing in a very early volume of the magazine, "Divorce: Apropos of Passing Events" (Fig 1.5) pictures a disgruntled couple who, although seated facing away from each other, are joined at the neck by a beribboned cord. Above them hovers Cupid, holding a tragic mask before his mischievous face, as he prepares to sever the bond between the couple. Around the soon-to-be separated pair swirl images suggestive of the forces in conflict over the divorce question: two "knights"—one of the church and one of the bar—joust over their respective positions on the permanency of the marriage contract, while Death points to a scroll which admonishes "Until death us do part" and asks, "Why don't you give me a chance, judge?" Two cupids duke it out wearing sandwich boards which proclaim, on the one hand, "Love cures all ills" and, on the other, "Divorce: no family should be without it." If this cartoon only hinted at the cause of the increased divorce rate, "The Society Flower (*Rapida Americana*)," like "The Education of the American Girl," ascribed marital failure to the same suspect motives that lead to pecuniary marriages. The illustration presents a Hogarthian progress of the flower of American womanhood (watered by Cupid): from the "Bud" stage in which she learns to accept young men's tributes with a reserve that never betrays real feeling, she "Blossoms" into a debutante and then a wife. Eventually, however, her loveless marriage bears the bitter "Fruit" of adultery, and discovered, she sues to "Leave" in the divorce court.[73]

At this stage, the American marriage promised to remain intact only when it continued to satisfy the desires and aspirations of its parties. In one cartoon, a lawyer asks his female client, "On what grounds, Madam, do you wish a divorce?" to which she draws herself up indignantly and answers, "Why, I married Barlow for money, and now he has lost everything." The piece is captioned with what must be taken as the modern motto for marriage: "For Better, not for Worse."[74] This sentiment grounds another marital vignette, "To Exchange," in which a business-savvy leisure-class wife, looking disdainfully at her gouty, overweight, snoring mate, determines to rid herself of "The husband with a past for one with a future." Indeed, the logic of exchange that encouraged disposal of old or unsatisfactory items in favor of new ones seemed to provide the perfect escape mechanism for the marriage market, guaranteeing risk-free "commitments." One young woman hints that "The Art of Matrimony" is in fact an art of cutting one's losses and moving on, explaining to her friend that should her impending marriage prove unhappy, her fiancé "has promised a divorce or a suicide" so that she is really "not running much risk." When in another cartoon vignette a young woman asserts to her suitor that "this country ought to have more liberal divorce laws" in order "to encourage matrimony," she employs the logic that certain means of escape via easy divorce might tempt her to try marriage on something akin to an "approval basis" with her unpromising beau.[75] Thus marital "Knots" (Fig. 1.6) are no longer permanent bonds if the ties have lost their attraction and begin to chafe.

*

The following chapters examine six Progressive Age novels of marital discord which specifically focus upon narratives of divorced and divorcing women within the context of their multi-valent social and economic value on the "marriage market." In some fashion, these works all trace their literary genealogy back to Embury's tale of feminine "extravagance," and each has a close relation in the contemporary works of social theory or cultural criticism which suggest that marriage and domestic management have become, instead of her vocation, a woman's particular (and peculiar) occupation. In shifting the ground from vocation to occupation, from essentialized to professionalized drives, these novels distance themselves from the emotionally charged domestic ideal and are thus better able to assert what Boone terms "counter-narratives" to the familiar plot trajectory. These novels work toward a "persistent 'undoing' of the dominant tradition," concealing within familiar forms contradictions, "slippages of logic," that undermine the representations of "love" and "life" codified by hegemonic culture.[76]

Henry James's *The Portrait of a Lady* (1881) and *The Golden Bowl* (1905) are notable for the way in which divorce is so studiously avoided for two heroines who would seem to have the moral, legal and—most significantly—the contractual grounds for leaving their erring husbands as well as the financial means to free themselves. Clearly troubled by the circumscribed position afforded women by traditional domesticity or in Veblenesque leisure-class marriages, James nevertheless takes issue with the notion that freedom and personal fulfillment can be won by repudiating one's choices and obligations, no matter how circumstance has altered them. By exploring the "uncertain textual realm of marital impasse and stalemate,"[77] James challenges the conventional marriage plot by positing a mode of conjugal partnership that resists stultifying stasis.

Chapter Three moves from James to Edith Wharton's *The Custom of the Country* (1913) and its examination of the manner in which divorce is deployed as a product that may enhance a woman's chance for social and economic advancement on the marriage market. Almost from the novel's outset, Undine Spragg demonstrates an awareness of the conspicuous display required of respectable households and of the benefits divorce might afford a "disappointed" wife. Husbands who "aren't in the right set" or who fail to provide sufficient tokens of their pecuniary power and thereby hinder a wife's ability to "really get anywhere" can be "got rid of," all to the wife's "credit" for wanting change. Undine's multiple marriages would seem faithful to the course plotted by the domestic ideal, particularly insofar as they represent "recognizable, repeating and contained structures."[78] However, by plotting dizzying repetitions of marriage and divorce which spiral out of control rather than toward closure, Wharton in fact undermines the conventional wisdom which looks to matrimony as the stable structure symbolizing personal and social well being.

Chapter Four takes up narratives which lead divorced wives from the domestic space and into the workplace, where they bypass the husband-provider and become earners and spenders in the culture of consumption. While during the decade 1910–1920 mass-circulation women's magazines warned against the dangers of extra-domestic careers, the novels *Roast Beef Medium* (1913) and *Emma McChesney and Company* (1915), by Edna Ferber, and *The Job* (1917), by Sinclair Lewis, seem to offer viable life trajectories for the single female protagonist beyond or outside marriage, thus interrogating traditional narrative conventions that define women's "natural" vocation. These chapters, then, examine both the plot and form of the marriage narrative in order to determine whether divorce functions as a strategy for containment and the preservation of old hegemonies, or as an authentic mode of liberation.

NOTES

1. Glenda Riley, *Divorce: An American Tradition* (New York: Oxford University Press, 1991), 3. A Puritan court awarded the first "American" divorce in Massachusetts in 1639.

2. Jay Fliegelmann, *Prodigals and Pilgrims: The American Revolution Against British Patriarchal Authority, 1750–1800* (New York: Cambridge University Press, 1982), 267.

3. Riley, *Divorce: An American Tradition*, 32.

4. Michael Grossberg, *Governing the Hearth: Law and the Family in Nineteenth-Century America* (Chapel Hill: University of North Carolina Press, 1985), 3–4.

5. Ibid., 10.

6. As Evelyn J. Hinz observes, "in the mainstream of our critical tradition . . . marriage has come to be regarded as one of the distinguishing aspects of the novel. . . ." "Hierogamy versus Wedlock: Types of Marriage Plots and their Relationships to Genres of Prose Fiction," *PMLA* 91 (1976), 900.

7. *Adultery in the Novel: Contract and Transgression* (Baltimore: Johns Hopkins University Press, 1979), 3–4.

8. Hinz, "Hierogamy versus Wedlock," 902–903.

9. Boone identifies the courtship, seduction (courtship's tragic variation) and wedlock plots. His discussion of the courtship plot essentially follows

Hinz's outline of comic wedlock; that is, a couple overcomes obstacles of outlook, attitude or disparate position to find bliss in marriage. The seduction plot inverts this trajectory, but social norms are nevertheless upheld in the recognition of the brutality and unseemliness of the seducer's actions. Boone's wedlock plot is either comic or tragic. In the comic variation, an already married couple faces, like the courting couple, hardship and/or threats to their union before happily re-uniting. The tragically married couple reaches an impasse and cannot recover happiness. See *Tradition Counter Tradition: Love and the Form of Fiction* (Chicago: University of Chicago Press, 1987), 9–10.

10. Boone, "Wedlock as Deadlock and Beyond: Closure and the Victorian Marriage Ideal," *Mosaic* 17 (1984), 65. Or, as Hinz says, both versions of the marriage plot symbolize "the entrance into society of the individual, the acquisition or restoration of a realistic attitude toward life, the movement from *romantic* illusion to a *novelistic* sense of reality." "Hierogamy versus Wedlock," 904.

11. Boone, *Tradition*, 66.

12. Hinz, "Hierogamy versus Wedlock," 904.

13. Boone, "Wedlock as Deadlock," 69.

14. *Beyond Egoism: Fiction of James Joyce, Virginia Woolf, and D. H. Lawrence* (Cambridge, Mass.: Harvard University Press, 1980), 86.

15. Between 1880 and 1900, the American divorce rate doubled, and by 1920 it had more than doubled again. It is no doubt the rhetoric of "doubling rates" that alarmed the public; the actual numbers hardly seem the harbingers of social doom. The divorce rate increased from .4 per 1000 persons in 1880 to .8 in 1900; in 1920, the rate was1.75 persons in 1000. See Nelson Manfred Blake, *The Road to Reno: A History of Divorce in the United States* (New York: Macmillan, 1962), 228. As Norma Basch has shown, divorce was primarily a marital remedy for the middle class. *Framing American Divorce: From the Revolutionary Generation to the Victorians* (Berkeley and Los Angeles: University of California Press, 1999), 35–40.

16. Roderick Phillips, *Putting Asunder: A History of Divorce in Western Society* (New York: Cambridge University Press, 1988), 135. The necessarily compressed discussion of some of the general tendencies in American divorce law is indebted to the following sources: Blake, *The Road to Reno*; George E. Howard, *A History of Matrimonial Institutions* (Chicago: University of Chicago Press, 1904); Frank Keezer, *The Law of Marriage and Divorce: Giving the Law in all the States and Territories with Approved Forms* (Boston: William Nagel, 1906); Phillips, *Putting Asunder;* Glenda Riley, *Divorce: An American*

Tradition; Lelia Josephine Robinson, *The Law of Husband and Wife* (Boston: Lee and Shepard, 1890); and Carrol Wright, *A Report on Marriage and Divorce in the United States, 1867–1886* (Washington D. C., 1889). For the history of divorce law in the United States, Phillips' *Putting Asunder* is invaluable in both its comprehensive discussion and its subtle analyses. Blake's work is both scholarly and readable, and considered a modern standard, although its discussion ends with the 1960s. Riley's book, like Blake's, is full of anecdotes and case studies, and brings the history of American divorce into the 1990s.

17. Conviction in Essex County of John Littleale of the offense of living "in a house by himself . . . whereby he is subject to much sin and inequity, which ordinarily are the consequences of a solitary life." Quoted in Phillips, *Putting Asunder*, 146.

18. Divorce was not mandatory in cases of adultery provided the wronged spouse could forgive and continue to live with the erring partner. However, if convicted of adultery, civil authorities could mete out harsh penalties, including death. See Phillips, *Putting Asunder*, 147.

19. Edmund S. Morgan, *The Puritan Family: Religion and Domestic Relations in Seventeenth Century New England* (1944; reprint, New York: Harper and Row, 1966), 35.

20. Connecticut's divorce statues were considered the most "liberal" in New England, defining adultery, desertion, fraudulent contract and seven years absence as grounds for absolute divorce; annulment was granted for impotence. But the Connecticut General Assembly also consented to hear petitions for divorce that did not fit those parameters on a case by case basis. A successful petition brought before the Assembly in 1677 alleged "heretical opinions" and "hard usage" against a husband, while cruelty complaints were often heard in conjunction with adultery and desertion charges. The Middle Colonies (New York, New Jersey, Pennsylvania, Delaware) were more restrictive during the seventeenth-century in granting divorces; the southern colonies (Virginia, North Carolina, South Carolina, Georgia and Maryland) made no provisions for divorce.

21. Howard, *Matrimonial Institutions*, vol. 3, 14.

22. Blake, *Road to Reno*, 56–57; Phillips, *Putting Asunder*, 156–157. In describing this trend, it is important to note that New York proved quite an exception. Although it transferred authority to its courts in granting divorce in 1787, adultery was the only ground recognized for absolute divorce. Southern states were more reluctant to relinquish legislative control in divorce matters, although by the late nineteenth century the courts handled most of the caseload.

23. Robert Griswold, "The Evolution of the Doctrine of Mental Cruelty in Victorian American Divorce, 1790–1900," *Journal of Social History* 19 (1986), 127.

24. Keezer, *Law of Marriage and Divorce*, 60.

25. Quoted in Griswold, "The Evolution of the Doctrine of Mental Cruelty," 135. In 1886, five states and two territories (Arkansas, Missouri, Oregon, Pennsylvania, Tennessee, Washington and Wyoming) granted absolute divorce for indignities and one (North Carolina) granted separation only. Louisiana granted absolute divorce for "public defamation." See Wright, *Report on Marriage and Divorce*, 113–117. Under the 1854 statutes, a husband could sue for divorce on the ground of cruelty (only wives could under the 1815 law), but only wives could sue for divorce for alleged indignities. See Griswold, "The Evolution of the Doctrine of Mental Cruelty," 145. Finally, Jane Censer found that the inclusion of indignities as a ground for divorce played a key role in expanding the traditional notions of marital cruelty in North Carolina, Tennessee and, especially, Arkansas. See "'Smiling Through Her Tears': Ante-Bellum Southern Women and Divorce," *American Journal of Legal History* 25 (1981), 27–32.

26. Morris v. Morris, 14 *California Reports* 77 (1859). Quoted in Griswold, "The Evolution of the Doctrine of Mental Cruelty," 136.

27. *The Outlook* 100 (February 24, 1912), 474.

28. Griswold, "The Evolution of the Doctrine of Mental Cruelty," 139.

29. In fact this "natural right" was impaired by marriage, a "state" exercising a sovereignty which superceded national claims. As Thomas Jefferson notes while preparing a brief to argue for Virginia's first absolute divorce decree, the severance of the marital tie "*restores* women to their natural right of equality." See Frank Dewey, "Thomas Jefferson's Notes on Divorce," *William and Mary Quarterly* 39 (1982), 216–19; emphasis added.

30. Arthur, *The Hand But Not the Heart; or, The Life Trials of Jessie Loring* (New York: Derby and Jackson, 1858), 74. Subsequent quotations are from this edition and will be cited parenthetically in the text as *HBH*.

31. Arthur, *Out in the World* (New York: Carelton, 1864), 58. Subsequent quotations are from this edition and will be cited parenthetically in the text as *OW*.

32. *Mary Lyndon; or, the Revelations of a Life* (New York: Stringer and Townsend, 1855), 120–121. Subsequent quotations are from this edition and will be cited parenthetically in the text as *ML*.

33. "Fanny Fern's *Rose Clark,*" *Legacy* 8.2 (Fall 1991), 92. Fern also addressed the question of marriage and divorce in her articles in the *New York Ledger*, arguing that is better for a woman to leave home and children than to remain in a brutalizing marriage: "Better let her leave them, than remain to bring into the world their puny brothers and sisters. Does she shrink from the toil of self-support? What could be more hopeless, more endless, *more degrading* than that from what she turns away?. . . Let a woman who *has the self-sustaining power* quietly take her fate in her own hands, and right herself. Of course she will be misjudged and abused. *It is for her to choose.*" *New York Ledger,* 10/24/1857; quoted in Joyce W. Warren, *Fanny Fern: An Independent Woman* (New Brunswick: Rutgers University Press, 1991), 291.

34. *Rose Clark* (New York: Mason Brothers, 1856), 231. Subsequent quotations are from this edition and will be cited parenthetically in the text as *RC*.

35. James Harwood Barnett, *Divorce and the American Divorce Novel, 1858–1937* (Philadelphia: University of Pennsylvania Press, 1939), 82. This appraisal is echoed in Everett Carter's estimate that *A Modern Instance* is the "first complete treatment of a broken home in serious American Fiction" [*Howells and the Age of Realism* (Philadelphia: J. B. Lippincott, 1954), 146] and repeated as recently as George R. Uba's "Status and Contract: The Divorce Dispute of the 'Eighties and Howells' *A Modern Instance"* [*Colby Library Quarterly* 19 (June 1983)]. Barnett, a sociologist, was not particularly concerned with literary aesthetics in his appraisal of some fifty divorce novels, but rather with the way these works reflected social conditions—a bias that clearly favors literary realism over the sentimental mode of the mid-nineteenth century.

36. "The Mistaken Choice; or, Three Years of Married Life," *Graham's Magazine* 19 (July 1841), 13–17.

37. For a discussion of the economic and social upheavals wrought by the Panic of 1837, see William Charvat, "American Romanticism and the Depression," *Science and Society* (Winter 1937); Peter Temin, *General Notes on the Panic of 1837: The Traditional Approach; The New Approach,* (New York: Norton, 1969); and Charles Grier Sellers, *The Market Revolution: Jacksonian America, 1815–1846,* (New York: Oxford U P, 1991).

38. Dixon Wexter, *The Saga of American Society: A Record of Social Aspiration, 1609–1937* (New York: Scribners, 1937), 175.

39. "Marrying a Beauty," in *Orange Blossoms Fresh and Faded* (Philadelphia: J. M. Stoddard & Co., 1871), 277. Subsequent references to

stories in this text are from this edition and will be cited parenthetically in the text as *OB*.

40. Harriet Beecher Stowe, *Household Papers and Stories* (Boston: Houghton-Mifflin, 1896), 43.

41. Gillian Brown, *Domestic Individualism: Imagining the Self in Nineteenth Century America* (Berkeley and Los Angeles: University of California Press, 1990), 32.

42. *My Wife and I* (Boston: Houghton-Mifflin, 1896), 3. Subsequent quotations are from this edition and will be cited parenthetically in the text as *MWI*.

43. Brown, *Domestic Individualism*, 47.

44. Stowe, *Household Papers*, 23–47.

45. Brown, *Domestic Individualism*, 52.

46. *Pink and White Tyranny* (New York: New American Library, 1988), 44–45. Subsequent quotations are from this edition and will be cited parenthetically in the text as *PWT*.

47. "The Ravages of a Carpet" tells the story of a housewife who foolishly purchases a hearth-rug for its beauty rather than for function; not only does it fail to do the job, it causes the other useful furniture in the room to look shabby. The primacy of the rug's beauty and fashion value requires that the whole room be refurnished, at an expense beyond what the household finances can bear. See Stowe, *Household Papers*, 1–22.

48. *H.I.T.* (New York: American News Company, 1871), 31; 22.

49. *The Theory of the Leisure Class* (New York: Penguin, 1979), 22.

50. *The American Code of Manner: A Study of Usages. Laws and Observances which Govern intercourse in the Best Circles, and of the Principles which Underlie Them* (New York: W. R. Andrews, 1880), 253.

51. Veblen, *Theory of the Leisure Class,* 68; 180–181.

52. *Society as I Have Found It* (New York: Cassell Publishing, 1890), 242–243.

53. Dorothy Dix, quoted by Robert S. and Helen Merrell Lynd in their pioneering 1929 study, *Middletown: A Study in American Culture* (New York: Harcourt Brace Jovanovich, 1957), 116.

54. *Woman and Economics*, ed. Carl Degler (New York: Harper & Row, 1966), 71.

55. Ibid., 170.

56. Ibid., 120.

57. Ibid., 93.

58. *American Code of Manners*, 257.

59. Gilman, *Women and Economics*, 93.

60. Veblen, *Theory of the Leisure Class,* 180.

61. Frank Luther Mott, *A History of American Magazines*, vol. 4 (Cambridge, Mass.: Harvard University Press, 1938–1968), 561.

62. Ibid., 557; 561–2.

63. *Life* 17, no. 420 (Jan. 15, 1891).

64. *Life* 10, no. 238 (July 21, 1887).

65. *Life* 63, no. 1630 (Jan. 22, 1914); 63, no. 1652 (June 25, 1914); 52, no. 1359 (Nov. 12, 1908); 14, no. 355 (Oct. 17, 1889); 19, no. 478 (Feb. 28, 1892); 7, no. 176 (May 13, 1886); 11, no. 272 (March 5, 1888); 53, no. 1372 (Feb.11, 1909)..

66. *Life* 8, no. 314 (Jan. 3, 1889).

67. See *The Complete Notebooks of Henry James*, ed. Leon Edel and Lyall H. Powers (New York: Oxford University Press, 1987), 73–74; and *The American Scene* (New York: St. Martins, 1987), 250.

68. *The American Code of Manners*, 263.

69. Gilman, *Women and Economics*, 118–119.

70. This figure was calculated by comparing two four-year periods: "The number of divorces for the four years 1921–1924 has increased 622 per cent. over the number of divorces in the county [in which Middletown is the chief city] in the four years 1889–1892." As the Lynds remark, Middletown "is no Reno"—that is, there was no appreciable influx of out of state traffic swelling the rolls of the divorced. *Middletown*, 121.

71. Ibid., 126.

72. Elaine Tyler May, "The Pressure to Provide: Class, Consumerism and Divorce in Urban America, 1880–1920," *Journal of Social History* 12 (1978), 182–183.

73. *Life* 10, no. 238 (July 7, 1887).

74. A column in *Life* 41, no. 1073 (May 21, 1903) commented further on this theme, noting the difference between the Episcopal Church's position on marriage and divorce and its parishioners who wished to be counted among the faithful but found it difficult in modern society to toe the official line: "There is only one form of the marriage ceremony in that Church, and that one unquestionably expects a permanent relation. There is no 'barring accidents,' or 'until further notice' clause in it." *Life* opined that wise business practice would dictate that either the Church offer a range of "products" to its consumer-parishioners, or they take their custom elsewhere: "It would be very much for

the accommodation of such persons if the Church kept different degrees of matrimony in stock, and was ready to supply holy matrimony, respectable matrimony, and better-than-nothing matrimony, as the exigencies of cases might demand. But as long as holy matrimony is the only sort it dispenses, it really seems both kinder and wiser for persons whom its rules make ineligible for matrimony of that quality to take their patronage elsewhere . . . ."

75. *Life* 49, no. 1266 (Jan. 31, 1907); 19, no. 475 (Feb. 4, 1892); 27, no. 437 (May 14, 1891).

76. Boone, *Tradition*, 2.

77. Ibid., 9.

78. Ibid., 19.

CHAPTER TWO

From Wedlock to Marriage: Revising Contracts and Resisting Divorce in Henry James's *The Portrait of a Lady* and *The Golden Bowl*

I

To a sketch of *The Portrait of a Lady* recorded in late 1880 or early 1881, Henry James appended a defense against the anticipated "obvious criticism" that he had "not finished" the plot, that he had "not seen the heroine to the end of her situation" but rather had left her *"en l'air"*:

> This is both true and false. The *whole* of anything is never told; you can only take what groups together. What I have done has that unity—it groups together. It is complete in itself—and the rest may be taken up or not, later.[1]

Critical appraisals of this now famous statement have focused upon its expression of Jamesian realism—of what can be known and hence represented in fiction—and his sense of an aesthetic, rather than merely formulaic, unity or completeness. However, the seemingly tagged-on and thus overlooked final phrase "the rest may be taken up or not, later" evokes the author's commitment to an ongoing process of revision, (re)presentation and choice and thus also forms a significant statement, providing important insight into James's artistry as well as his evolving views on marriage and divorce. For if James came to represent the artist's craft in terms of "marriage,"[2] a dynamic union of form and vision, so he envisioned marriage as a process requiring ongoing negotiation between wedded partners. Indeed, *The Golden Bowl* "takes up" and (re)presents what James did not—or could not yet—image at the "end" of *The Portrait of a Lady*: the (re)negotiation of the terms of a marriage contract in Maggie Verver's re-seeing and re-animating the private possibilities inherent in the social form. Thus *The Golden Bowl* also affords James the opportunity to return to unresolved formal matters and craft an unconventional marriage narrative, ostensibly within the confines of the traditional plot trajectory.

Central to James's conception of marriage, whether understood as metaphor or as social fact, is struggle: the struggle to accommodate complex ideas within narrowly defined forms, the struggle to accommodate individuals' multiple and shifting desires within a stubbornly restrictive institution. In social terms, "successful" marriages remain true to this dynamic process of struggle and resist the idealized, comedic formulation of matrimony as a "happily ever after"—an achieved and therefore static equilibrium. Similarly, the concept of contract as expressive of the fixed values of exchange— particularly in the Veblenesque age of the "marriage market"—denies process and thus must be rejected. Importantly, both Isabel Archer and Maggie Verver eventually eschew the fairy-tale constructions as well as the strict contractual basis of marriage and choose to remain in compromised marital relationships, keeping them viable with their dedication to engagement, negotiation and change. For either to opt for divorce would mark not only the end of a marriage, but also the abandonment of hard-won vision integral to each woman's sense of selfhood. Divorce came to signify for James far more than a legal convenience employed by dissatisfied spouses; it also metaphorized any number of modern social ills: the gulf between personal vision and agency; the split between traditional obligations and personal independence; the growing distance between men and women originating in separate sphere ideology but exacerbated by the burgeoning consumer culture. And, by cutting short marriage, divorce also spelt the end of process. To be sure, the traces of divorce as a legal remedy for an ailing social institution exist in both *The Portrait of a*

Lady and *The Golden Bowl*: Henrietta Stackpole counsels Isabel to use the convenient divorce statutes of the American West and free herself from suffocating wedlock, and Mrs. Rance seems willing to follow just such advice and jettison *her* husband in order to become an eligible candidate for Adam Verver and his fortune. However, these proponents and practitioners of divorce tend to be lesser characters (and *of* less character) for whom the burden of struggle would be too great or upon whom its rewards would be lost.

In consigning these "lesser" types to "the great alkali desert of cheap Divorce,"[3] James's position—at least initially—bears a striking resemblance to his father's, Henry James Sr., who had for thirty years "made the philosophy of marriage . . . a special study."[4] For the elder James, marriage was essentially a spiritual union which had lost its original force and significance when reduced to the status of a civil contract in the law. Thus he argued in his enthusiastic preface to the Fourierist tract *Love in the Phalanstery* that the *law* of marriage encouraged promiscuity because it inexorably bound together individuals whose mutual affection had long ceased.[5] Divorce, he reasoned, should be made more rather than less accessible to allow those "to whom marriage was hateful or intolerable to leave its ranks as soon as possible, and so close them up to its undefiled lovers alone." [6] Responding to Horace Greeley's attack asserting that he was anti-marriage, James wrote that, indeed, he had

> invariably aimed to advance the honor of marriage by seeking to free it from certain purely arbitrary and conventional obstructions in reference to divorce. For example, I have always argued against Mr. Greeley that it was not essential to the honor of marriage that two persons should be compelled to live together when they held the reciprocal relation of dog and cat, and that in that state of things divorce might profitably intervene. . . .[7]

By "freely legitimating divorce," he continued, "you place an inducement to mutual fidelity no longer in the base legal bondage of the parties merely, but in their reciprocal inward sweetness or humanity."[8]

Nearly twenty years later, James Sr. reprised these sentiments in a private letter to Harvey Y. Russell of Minnesota's *Saint Paul Daily Press* after Henry Ward Beecher had been accused in the pages of the feminist journal *Woodhull & Clafin's Weekly* of seducing Mrs. Elizabeth Tilton, the wife of the pro-divorce editor of *The Independent*.[9] In it, James Sr. again notes the problematic disjunction between matrimony's spiritual and civil aspects, distinguishing those who come to marriage as a "divine education or discipline" from the "other people" who do not. Yet for the first time it is apparent that even marriage's true devotee might chafe in his marital bonds:

> I marry my wife under the impression that she is literally perfect, and is going to exhaust my capacity of desire ever after. Ere long I discover my mistake . . . I know that it would be possible to make a compromise or enforce a truce between the two interests by clandestinely pursuing pleasure and openly following duty. But my heart revolts from this. . . . The law is holy, just and even good, though it slay me. Yes, death at its hands were better than life at the risk of dishonor at my hands; so I abide by my marriage bond. I see very well that the bond ought to be loosened in the case of other people; that divorce should be allowed more freely than it now is, so that multitudes of people to whom marriage as a divine education or discipline is mere derision and mockery, might become free from its bondage as a civic institution, and so no longer profane it and their souls by clandestinely violating it. But as for me, I will abide in my chains.[10]

The choice to "abide in . . . chains" nevertheless yields compensations which arise from the "natural" differences between male and female. Because she is "the very opposite of everything [he] find[s] in [him]self," "yielding" where he is "obstinate," "patient" where he is "self-willed," and "unconscious" where he is "morbidly self-conscious," he is drawn to his wife in the physical embodiment of a spiritual allegory of enlightenment:

> I see that there is no other way for the Divine to get hold of me, at all events, but by first binding me in sensuous love to this noble woman, and then letting into my interiors from the *camera obscura* of her person the accommodated blaze of his eternal purity and beauty, that I might see myself as I truly am, and know Him. . . . Thus marriage is to me my truest divine revelation." [11]

Surely, however, this is marriage as wed*lock*. Having discovered his "mistake," marriage's "true devotee" finds no possibility of "truce" or "compromise"; "pleasure" is invariably at odds with "duty" rather than something which might be derived from it. The holy law of marriage in fact exacts a figurative death from its devotee by denying the very human, pleasure-seeking aspect of his personality. Although marriage leads to "divine revelation," the image of physical bondage prevails—a bondage implicitly figured in the male-female hierarchy, itself a "chain" of being, conveying the overwhelming sense of enclosure, fixity and entrapment.[12]

It is here, then, that the son takes issue with the father, rejecting the stoic stance which creates wedlock out of marriage and deadlocks spouses within a sexual hierarchy which by its very nature denies the potential dynamism within the form. For the younger James, the rewards of remaining intimately and thus difficultly wed are won not by mere endurance, but by developing a consciousness that keeps matters between spouses constantly in play. And though this commitment to process exacts a toll at least as costly as that paid by those in marital chains, self-possession—rather than possession by the spirit or by others' plots and plans—rewards characters of the magnitude of an Isabel Archer or Maggie Verver.

II

Surely, to observe that Isabel Archer's choice of the "very straight path" back to Rome and the detestable Gilbert Osmond fails to evoke much sympathy in modern readers is to be guilty of understatement.[13] How, we wonder, could "one so fond of [her] liberty" (PL 30) and so confirmed in her desire to "do great things" (PL 101) seem, in the end, to renounce her freedom and retreat from her fate, defined initially as congress in a world "of brightness, of free expansion, of irresistible action" (PL 53)? James's aesthetic determination to leave his heroine "*en l'air*" at this most critical juncture because "the whole of anything is never told" leaves her also at the mercy of many, often punishing, explanations for her return. Thus Isabel's "knowing" ("She had not known where to turn; but she knew now. There was a very straight path") is discounted by critics, her agency transformed instead into a variety of personal and moral infirmities: her "fear" of sexuality, her "treacherous servility," her fastidious aversion to publicity, her inability to grapple with the difficulties of divorce law.[14] But to read defeat—whatever its source—into Isabel's action is also to assume that Osmond and the ancient city of Rome function inevitably as the loci of subjection and adherence to empty form and, more importantly, that Caspar Goodwood and America represent her best chance for freedom and personal fulfillment. Instead, I would like to suggest a reading of *The Portrait of a Lady* as James's critique of America's celebrated tendency to elevate individual liberty over obligation or tradition and its faith that radical breaks—for which the American War for Independence is paradigmatic—are sufficient to secure such liberty. Thus viewed, Henrietta Stackpole's counsel to make use of the western states' divorce laws and Goodwood's assertion that "a woman made to suffer is justified in anything" to free herself in fact offer Isabel only illusions of freedom. Their "solutions" neglect her abiding sense of responsibility in the matter of her marriage, and fail to recognize that marriage itself, with its institutionalized inequalities, is the focus of her concern, and not the proprieties of escaping its claims. What Isabel "knows" as she returns to Osmond is that personal liberty cannot be gained by disengagement from struggle, nor can equality in marriage be won by divorce.

*

As Adeline Tintner points out, only one date is mentioned in *The Portrait of a Lady;* the date, 1876, which appears twice within the space of a few paragraphs, effectively divides the novel in half, marking as it does the end of James's focus on Isabel's several opportunities for love and adventure and the beginning of his attention to the singleness of her fate in marriage. As the date of the official Centennial, the celebration of American independence from Great Britain, the reiteration of 1876 at this point in the narrative marks the irony of Isabel's situation: the freedom-loving heroine finds herself after a few short years of marriage to be trapped in the "house of darkness, the house of dumbness, the house of suffocation" (*PL* 353). Indeed, Alfred Habegger goes so far as to characterize *Portrait* as a "countercentennial novel" insofar as it reveals that the much heralded freedom accorded American women was but an illusory one.[15] Certainly, Tintner's argument that James thought of this novel in terms of the Centennial and of his heroine as the representative American female is persuasive:

> James seems to have begun to think about *The Portrait* in the very year of the Centennial (although he was not actually to write it until 1880), for we have a letter to Howells, dated October 24, 1876, in which he writes, "My novel is to be an *Americana,*—the adventure in Europe of a female Newman." James continues to think of Isabel Archer as "an *Americana"* for he calls her that again in a letter to his brother William dated July 23, 1878, at the time he is "just completing, by the way, a counterpart to D[aisy] M[iller] for the *Cornhill."* The counterpart is, of course, "An International Episode," a specifically Centennial story. James goes on to say, "The 'great novel' you ask about is only begun; I am doing other things just now. It is the history of an *Americana*—a female counterpart to Newman . . . and I hope to be able to get to work on it this autumn."[16]

Tintner also notes the parallel between the pervasive Centennial image of a young woman dressed in the stars and stripes and James' own representation of Isabel—through Ralph Touchett's hastily sketched caricature—as Columbia draped "in the folds of the national banner."[17] Indeed, with her frequent declarations of personal independence and her determination "to be as happy as possible," Isabel embodies, at least initially, the Revolutionary spirit commemorated by the 1876 Exposition. Yet to attribute James' interest in and foregrounding of the Centennial year merely for the ironic accent it adds to our appreciation of Isabel's plight overlooks the extent to which the rhetoric and ideals of the 1776 Revolution shaped marital expectations and informed, well into the nineteenth century, America's divorce debate.

The American Revolution against British patriarchal authority, grounded as it was in contractual terms that highlighted voluntary consent, reciprocal duties and the possibility of dissolution, "provided a paradigm by which Americans for the next two hundred years would understand and set forth the claims of both individual and national independence."[18] Perhaps because Thomas Paine and his pamphleteering brethren tended to describe the crisis with England in terms of a domestic dispute, revolutionary ideals found almost simultaneous expression in petitions for and legal writings about divorce, an argumentative strategy which continued long after national independence had been won.[19] The notion of companionate marriage based in reciprocal duties and satisfactions was in accord with the period's republican sentiments; divorce petitioners maintained that an individual was morally justified in breaking away from a marriage partner if the union lacked mutual fulfillment and happiness. Concepts such as "tyranny," "misrule," "injustice," and the "happiness of the individual" were employed by republican divorce seekers in proclaiming their rebellion against the unjust rule of a spouse.[20] Thus a Connecticut petitioner, Abigail Dayton, asked for divorce on the grounds that her husband of twelve years destroyed her "sanguine Expectations of enjoying the Happiness that usually attends the Marriage states," and had become "instead of a Bosum friend . . . an inveterate Enemy." According to Abigail's petition, Israel Dayton had thereby "dissolved the Marriage Covenant . . . every valuable Purpose, for which the marriage Relation was originally intended, is under present Circumstances, defeated."[21] Thomas Jefferson, while preparing a brief for Dr. James Blair of Williamsburg, argued that the Virginia legislature should grant the state's first absolute divorce because contracts which opposed the will and desire of the parties involved were "unproductive" and thus "dissoluble." He maintained that "to chain a man to misery till death" was as cruel to the individual as it was damaging to the institution of marriage itself. While Jefferson obviously had a particular man in mind, his arguments for divorce also attend to the interests of the generic man—and woman. Indeed, according to Jefferson's notes on the subject, "divorce prevents and cures domestic quarrels," "preserves the liberty of affection," and, by nullifying their *feme covert* status, "restores women to their natural right of equality."[22] Although Jefferson implicitly acknowledges that there is something in the marriage contract which alienates a woman from her "natural" sovereign self, he did not propose a revision in marital roles or rights. Instead, keeping faith with the model which secured national freedom and sovereignty, he proposed that a married woman's abridged rights could be regained only by dissolving matrimonial bonds.

The displacement of patriarchalism with contractualism in American ideals and jurisprudence also marked a shift in emphasis from the public function and utility of marriage as a institution which provided accessible local models of authority and order to its private aspect as a domestic partnership. English legal tradition had defined marriage as a civil contract, stressing "the secular, contractual nature of matrimony while at the same time endorsing strict public nuptial vigilance."[23] Although post-revolution domestic law continued to portray matrimony as a civil contract, the emphasis was increasingly on the word "contract" and the mutual consent thus implied. Society was thought to be best served by the family when the individuals comprising it fulfilled their obligations willingly rather than by compulsion. In the following passage from a 1791 divorce petition brought by John Christian Smith, the claims of the individual and society regarding marriage seem balanced, placed as they are on either side of the coordinating conjunction "and." However, their relative position as sentence elements foregrounds the individual's plight and thereby establishes the argumentative drift:

> Since Marriage was instituted for the purpose of promoting the happiness of individuals and the good of society and since the attainment of those objects depends entirely on the Domestic harmony of the parties connected and their living together in a perfect union of inclination interests and affections, when it becomes impossible for them to remain longer united when mutual wretchedness must be the consequence of continuing their connection or the purposes for which marriage was instituted entirely faile in its influence and the good of Society no less than the well being of individuals requires that it should be dissolved and that the parties should be left free to form such other domestic connections as may contribute to their felicity.[24]

The prominence given to contractualism signaled a challenge to the traditional gendered hierarchies of family by models which stressed reciprocal obligations and, in some instances, advocated even egalitarian domestic relations. A self-proclaimed "Matrimonial Republican" defined this perception in the 1792 *Ladies Magazine*, objecting to the word obey in the marriage service because "it is a general word, without limitations or definitions." Counter to law and custom, she extended to marriage the concept of contract as an exchange between equals, insisting that "obedience between man and wife ought to be mutual. Marriage ought never to be considered a contract between superior and inferior, but as the reciprocal union of interests, and implied partnership of interests, where all differences are accommodated by conference; and decision admits of no retrospect."[25] However, this strategy of extending the terms which governed public business contracts to erase the inequalities of status between husband and wife proved ineffective. As Mary L. Shanley has observed, "the 'contractual' element in marriage [was] simply the *consent* of each party to marry the other. . . . To contract a marriage was to consent to a status which in its essence was hierarchical and unalterable."[26]

Without any change to the existing laws governing marital dissolution, the overall numbers of divorce petitions increased with the onset of the War for Independence, and women—in the spirit of a Philadelphia patriot who declared herself "born for liberty"—filed for matrimonial freedom in greater numbers than ever before. As Nancy Cott has observed, "[t]he growth of petitions seems to indicate that more individuals were asserting control over the direction their lives and were refusing to be ruled by unhappy fates. . . . In the Revolutionary period, this kind of self-assertion may have gone along with an enhanced sense of citizenship and legal rights."[27] By the mid-nineteenth century, women's petitions initiated the majority of divorce proceedings, a trend which continued into the twentieth century.[28]

By the mid-nineteenth century, however, a different ideology, formed in reaction to the forces of industrialization and sectional discord, challenged the discourse of republican individualism within the family, asserting the permanency of the marriage tie, the sanctity of the home and the dependence of civilization and nationhood upon the united family.[29] Indeed, as historian William O'Neill has suggested, none of these ideas was new, but they did not become so widely accepted until the Victorian era "when they quickly received such general support that men found it impossible to believe that customs had ever been otherwise."[30] Nevertheless, the mid to late nineteenth-century still found social reformers eager to counter the period's moralists with republican arguments for "decreasing [the impediments] to divorce."[31] In the same month that Henry James wrote to his brother about the projected "history of an *Americana*," D. A. Gorton published "The Ethics of Marriage and Divorce," a review of John Stuart Mill's *The Subjection of Women* and Ernest Legouve's *Histoire morale des femmes* in which he reprises familiar republican sentiments, arguing that "the only quality of wedlock of abiding concern to the State [is that] which promises the individual enduring satisfaction."[32] Although I can claim no evidence that James was familiar with the particular essay, it nevertheless addresses the very issues which would figure prominently in *Portrait*: individual happiness in conflict with social claims and equality between partners in marriage. Certainly, Gorton's essay would have interested James, for not only had Henry James Sr. written extensively on the "divorce problem," both father and brother had responded to Mill's *Subjection*—and dismissed it for its "sentimental" ideal of equality between husband and wife.[33]

Gorton's essay, guided by secular rather than spiritual concerns, typifies the arguments widely circulated by the period's pro-divorce contingent. Recognizing mutuality and individual fulfillment as "essential" to marriage, he argues that any union bereft of such values is not a marriage at all "except in the fiction of [the] law."[34] Like his revolution-minded forefather Jefferson, he affirms that it is the consenting individual will alone which actuates, and thus validates, the marital contract, and not the authority of the state. Also in keeping with Jefferson's apparent concern for female equality, Gorton notes that a woman's subject status in marriage "is a serious offense to justice and morality" and concurs with Legouve's declaration that "divorce will be necessary to [teach] her liberty."[35] Even as Gorton bows to Victorian preoccupations, strategically seeming to focus upon the deleterious effect of bad marriages upon society, his abiding concern for the individual is much in evidence:

> To bind two souls with indissoluble bands who insist on hating each other, and that, too, by reason of causes independent of their control or responsibility . . . leads to aggravations of the evils of domestic dissentions and crime under which society suffers, and against which the moralist idly prays. It conduces directly to the practice of deceit and the nurture of hypocrisy. That the parties to such a bond may not appear disreputable, they live in discord at home and wear the garb of felicity abroad. Nor is this, demoralizing as it is, the worst. There are those who maintain the semblance of conjugal fidelity to the public, but who practice conjugal infidelity in secret; who, in other words, do in private and concealment that which would be considered unlawful

and wrong if done openly—to the end that private morality may appear to be that which in reality it is not, and can never be under the current inflexible rule of divorce. . . . The scandals of the day are but ripples on the social wave; the incidents on life's stage, which by the accidents of indiscretion appear on the surface now and then, to indicate the character of that which subsists behinds the scenes, and is acted between the plays. It is all wrong, but it is as inevitable as it is wrong and disreputable, so long as the law compels people to become infamous before they can become divorced. [36]

With its portrayal of desperate spousal discord, the dissimulation exacted in response to customary notions of marriage, and the threat of public infamy attached to dissolving that private relation, this passage seems to foreshadow Isabel Archer's own marital situation. Although in the beginning she places supreme value on her independence and an inner life "always in harmony with the most pleasing impression she should produce" (*PL* 55), she finds herself bound to a thoroughly unsympathetic husband, hiding her hurt behind a mask of studied serenity so that her expression seems perpetually "fixed and mechanical" (*PL* 323). As she asks herself, "what ought *she* to do? When a man hated his wife, what did it lead to? . . . They were strangely married, in all events, and it was a horrible life" (*PL* 356).

*

From the novel's outset, Isabel clearly embodies the idea of liberty. The ambiguous assessment of her as "quite independent" (*PL* 24) in Mrs. Touchett's staccato telegram launches a lively discussion around the possible constructions the phrase might bear and the disposition of a young woman so characterized. Indeed, fearing her niece's freedom-loving manners might lead to some breach of propriety, Mrs. Touchett takes it upon herself to warn Isabel against "taking . . . too much liberty" (*PL* 67) in her relations. But because "the idea of diminished liberty was particularly disagreeable to her" (*PL* 104), Isabel is wary of the infringement upon her independence that marriage might bring. As she tells Ralph, "I don't see what harm there is in wishing not to tie myself. I don't want to begin life by marrying. There are other things a woman can do" (*P L* 132). She rejects both Warburton's and Goodwood's proposals, asserting "I like my liberty too much. If there's a thing in the world I'm fond of . . . it's my personal independence" (*PL*

140). Ironically, although she marries Osmond believing she has found the man with whom she might achieve "the union of great knowledge with great liberty" (*PL* 397), she is deprived of both. After three years of marriage, Ralph finds "the free keen girl had become quite another person" (*PL* 324) and wonders "what had become of her high estimate of her independence?" (*PL* 325).

Thwarted in her relationship with Osmond, Isabel must re-examine the nature of her much-advertised liberty and her characteristically American belief in the exercise of agency free from external influences. Although she maintains that "she had married to please herself"(*PL* 289), Isabel at last concedes that she has been trapped in a web of others' interests and used, "a dull unreverenced tool," to advance their causes and satisfy their desires. Confirmed in this knowledge, Isabel nevertheless cannot countenance a break with Osmond; she reverences her marriage vow even as she dreads the authority it grants her husband over her:

> She had not yet undertaken to act in direct opposition to his wishes; he was her appointed and inscribed master; she gazed at moments with a sort of incredulous blankness at this fact. It weighed on her imagination, however; constantly present to her mind were all the traditionary decencies and sanctities of marriage. The idea of violating them filled her with shame as well as dread .... Almost anything seemed preferable to repudiating the most serious act—the single sacred act— of her life. (*PL* 379)

Osmond, with his appeal to the "decency" and the "honor of the thing"—concerns which arise from his passion for maintaining appearances—also insists on the "us" and "we" of their marriage, arguing as Isabel herself had that "we should accept the consequences of our actions" (*PL* 438).[37] However, Osmond's use of the plural pronoun does not signify a unity of purpose or will, but instead invokes the fiction of marital unity upheld by law and custom in which the wife's personality and interests are subsumed by her husband's. In this context, the "we" connotes no more than "I," and represents a unilateral pronouncement of Osmond's desire. Thus the consequences of which he speaks are distinctly different: for Osmond, the cost of living "decently" with his wife means the vigilant governance of a will no longer in sympathy with his own; for Isabel, it means a bondage and submission every bit as complete as that exacted from his daughter, Pansy.

Certainly, if anyone would seem justified in seeking divorce based on republican principles of an individual's sovereignty, Isabel would—and so her friends tell her. Twice Henrietta exhorts Isabel to remedy her unhappiness and save herself ("before her character gets spoiled") by leaving Osmond in order to make use of the liberal divorce codes common to the states and territories of the American West. "Nothing," Henrietta assures Isabel, "is more common in our Western cities, and it's to them, after all, that we must look in the future." James, however, suggests the answer lies elsewhere, for Henrietta is silenced, "her argument . . . not concern[ing] this history" (*PL* 410).[38] Goodwood similarly appeals to Isabel's native instincts about the sanctity of the individual's right to happiness and the need to answer only to oneself for steps taken toward that end:

> Why should you go back—why should you go through that ghastly form? . . . Why shouldn't we be happy—when it's here before us, when it's so easy . . . You must save what you can of your life; you mustn't lose it all simply because you've lost a part. . . . I swear, as I stand here, that a woman deliberately made to suffer is justified in anything in life—in going down into the streets if that will help her! I know how you suffer, and that's why I'm here. We can do absolutely as we please; to whom under the sun do we owe anything? What is it that holds us, what is it that has the smallest right to interfere in such a question as this? Such a question is between ourselves—and to say that is to settle it! Were we born to rot in our misery—were we born to be afraid? (*PL* 481)

Entreaties so constituted well might strike a responsive chord in Isabel, for if at times she conceives of marriage as an irrevocable "sacred act" independent of personal circumstances and concerns, she also thinks of it in terms of a contract from which she might withdraw, given the particulars of its origin and the unhappiness generated by its consummation. Indeed, feeling herself the very type of the "woman deliberately made to suffer," Isabel "seemed to see . . . the rapid approach of the day when she would have to take back something she had solemnly bestown" (*PL* 379)—the vow validated by her consenting will. In demanding of Osmond, "[h]ow can you speak of an indissoluble union . . . when you accuse me of falsity?" (*PL* 439), Isabel employs the language of reciprocity to suggest—much as Abigail Dayton had in her own divorce petition—that the terms of their contract had been abridged.

Faced with Goodwood's entreaties, however, Isabel at the last places marriage into a category where no appeal to formal legal "repair" (*PL* 334), "redress," (*PL* 350), or "remedy" (*PL* 353) may be made for the violated marital relation; indeed, she—and James—rejects a simple contractual basis for marriage, realizing instead that "[c]ertain obligations were involved in the very fact of marriage . . . [that] were quite independent of the quantity of enjoyment extracted from it" (*PL* 473). Thus Goodwood's passionate plea goes down to defeat; as Isabel had earlier observed to Henrietta, "one can't change" (*PL* 400) by repudiating one's choices and obligations, no matter how circumstances have altered them.

That Isabel does painfully inch toward authentic, internal change might be charted in terms of both the literal and figurative thresholds upon which she stands during the course of the novel. In her childhood conduct, Isabel's flirtation with the threshold, with the outskirts of new or forbidden experiences [Rosier recalls that she "would persist in going so near the edge" (*PL* 183)] betokens a precocious independence as well as a determination to decide for herself; in adulthood, however, such a posture signals a mood akin to disengaged spectatorship—a freedom *from* entanglement rather than a freedom *for* exploration, choice and commitment. Indeed, just like "The Transitional American Woman" Kate Gannet Wells describes in her December 1880 *Atlantic Monthly* essay (running, therefore, simultaneously with *Portrait's* serialization), Isabel finds herself the inheritor of her country's "progressive desire," a mood that has brought about "emancipation from the old lines of conduct" without defining new paths. Thus liberated, Isabel, along with her American sisters, exhibits a "restlessness, wandering purpose and self-consciousness" and feels the impulse to always be "'in' or 'at' something" new.[39] Like so many of her countrymen—indeed, like James's quintessential American, Christopher Newman—that impulse is answered by deciding to "see for herself," and so Isabel begins her new life poised "in the ample doorway"(*PL* 25) at Gardencourt, "constantly staring"(*PL* 41), "looking at everything," but refraining from participation:

> She had been looking all around her again ... with a comprehensiveness of observation ... her head was erect, her eye lighted, her flexible figure turned itself easily this way and that, in sympathy with the alertness with which she evidently caught impressions. Her impressions were numerous, and they were all reflected in a clear, still smile. (*PL* 26)

James goes to great lengths to demonstrate that Isabel has an "idea" about rather than an understanding of "seeing"; for although she looks at everything about her, she fails to incorporate those sights into herself as experienced things. Rather, she is like a sapling swaying in the breeze or a lovely pool—clear and still—that does no more than reflect that which moves across its surface, preferring to see "without judging" (*PL* 39) and, as Ralph observes, without feeling (*PL* 132). Rather, Isabel maintains her position at the edge of experience, never wholly committing herself to the new paths in which she professes an interest. Even her initial entrance into Osmond's hilltop villa reveals this reticence; despite the enticing influences of her host's charm and the "soft" Tuscan spring, Isabel's first thoughts center vaguely upon escape, sensing that "once you were in [Osmond's house], you would need an act of energy to get out" (*PL* 213). Significantly, this feeling persists, and although she ostensibly commits herself to Osmond, to participation in the "magnificent form" of marriage, Isabel remains on the threshold: "What had happened was something that for a week past her imagination had been going forward to meet; but when it came, she stopped—that sublime principle somehow broke down. . . . Her imagination . . . now hung back: there was at last a vague space it couldn't cross . . ." (*PL* 260). When Rosier encounters Isabel some years after her marriage, he again finds her in her accustomed position near the edge, "framed in the gilded doorway" of her resplendent Roman apartments with the arrested air of someone "able to wait" (*PL* 303). Throughout, then, Isabel's aloofness—her willingness, if you will, to stand at the brink of any number of thresholds without actually occupying the "rooms" to which they lead—is conflated with her sense of independence, so that it denotes the failure to fully engage with experience as well as a carefully maintained absence of the past:

> She had a desire to leave the past behind her and, as she said to herself, to begin afresh. This desire indeed was not a birth of the present occasion; it was as familiar as the sound of rain upon the window and it had led to her beginning afresh a great many times. (*PL* 39)

By the novel's end, however, Isabel has markedly changed. As she breaks away from Goodwood's seductive embrace and regains the Gardencourt threshold on which she began, she makes the essential transition from "looking" to "knowing," from the literal darkness of her surroundings to what must be termed enlightenment:

> She never looked about her; she only darted from the spot. There were lights in the windows of the house; they shone far across the lawn. In an extraordinarily short time—for the distance was considerable—she had moved through darkness (for she saw nothing) and reached the door. Here only she paused. She looked all about her; she listened a little; then she put her hand on the latch. She had not known where to turn; but she knew now. There was a very straight path. (*PL* 482)

Isabel's refusal of Goodwood's offer, rather than a capitulation to tradition or a flight from sexuality, constitutes a rejection of that restless desire to discover yet another threshold so as to "begin afresh." Divorce—which Goodwood's solution demands and which Henrietta advises—is but another version of that threshold in that it would allow Isabel to repudiate her marital commitment before she had fully grappled with its problems—or its possibilities. The fact that by the 1870s liberal divorce law had become a well-known feature and attraction of the West suggests that the tendency to achieve "freedom" by means of a break with the old life was more than an episode in the national history, but had become a prevalent mode in the conduct of American life.[40] The West thus suggests but another threshold, a place where one could conveniently break free of one's obligations and past. By adopting such a model and jettisoning her history, Isabel would rid herself not only of Osmond and their "horrible life," but would also stand to lose Ralph and the hard-won realization they shared about the nature of their bond. For Isabel's (re)union with Ralph, after so much hurt and misunderstanding, suggests her readiness to abandon the threshold, to "know" and to act upon the knowledge that a union of hearts and minds is not a static achievement, but a process requiring continual effort and engagement; significantly, their rapprochement also prefigures the emotional struggle and negotiation which must be the result of her return to Rome.

*

I would like to focus once again on Philadelphia's Centennial Exposition in order to discuss several features of the 1876 celebration that bear upon Isabel's status as James's *Americana*, his representative American woman. Although James was living in Paris at the time of the United States Centennial, we need not suppose he was unaware of its proceedings; indeed, he evinced a hearty interest in the celebration, enjoining his brother William to write of his "adventure" in Philadelphia and, later, thanking him for doing so: "Your long and charming letter of July 5 [1876] . . . with its superior criticism of so many things, the Philadelphia Exhibition especially, interested me extremely . . . . What you said of the American pictures there gave me great pleasure . . . ."[41] Not content to receive only his brother's account, James also wrote to William Dean Howells of his interest in the fair: "I suppose you will write something about Philadelphia—I hope so, as otherwise I am afraid I shall know nothing about it" (*HJL* 54). James's concern proved unfounded: there was much to read about the Centennial on both sides of the Atlantic. In the July, 1876, *Atlantic Monthly* (in which an installment of *The American* is featured), Howell's essay "A Sennight of the Centennial" appeared, and through December the magazine also ran, in substantial monthly installments, an essay detailing the "Characteristics of the International Fair." The opening and closing ceremonies of the fair as well as the Fourth of July festivities were reported in the Paris and London papers, giving James ample opportunity to read for himself the events celebrating his country's centennial.[42]

The Centennial Exposition aimed to fulfill a dual purpose: first, it was to commemorate one hundred years of independence from Britain; second, it was meant to showcase for the world the young nation's vast material wealth and technological achievement. To carry out this latter goal adequately, a range of exhibit halls was erected on the grounds of Philadelphia's Fairmount Park, including the Machinery Building, the Agricultural Hall, the Horticultural Hall, the Memorial Hall (a gallery for painting and sculpture), the Main Building (devoted to both American and international exhibits), and smaller buildings sponsored by individual states to display their distinctive natural and human resources and achievements. Among these more modest structures was the Woman's Pavilion, "originated and paid for by the women of America, and devoted to the exclusive exhibition of the products of woman's art, skill and industry."[43] Period accounts of these products tended to focus on items which reinforced women's essentially domestic character—needlework displays, sewing machines, a cooking school, even sculptures formed of creamery butter; the Pavilion itself, like a well-bred lady, was reported to be "a very neat and tasteful edifice,"[44] "distinctly noticeable, without being pretentious."[45] Despite the well-mannered appearance and the well-intentioned exhibits of the Woman's Pavilion, Howells could not conceal his anxiety over this display of female independence: "Those accustomed to think of women as the wives, mothers, and sisters of men will be puzzled to know why the ladies wished to separate their work from that of the rest of the human race. . . . It seems not yet the moment for the better half of our species to take their stand apart. . . ."[46] Howells was most likely unaware of the facts which led to the separate women's building—facts that even recent histories of the Centennial often fail to mention: the women had not sought a space apart, but had from the first intended to be part of the general display of American arts and inventions housed in the Exposition's Main Building. Rather, they had been forced out by the fair's organizers; as Elizabeth Cady Stanton wryly observed, "[t]he Woman's Pavilion upon the Centennial grounds was an afterthought, as theologians claim woman herself to have been."[47]

In 1873, thirteen Philadelphia women (one for each of the original thirteen states) were invited by the Citizen's Centennial Board of Finance "to cooperate with them in the endeavor to create popular enthusiasm and to add to the subscriptions for Centennial stock."[48] The Women's Centennial Executive Committee, with Mrs. E. D.. Gillespie as its head, was thus formed. This Committee, motivated by "love for our land and . . . ambition for our sex," secured a promise for ample exhibit space in the planned Main Building in exchange for its fundraising efforts. In the next two years, the Women's Committee sponsored several remunerative events and succeeded well enough to contribute over $100,000 for the centennial fair—more than any other group. But in June, 1875, Mrs. Gillespie received a letter from A. T. Goshorn, the Director-General of the Centennial Committee, informing her that there would be insufficient space to accommodate a "Woman's Department" within the Main Building because

> [i]t is now obvious, from the demands that have been made by foreign countries for space in the Main Exhibition Building, that the space allotted to the United States in this building will be insufficient for all the articles that were originally intended to be displayed in it . . . recognizing the noble and efficient work the women of the country have already accomplished in behalf of the centennial celebration, we feel encouraged to make the suggestion that it would be a most worthy and attractive feature of the Exhibition if they could secure a sufficient sum for the construction of a separate building in the Park which . . . would most fittingly represent the position, energy and accomplishments of the women of America.[49]

Discouraged by such treatment but unwilling to be left out of the historical proceedings, the Women's Committee raised the money and erected a separate structure—emblematic indeed of the "position . . . of the women of America."

The status of women as outsiders—whether in regard to the Exhibition's Main Building or the country's mainstream affairs—was further illustrated when Stanton, "representing 20,000,000 disenfranchised citizens of America" as president of the National Woman Suffrage Association (NWSA), asked the Centennial Committee for permission to present, after the Declaration of Independence had been recited in the Fourth of July ceremonies, a Woman's Declaration of Rights: "We do not ask to read our declaration, only to present it to the President of the United States, that it may become an historical part of the proceedings."[50] The request was denied, and the terms of the refusal leave little doubt that women's participation—an exercise of "citizenship" in the day's events— was at odds with both national and patriarchal interests:

It seems a very slight request, but our programme is published, our speakers engaged, our arrangements for the day decided upon . . . we propose to celebrate what we have done in the last one hundred years, not what we have failed to do . . . I understand the full significance of your very slight request. If granted, it would be the event of the day—the topic of discussion to the exclusion of all others.[51]

Stanton reflected bitterly that while "foreign potentates and the myrmidons of monarchical institutions . . . found no difficulty in securing recognition and places upon that platform," "representative womanhood was denied." An editorial in the Toledo *Ballot Box* used the incident to demonstrate that "the women [of the United States] have no country—their rights are disregarded, their appeals ignored, their protests scorned, they are treated as children who do not comprehend their own wants, and as slaves whose crowning duty is obedience."[52]

Disobedience, however, proved the watchword for women on July 4, 1876. After making "a very discourteous interruption" (which, as the New York *Tribune* went on to predict, "prefigure[d] new forms of violence and disregard for order which may accompany the participation of women in . . . politics"), representatives of the NWSA led by Susan B. Anthony seized the platform and read to the assembly their Declaration of Rights. These protesters must have born a striking, if ironic, resemblance to a commemorative medal struck for the Centennial which employed the familiar icon of Columbia as a young female figure, for the design on the medal's obverse "represents the Genius of American Independence rising from a recumbent position, grasping with her right hand the sword which is to enforce her demands, and raising her left in appealing pride to . . . the original colonies. . . ."[53] Thus embodying the spirit for which they provided the form but which social propriety had always denied them, these women observed that "the history of our country . . . has been a series of assumptions and usurpations of power over women." The authors of the protest followed the familiar structure and wording of the Declaration of Independence, enumerating the wrongs suffered by American women whose rights as citizens had been abridged on the basis of sex and "in direct opposition to the principles of just government, acknowledged by the United States as its foundation." Significantly, this declaration explicitly links women's lack of social, economic and civil power with her subject status in the domestic hierarchy, arguing that by "establishing an aristocracy of sex" that aligns public policy with private sphere ideology, the government had "impose[d] upon the women of this nation a more absolute and cruel despotism than monarchy." To redress these wrongs, the declaration demands—not independence in accordance with historical precedent—but freedom, freedom for women to exercise their citizenship as equal partners in the life of the nation:

> . . . we declare our faith in the principles of self-government; our full equality with man in natural rights; that woman was made first for her own happiness, with the absolute right to herself—to all the opportunities and advantages life affords for her complete development; and we deny the dogma of the centuries, incorporated into the codes of all nations—that woman was made for man—her best interests, in all cases, sacrificed to his will . . . . We ask justice, we ask equality, we ask that the civil and political rights that belong to citizens of the United States, be guaranteed to us and our daughters forever. [54]

This statement, the Declaration's closing salvo, seeks to overturn the model of domestic relations which, by denying a wife self-sovereignty, served as the basis of women's civil and political disenfranchisement. Thus in considering women's enforced position as "outsiders" in 1876 and their demand to be taken "inside," so to speak, as equal participants in the national enterprise, it becomes apparent that reform must occur in the home, that for the sake of the nation's republican principles domestic hierarchy must give way to domestic partnership.[55]

If the public nature of the women's protest would have troubled James, he nevertheless might well have agreed with their urging greater equality between men and women and between husbands and wives, for his works repeatedly focus upon the lack of spousal partnership as the central feature and problem of American marriages. In "An International Episode" (1878), a story which has generally been read as a celebration of the social freedom possible for American women which is denied their English counterparts (Tintner calls it a "specifically Centennial story" for this reason), the separate spheres inhabited by husbands and wives are evident and seemingly irreconcilable. While Mrs. Westgate takes care of the social front, entertaining her husband's British acquaintances at fashionable Newport, Mr. Westgate remains in town, "dreadfully confined to New York" and business.[56] Westgate's arrival in Newport becomes a matter for daily speculation, but he remains tied to the office:

> Mr. Westgate, all this time, hadn't, as they said at Newport, "come on." His wife more than once announced that she expected him on the morrow; but on the morrow she wandered about a little, with a telegram in her jeweled fingers pronouncing it too "fiendish" he should let his business so dreadfully absorb him. . . . And she went on to explain, while she kept that slow-paced circulation which enabled her well-adjusted skirts to display themselves so advantageously, that unfortunately in America there was no leisure-class and that the universal passionate surrender of the men to business-questions and business-questions only, as if they were the all in life, would have to be stemmed. (*IE* 326–327)

If husband could be incorporated, albeit somewhat infrequently, into the domestic/social territory, wives were irrevocably outside their spouses' world. In 1892 James again remarked on the lack of common ground between men and women, between husbands and wives, characterizing the distant relation as one of "divorce [which] is rapidly becoming a gulf—an abyss of inequality, the like of which has never before been seen under the sun" (*NB* 73–74). James reprises this theme once more in *The American Scene* (1907), imaging the schism at the heart of American marriage in terms of the woman whose "freedom" results from being left outside to do as she will, "after watching the Man, the deep American man, retire into his tent and let down the flap."[57]

Of course, the failure of partnership in marriage is at issue in *Portrait* as well, from the Touchett's "unhappy experiment in matrimony" (*PL* 23)[58] to the "horrible life" endured by Isabel at the hands of her "appointed and inscribed master." It has been suggested that because Isabel is "refined by her oppressive life with Osmond,"[59] her return to Rome—tantamount to an acceptance of the domestic hierarchy which would place her under the sway of her master-husband—validates Henry James Sr.'s views on marriage. While Henry

James Sr. argued for a greater freedom of divorce for those who failed to acknowledge marriage's spiritual significance, he was sure that those who recognized marriage as a divine discipline would resist the idea of divorce as inimical to its sacred aspect. Certainly, James Jr.'s depiction of Isabel as one subject to a "master" invokes his father's proclamation, "I shall abide in my chains"; however, I believe he does so in order to interrogate the male-centered ideology in which the spiritual benefit resulting from such marital discipline accrues to the husband alone; the wife—a being essentialized by her dependent, yielding nature—exists merely as the conduit for her husband's enlightenment. Indeed, a husband's rewards were not only spiritual, but social, economic and political as well. Disadvantaged according to the law and custom of marriage, women bore much different consequences than did men in "choosing" their marital chains.

Given the sympathetic treatment Isabel receives (emphasized by narrator's reiterated appeals *not* to take her lightly), *Portrait* might well be the son's critique of his father's (and the patriarchal) tendency to exclude women from his formulations or to deny them anything but contingent reality. After all, what Isabel aspires to in marriage—and what she is so effectively denied by Osmond—is participation, partnership, and in this she echoes the theme struck by the "Matrimonial Republican" and reiterated by the women of the centennial. From the first, Isabel images her marriage as "a magnificent form" based in a symmetry of spousal accord and effort. Indeed the traditional wifely position of dependence, of subjecthood, seems overturned in Isabel's conception, for she believed "she could marry [Osmond] with a kind of pride" in that "she was not only taking, she was giving" (*PL* 292). When, after her nightlong vigil before the parlor fire, Isabel recognizes how drastically her own domestic situation has deviated from her ideal, the vision of marriage as a reciprocal relation reasserts itself. She remembers thinking that

> She would launch his boat for him; she would be his providence; it would be a good thing to love him. And she had loved him, she had so anxiously and so ardently given herself—a good deal for what she found in him, but a good deal also for what she brought him and what might enrich the gift . . . [she felt] the happiness of a woman who felt

that she was a contributor, that she came with charged hands. (*PL* 351)

Thus Isabel must be seen as something more than an ironic Columbia, for when she turns away from Goodwood to recross the threshold leading back to Rome and Osmond, she reclaims her vision—albeit cleansed of its rosy idealism—of participatory union. Her return promises the sort of engagement and negotiation that might win an equality within marriage commensurate with that guaranteed to Americans as their birthright, a status *within* marriage that divorce can never secure. Certainly James's representation of marriage in *Portrait* owes much to Jefferson's observation that to be a wife is to lose the otherwise unalienable "natural right of equality," for marriages are repeatedly portrayed as requiring a woman's "giving up" of "country." When Goodwood discovers Warburton's proposal to Isabel, he asks her "Do you intend to give up your country?" (*PL* 140); similarly, upon Henrietta's betrothal, Isabel echoes this question and inquires "are you going to give up your country?"(*PL* 462). Such questions stem from something far deeper than the international aspect these marriages bear and suggest a forfeiture of rights parallel to giving up one's American citizenship. Clearly, according to both law and custom a wife must give up any allegiance that detracts from her husband's authority, as when Osmond insists, "I've an ideal of what my wife should do and not do. She should not travel across Europe alone, in defiance of my deepest desire, to sit at the bedside of other men. Your cousin is nothing to you; he's nothing to *us*" (*PL* 438). But if Jefferson believed that divorce, as a solution paralleling America's rebellion from British patriarchal authority, could repair the problems inherent to marriage itself, James did not, and in Isabel's return he holds forth the possibility of a future imaginatively fashioned from the traditions and obligations of a usable past as well as the ideals championed by the new nation. What Isabel comes *to know* opens the door for revising the self-erasing "we" and "us" Osmond so frequently deploys to his own advantage, so that these pronouns truly represent, rather than merely imply, partnership, union and the freedom for shared responsibility. For as we are told, Isabel had not "given up" her country or its promises, but had only "relaxed her hold of it" for awhile (*PL* 462).

III

In 1892, James recorded in his notebooks an incident, the "simultaneous marriage, in Paris . . . of a father and a daughter—an only daughter" (*NB* 74), that serves as the germ for the novel *The Golden Bowl*. Like *Portrait*, the plot which evolves is "intensely international," "dramatic," and "ironic" (*NB* 115) in its treatment of marriage and spousal relations, especially those containing the explosive potential of undisclosed former ties. In teasing out the ramifications of this Paris incident, James suggests the manner in which "the whole situation works in a kind of inevitable rotary way—in what would be called a vicious circle":

> The daughter—American of course—is engaged to a young Englishman, and the father, a widower and still youngish, has sought in marriage at exactly the same time an American girl of very much the same age as his daughter. Say he has done it to console himself in his abandonment—to make up for the loss of the daughter, to whom he has been devoted . . . . they all shall have married, as arranged, with this characteristic consequence—that the daughter fails to hold the affections of the young English husband, whose approximate mother-in-law the pretty young second wife of the father will now have become. The father *doesn't* lose the daughter nearly as much as he feared, or expected, for her marriage . . . leaves her *des loisirs*, and she devotes them to him and to making up, as much as possible, for having left him. They spend large parts of their time together, they cling together . . . and are even *more* thrown together than before . . . [the daughter's] very alienation in this manner from her husband gives the second wife, the stepmother, her pretext, her opportunity for consoling the other. From the moment she is not so necessary as the father first thought she would be (when his daughter seemed wholly lost), this second wife has also *des loisirs*, which she devotes to her husband's son-in-law. Lastly, the son-in-law, with the sense of his wife's estrangement from him, finds himself at liberty and finds it moreover only courteous to be agreeable to the other lady in the particular situation that her 'superfluity,' as it were, has made for her. (*NB* 74–75)

The young husband, who in *The Golden Bowl* becomes an Italian prince, finds it only too easy to be "courteous" to his mother-in-law since he "has known her before, has liked her, etc.—been attracted by her, and would have married her if she had had any money" (*NB* 74). Left at loose ends by the "exceptional degree of attachment" of their respective spouses, they become lovers. Thus, if Isabel Archer would seem to have had a moral basis for ending the "ghastly form" of her marriage, then Maggie Verver, the daughter in this scenario, is in certain possession of the legal grounds for divorce. Yet, having discovered her husband's adultery, she never even considers the option for legal redress of this wrong against her. Indeed, once Maggie "sees" Prince Amerigo's infidelity and the "funny form" of their marriage which engenders it, she acts to repair the "divorce" which is already between them. By destabilizing the economic language of contract and converting its terms—"price" into "worth," "reputation" into "character," and "use" into "need"—Maggie renegotiates and thus redeems her matrimonial bond. In so doing, she approaches the "magnificent form" once imagined by Isabel—the union of private interests and value within the public institution.

The Golden Bowl commences with a nuptial agreement between an American heiress and her handsome Prince; that this relation should be represented as an "inspired harmony" reached by a contingent of the Verver's "London lawyers" and Prince Amerigo's "man of business" foregrounds the contractual basis of marriage which, like the big Wall Street deal, is rooted in exchange, in "reciprocity," on the market (*GB* 4). Brook Thomas remarks that the eighteenth-century tendency to assume property's intrinsic and thus relatively stable worth was overturned when, "in the highly developed market economy of the late nineteenth century[,] value was determined by contractual"—and quite public—"exchanges in the marketplace."[60] This principle similarly guided calculations of value in the marriage market and gave rise to what James termed "the endless spectacle" (*NB* 73) of wealthy American girls' eastward migration to England and the Continent where they hoped to secure the best value and, with it, the highest status via the "purchase" of a titled husband. Thus when the Prince protests that neither Maggie nor her father knows anything about his "personal quantity" (*GB* 7), she explains that their interest in him is secured by virtue of his unique social position, by "the generations behind you, the follies and the crimes, the plunder and the waste" which "so many volumes in your family library are all about." Indeed, she asks him, "where . . . without your archives, annals, infamies, would you have been?" (*GB* 8). Acquisition of a foreign Prince and his documented, ancient associations proves far superior to any asset a member of the domestic "Four-Hundred" might tender and testifies to the Ververs' "rare power of purchase" (*GB* 561) as well as their ability to discern the genuine article:

> You're . . . one of the things that can only be got over here. You're a rarity, an object of beauty, an object of price. You're not perhaps absolutely unique, but you're so curious and eminent that there are very few others like you—you belong to a class about which everything is known. You're what they call a *morceau de musée*. (*GB* 10)

Although Maggie eventually revises the perception which grounds value in contract and the publicity of its transaction, her initial nuptial relation reproduces the conquest of Europe by a generation of American girls—of which the shining example is Consuelo Vanderbilt—who (were) traded (as) wealth for the status conferred by "the real thing."

As Miles Orvel has argued, "authenticity" became a "primary value" in the late nineteenth century as a response to the mass market's overwhelming production and reproduction of "things."[61] Whereas social status could once be determined on the basis of an individual's possession of a few choice items, the mechanization of production democratized consumption by flooding the market with affordable goods. Possession of things could thus make one of a certain "type" *appear* to be in possession of a certain status as well, especially when America's lack of a rigid class structure made social mobility at least theoretically possible.[62] The potential for counterfeit social appearances generated considerable anxiety for which "the real thing" offered the only cure: "One might imagine that the concept of authenticity begins in any society when the possibility of fraud arises, and that fraud is at least possible whenever transactions—whether social, political, commercial or aesthetic—routinely occur, especially when society becomes so large that one usually deals with strangers, not neighbors."[63] Ward McAllister's declaration that New York society consisted of "'the' Four Hundred" is just such an attempt to identify definitively the genuine article from the ranks of the merely ambitious.[64] The desire for and procurement of the authentic thus becomes a move in the game of consumer one-up-manship described by Thorstein Veblen: social status is validated not in the mere accumulation of things, but in the exclusivity of consumption of "real" things.[65] Not coincidentally, authenticity becomes an issue just at the moment that contracts, forged in the public marketplace, become at once a means of securing and validating that quality.

If Henry James and *Life Magazine* were famously at odds in matters of literary taste,[66] these wry observers of American manners were in greater accord when it came to the "spectacle" of the American girl in pursuit of "the real thing" in the European marriage market. From the mid-1880s to the mid-1890s—a period which culminates in the nuptials of Conseulo Vanderbilt and the Duke of Marlborough—*Life* documented the peculiar American anxiety over social position and its relief in the purchase of authenticity. In one cartoon, a young woman who possesses "the recip[e] for success" on the marriage market in the form of "a father worth $1,000,000" is warned to "Beware of Counterfeits": the fortune-hunting "birds of prey" who counterfeit love to gain money and whose counterfeit status rests upon a stack of unpaid bills. Heeding just such a warning to accept only the real thing, another woman turns down a proposal from a suitor she acknowledges to be "one in a thousand" because he "[is] not in the Four Hundred." As a reliable aid to fixing social position, another cartoon caption asks the loaded question, "Why Not Use Our Titles?", valorizing that which immediately telegraphs distinction even as it winces with the paucity of such "titles" in a democracy where you are what you (or at least what your husband) do[es] (Fig. 2.1). Thus the marriageable American girl in an 1889 illustration wonders "which" to choose, "Native or Foreign": love in the form of a Yankee Doodle cupid on bended knee or status from the haughty British Eros whose minion advertises his value on an armorial shield.[67]

In the New York Edition Preface to "Lady Barbarina," James recalls that the American Girl seemed set on the foreign candidate:

The international relation had begun to present itself "socially," after the liveliest fashion, a quarter of a century ago and earlier, as a relation of intermarrying; but nothing was meanwhile so striking as that these manifestations took always the same turn. The European of "position" married the young American woman, or the young American woman married the European of position—one scarce knew how best to express the regularity of it; but the social field was scanned in vain for a different pairing. No American citizen appeared to offer his hand to the "European" girl, or, if he did so offered in vain. The bridal migrations were eastward without exception—as rigidly as if by statute. Custom had clearly acquired the force of law; a fact remarkable, significant, interesting and even amusing.[68]

Although the American Girl as Columbia—an Isabel Archer figure to be sure—strenuously resists "The Invasion . . . by the British" (Fig. 2.2) from behind her accumulated wealth (which paradoxically both protects her from and entices fortune hunters) or, in a less militant mood, happily procures a fine specimen of the Chicago Millionaire (Fig. 2.3), the savvy American shopper finds her "best buy" in Europe (Fig. 2.4) with a regularity that alarms "Mrs. Britannia" (Fig. 2.5). The fit between the parties' interests seemed a perfect one, and *Life* found itself regularly reporting that, again, "a portion of the very abundant means of another American heiress is to be devoted to the maintenance of a titled foreigner," or that "a new exportation of American gold" to Europe was imminent.[69] The text of a cartoon entitled "Reciprocity" echoes such announcements when "Lord Fitzerston" exclaims to "Miss A[merica]," "GAD! British noblemen furnish the money to run your American industries" and receives the reply, "Yes, but American wives furnish the money to run your British noblemen."[70] While this exchange foregrounds the mutual benefit derived from trans-Atlantic marital ties, it also suggests that the American heiress walks a fine line between consuming and being "sold." The question "what price status" thus inevitably arises, and Charles Dana Gibson's 1890 cartoon "America's Tribute" presents both the irony of democratic misses' prostration before Old World aristocracy and the ambiguity of their position: are American lovelies offered as a fitting acknowledgment of the British Lion's majesty, or—given the Coliseum-like setting—are they sacrificed to its moribund values?[71]

WHY NOT USE OUR TITLES?

Mrs. Robinson: WHY, MY DEAR MRS. DOCTOR SMITH, I AM SO GLAD TO SEE YOU! WHERE HAVE YOU BEEN ALL THESE MONTHS?

Mrs. Smith: THANK YOU, MRS. RETIRED GROCER ROBINSON. I HAVE BEEN TRAVELING ABROAD WITH MR. DOCTOR SMITH AND MY DEAR OLD FRIEND MRS. MERCHANT TAILOR JONES. HOW IS YOUR HUSBAND?

Fig. 2.1 "Why Not Use Our Titles?" [*Life* 11, no. 265 (June 26, 1888)]

THE INVASION OF AMERICA BY THE BRITISH.

FORCING AN ENGAGEMENT.

Fig. 2.2 "The Invasion of America by the British" [*Life* 9, no. 216 (Feb. 17, 1887)]

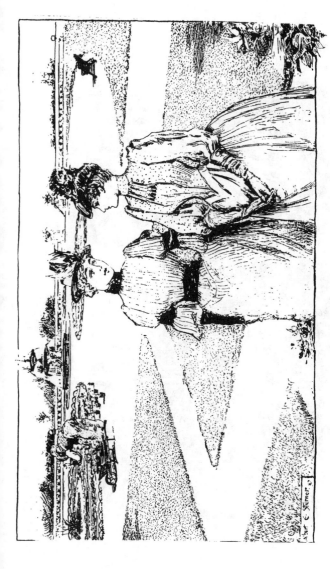

GOOD FISHING.

"I'VE JUST RETURNED FROM A FISHING EXCURSION IN THE ADIRONDACKS. I HAD A LOVELY TIME!"

"YOU HAD GOOD LUCK, THEN?"

"OH MY, YES. I CAUGHT A CHICAGO MILLIONAIRE!"

Fig. 2.3 "Good Fishing" [*Life* 10, no. 247 (Sept. 22, 1887)]

SOME AMERICAN GIRLS GO ABROAD AND RETURN EMPTY HANDED. OTHERS PICK UP SOMETHING.

Fig. 2.4 "Shopping Europe" [*Life* 25, no. 628 (Jan.10, 1895)]

· LIFE ·

THE LION IN LOVE.

MRS. BRITANNIA: DEAR ME! SOMETHING MUST BE DONE, THAT AMERICAN GIRL IS GETTING DANGEROUS. —OLD FABLE.

Fig. 2.5 "The Lion in Love" [*Life* 13, no.326 (March 27, 1889)]

· LIFE ·

ANOTHER NOBLEMAN AMONG US.

HURRAH FOR OLD ENGLAND!

Fig. 2.6 "Another Nobleman Among Us" [*Life* 12, no. 306 (Nov. 8, 1888)]

Life's portrayal of the European aristocracy implies that these women were indeed sacrificed, for in a series of cartoons a representative "type" of the aristocratic "real thing" emerges: a figure who is old, short, pot-bellied, slack-jawed and seemingly without the vitality to equal that of the robust American Girl. Unmindful of Ward McAllister's concern for the quality of the "native stock" and his warning against the "import[ation of] . . . broken-down titled individuals from abroad,"[72] American girls continued to swoon when "Another Nobleman Among Us" (Fig. 2.6) came up for sale. Since, as another caption announced, "damaged goods still command first-class prices in the American market,"[73] "The Same Job Lots" are left for prospective bidders in the marriage market, and the derelict aristocracy is auctioned off to the American Heiress. The cartoon's insert, showing a lion plucking the tail-feathers of an eagle, suggests that Britain gets the best of the deal: rid of its impoverished titles, it gains "revenge for that affair of '76."[74]

If international revenge was not the specific motive, Consuelo Vanderbilt nevertheless became the certain victim of the neatly meshed needs uniting her prospective husband, the Duke of Marlborough, and her estranged parents. In a real-life version of Gibson's "America's Tribute," she was sacrificed to Alva Vanderbilt's ambition to regain her position, after a scandalous divorce, among "the Four-Hundred"; to William K. Vanderbilt's willingness to "pay up" rather than face his ex-wife's notorious temper; and to the Duke's chronic lack of funds sufficient to maintain the trappings of his position. A *Life* cartoon running in the summer of the Duke's well-documented courtship of the Vanderbilt fortune notes his infamous "lack": facing the formidable father who challenges the suitor's fitness to marry his statuesque daughter, Marlborough presses the potential for linguistic confusion between his diminutive physical stature and his reduced economic circumstances and asserts that he won't "be so short" after his marriage when, presumably, he would be more amply endowed.[75] All in all, it seemed a perfect remedy for "a man of, and in, his position," and *Life* congratulated the Duke

on his prospective alliance with the American house of Vanderbilt. So far as appears, the young Duke is a man of parts and of engaging personal qualities. He is heir to a famous, though somewhat impoverished, estate. He has excellent facilities for spending money, and he needs the money to spend. He also needs a wife, and nothing is more natural to a man of, and in, his position than to seek to gain a good wife and good money by one and the same operation. In the opinion of the average worldling, he is entitled to marry a great heiress if he can find one to suit him, and there is no reason why even so great an heiress should not be content to marry him, provided he suits her.[76]

Unfortunately, the Duke did not suit Consuelo, who was in love with and secretly engaged to Winthrop "Winty" Rutherfurd, an American youth of "outstanding looks" and respectable means.[77] The bride's tastes, however, were quite beside the point. The marriage contract "to profit the illustrious family" settled and the wedding concluded, the gossip sheet *Town Topics* quipped, "Winty outclassed. Six-foot-two in his golf stockings, he was no match for five-foot-six in a coronet."[78] In the drive to acquire a prime example of "the real thing," the economics of status overmasters "the personal quantity." Nevertheless, in the days following the Vanderbilt-Marlborough alliance, it was business as usual. The *New York World* published, for the benefit of American heiresses, pictures of all twenty-seven of England's dukes, highlighting in white the still-eligible prospects, and asked, "What will you bid?"[79] Even *Life* opined, only half ironically, that the foreign suitor, because "the business end of his enterprise is frankly acknowledged," stood to make the better husband because he was "likelier . . . to live up to his matrimonial contract." Thus "it is not safe to conclude that a husband gained at a great price may not be worth all that cost."[80]

To be sure, Prince Amerigo "costs" the Ververs a great deal in living up to the terms of his matrimonial contract, and in *The Golden Bowl* James employs the language of exchange to tally the financial as well as the emotional price that must be borne for the acquisition of so rare a Prince. Like the Duke of Marlborough, part of the Prince's purchase price consists in offsetting "the boundless *bêtises* of other people—especially their infamous waste of money" (*GB* 7) with Adam Verver's generous "principle of reciprocity"(*GB* 5). But if Verver's millions are little "taxed" in the transaction, Maggie in effect offers a blank check on her affections, pledging "to pay rather than to lose" her Prince (*GB* 10). Of course, all parties to the bargain receive a return on their respective investments. In exchange for his financial backing, Adam Verver adds to his collection of rarities a son-in-law who, as "a representative precious object," shows "the great marks and signs . . . the high authenticities, he had learned to look for in pieces of the first order" (*GB* 103). If for a specimen "deep Italian" the Prince "spoke English too well[,] it was his only fault" (*GB* 5), and this newest addition to the collection testifies to Verver's pecuniary prowess, his "rare power of purchase." In inspiring the appreciative gaze of other women, the Prince also provides a handsome return for Maggie, for in "the exhibition of him" before other desiring eyes, she experiences a "sovereign charm" (*GB* 122) that attests to her own "power of purchase" as one who both holds and has hold over a precious possession. The Prince thus proves to have a considerable use value for the Ververs, and seems truly "worth all that cost."

In exchange for alienating the "cluster of his attributes" (*GB* 19), the Prince gains—or so he believes—the opportunity to establish a value beyond his associations, beyond the infamous familial "doings" which constitute his "antenatal history." Indeed, by means of the fortune dedicated to his purchase, he hopes to turn that history around, to convert it into something expressive of his personal rather than his public quantity:

> What was this so important step he had just taken but the desire for some new history that should, so far as possible, contradict, and even if need be flatly dishonour, the old? If what had come to him wouldn't do, he must *make* something different. He perfectly recognized—always in his humility—that the material for the making had to be Mr. Verver's millions. There was nothing else for him on earth to make it with; he had tried before—had had to look about and see the truth. (*GB* 13)

In order to change the history that he finds "won't do" for him, the Prince must himself "do" and thereby prove the worth of the unevaluated "personal quantity," the "unknown, unimportant" "single self" (*GB* 7). However, as he is first puzzled and then frustrated to discover, his contract precludes such "doing." As a "real thing"—a purchased quantity with a unique use value—he is expected merely "to be."[81] Having "sold himself for a *situation nette*" (*GB* 262), the Prince pays with more than his history and sacrifices the chance to validate the worth of his latent private self:

> It was as if he had been some old embossed coin, of a purity of gold no longer used, stamped with glorious arms, medieval, wonderful, of which the 'worth' in mere modern change, sovereigns and half-crowns, would be great enough, but as to which, since there were finer ways of using it, such taking to pieces was superfluous. That was the image for the security in which it was open to him to rest; he was to constitute a possession, yet was to escape being reduced to his component parts. What would this mean but that, if they didn't 'change' him, they really wouldn't know—he wouldn't know himself—how many pounds, shillings and pence he had to give? (*GB* 18)

Unable to be "changed," to be converted from a public to a private value or to establish some congruence between these "quantities," the Prince feels "cut . . . in two" (*GB* 240), a phrase which suggests not only the split between his selves, between his "use" and his desire, but also a diminishment by the fact of this division into a role traditionally assumed by the woman in marriage. Indeed, the Prince pays the price for his *"situation nette"* with his masculine pride, feeling himself "reduced," "practically held cheap and made light of" because "of the very relinquishment, for his wife's convenience, of his real situation in the world" (*GB* 259).

The acquisition of the prince, disruptive as it is in unbalancing the long-standing intimacy of father and daughter, necessitates another useful purchase to restore at least the outward form of equilibrium. If Charlotte Stant cannot be counted among the "real things" of the world, she nevertheless constitutes a "special type" whose value resides in her ability to assume any role—an ability which stems in part from her *lack* of associations:

> Nothing in her definitely placed her; she was a rare, a special product. Her singleness, her solitude, her want of means, that is her want of ramifications and other advantages, contributed to enrich her somehow with an odd, precious neutrality, to constitute for her, so detached yet so aware, a sort of small social capital. (*GB* 41)

Believing that Charlotte's social capital "mustn't be wasted" (*GB* 137), Maggie comes to regard her former schoolmate as a quantity who might, by becoming one of a pair with Adam, fulfill a dual function: she will relieve Maggie of the guilt felt at seeming to have abandoned her father in favor of a husband, and she will keep at bay those who, like Mrs. Rance, had noticed Maggie's position at Adam's side vacant. In the second of these tasks, she proves remarkably efficient; as Fanny Assingham observes, Charlotte's arrival at Fawns, the Verver country estate, "simply cleared them out" (*GB* 142). Adam, too, sees a multiplicity of uses to be got for the small cost of taking the exquisite Charlotte as his wife, the chief being that she will "put . . . his child at peace" because then Maggie "would less and less appear to herself to have forsaken him" (*GB* 154). Although no lawyers dance in attendance, Adam nevertheless forges a contractual understanding with Charlotte that is to form the basis of their union: in exchange for relief of "her singleness, her solitude, her want of means," she will "do" to put Maggie at peace. If at first Charlotte doesn't "see why . . . for a mere escape from [her] state—[she] need do quite so *much*" (*GB* 162), she does at last agree to Adam's terms and "their understanding sealed itself . . . as with the click of a silver spring" (*GB* 177).

If the Prince's value resides in the rather vague occupation of simply "being," Charlotte's demands an active "doing." Meeting her husband's "preferences . . . absolutely, as a fixed rule, *all* his preferences"(*GB* 188) to put Maggie at peace comes to entail "the act of representation at large and [in] the daily business of intercourse" (*GB* 232) of both father and daughter. Charlotte's brilliant social facility makes it possible for the Ververs to withdraw ever more completely from their public obligations into their private world. Although she is well aware that "they had brought her in . . . to do the 'worldly' for them" (*GB* 233), Charlotte nevertheless attempts to exceed her contractually defined use value and take her wifely place in Adam's affections. Her hope that a child of her own might "ma[ke] perhaps some difference" in Adam's regard and, thus, in her position is not to be realized. Indeed, she discovers that her husband's matchless pecuniary power does not figure sexual or emotional potency but rather masks its absence, and consummation of the contractual relation is all he can produce. As Charlotte tells the Prince, "it's not, at any rate . . . my fault. There it is. . . . And now I'm too sure. It will never be" (*GB*

225). Thus, having "done, earnestly, everything" and "made it, month after month, [her] study" to make Adam "capable" of an affection "greater" than that commanded by his daughter, Charlotte resigns herself to failure and accepts—one might almost say with a vengeance—both her "use" and her "place." Because Maggie "thinks more, on the whole, of fathers than of husbands" (*GB* 188) and Adam likewise sets his paternal bonds above the nuptial one, Charlotte asserts to Fanny that "the only thing" her "situation" demands is that one "know one's place" (*GB* 191). Noting the similarity between her contracted relation and the Prince's—a similarity which renews a common bond that will, of course, draw these former lovers back together—she adds, "Doesn't it strike you . . . as rather placing the Prince too?" (*GB* 189).

By portraying the "contracted" nature of these unions—that is, their narrowed, circumscribed scope, their tendency to "place" partners in the fixed hierarchical relation of buyer and seller, of capital and labor—James addresses the inadequacy of contract to structure the complex dynamic suggested by marriage. Indeed, the very feature which makes contract a boon in business dealings creates wedlock of the nuptial relation because its restrictive definitions of the parameters governing an exchange deny vital process. Clearly, the Prince suspects what his marriage contract will mean, for as he wanders London's Bond Street and peers at the precious objects displayed behind shop windows, he feels that "the moment" in which "his fate had practically been sealed" had "something of the grimness of a crunched key in the strongest lock that could be made" (*GB* 4). As "charming" and "extraordinary" as the Prince finds Maggie, his sense of impending finality in his situation gives rise to a desire "to do something or other, before it was too late, for himself" (*GB* 15). The Prince's near panic at the prospect of wedlock recalls Henry James Sr.'s view of the marital state as one which admits no compromise nor negotiation, and leaves no room for the expression of individual desire.

Ironically, because the marriage contracts represented in The *Golden Bowl* delineate such specific exchanges, a space is created for the adultery and, thus, the grounds established for divorce. Although both the Prince and Charlotte intend the most traditional fidelities to their respective spouses, they are equally determined to be faithful to the terms established by their nuptial agreements, so that the "being" and "doing" required of them ultimately undermines their best intentions. After all, Adam purchases not the personal quantity in the Prince, the self which wishes to be tested and found worthy of the value invested in him, but the history rife with "folly" and "duplicity." Is it not, then, perfectly in keeping with "being" a Prince with such a history to find adultery among the family "infamies" that might be performed per contract? One rainy afternoon, the Prince enters Maggie's parlor ardently desiring her company and, finding it empty, resolves to wait for her return. When the door at last opens to reveal not Maggie but Charlotte, the "quantity" "brought in" to relieve his wife of that which interferes with her filial devotions, the circumstances are over-ripe for adultery: the former lovers find mutual solace and private recompense in the strict performance of their respective use values. Possessed by the logic which rationalizes this move, Charlotte asks, "What could be more simple than one's going through with everything . . . when its so plain a part of one's contract?" (*GB* 233). To the Prince she explains the beautiful simplicity of the situation: "keeping you company in your solitude . . . is what they must like to think I do" (*GB* 224). Besides, their renewed relation may not be condemned as something they do at their spouses' expense, but justified as "a matter of what they've done to us":

> And she showed how the question had therefore been only of their taking everything as everything came, and all as quietly as might be. Nothing stranger surely had ever happened to a conscientious, a well-meaning, a perfectly passive pair: no more extraordinary decree had ever been launched against such victims than this of forcing them against their will into a relation of mutual close contact that they had done everything to avoid. (*GB* 211)

Their intimacy thus rationalized, Charlotte and the Prince take as the "sovereign law" of their rekindled relationship the "vigilance of 'care' . . . never rashly to forget and never consciously to wound" (*GB* 239), hoping thereby to "protect" their spouses—and themselves—from painful discovery.

The rearrangement of couples in the marriages to maximize father's and daughter's privacy as well as the Prince's and Charlotte's social utility raises at least Fanny Assingham's eyebrows, but it is the very publicity of the illicit lovers' togetherness which creates for them a cloak of assumed propriety. As on the secret excursion which leads to the Bloomsbury shop and the golden bowl in the days just before the Prince's wedding, "the note of publicity struck [them] as better than any other" to obscure their purpose (*GB* 46). Indeed, such "simplicity . . . would cover everything" (*GB* 71) in their dealings: whether at the gala diplomatic reception where Charlotte *wants* Fanny to see her with the Prince and witness their "public juncture" (*GB* 185), or at the Matcham house party where "they were exposed . . . to its being pronounced funny that they should, at such a rate, go about together" (*GB* 242), they find both safety and privacy in cultivating publicity as they fulfill their respective use values. Ironically, while Adam Verver would seem to pose the greatest threat to the lovers should their adultery be discovered, he actually proves their greatest ally because he cannot afford to see beneath the appearance created for him at his expense. His vision limited by the economics of invidious consumption which requires display to gain or maintain status, Adam's greatest concern is that things "of price" should be "visibly perfect" (*GB* 146), that they "look like" (*GB* 108) what they are purchased to be. It is Maggie—misprized as "too unequipped or too indisposed" (*GB* 232) to function in the social whirl—who unexpectedly penetrates the elaborate public spectacle shielding the lovers. Finding at last the visible form of her marriage unsatisfactory, she renegotiates "need" for "use" as the basis of value in her relationship to the Prince and thus—at considerable cost—redeems their union.

*

Like his more famous work "The Real Thing," James's 1900 short story "The Special Type" provides an ironic glimpse of the Darwinian struggles waged between the "kinds" of individuals comprising particular social categories in order to interrogate the system of value that governs their divergent fates. A sketch of the projected action, at once "a comedy, a little drama, of a fine colour" (*NB* 145), tells the tale of a wealthy American who engages a woman of a certain "type" to help create the appearance of adultery and thereby "force his virago of a wife to divorce him." There is, of course, a third woman waiting in the wings whose future quite depends upon the outcome of this tableau; she is *the* woman, the "real thing," who the wealthy American loves, "but . . . loves too much to compromise . . . . [and] be divorced on *her* account" (*NB* 145). The story, which has as its basis the details surrounding the 1895 divorce of Alva and William K. Vanderbilt, is classed by its artist-narrator as " a wonderful case of its kind" in its depiction of "service and sacrifice" for love.[82] Ostensibly, this selfless performance is carried out by the husband, Mr. Brivet, who agrees to allow scandal to attach itself to his name in order to be free to marry his lady-love, Mrs. Cavenham; however, it is Alice Dundene, the "special type" hired for the occasion, who in fact bears the burden of sacrifice in service of the "lovely, lonely, untouched" (ST 176) real thing. Thus in its representation of the play of social appearances to mask private desires and the hierarchy of value which assures the survival and, indeed, the prosperity of "real things" at the expense of "special types," the story resonates with themes later struck in *The Golden Bowl* and forecasts the fate of Charlotte Stant.

Faced with the delicate operation of giving his "odious" wife the grounds to divorce him while at the same time keeping Mrs. Cavenham "on a pinnacle" where the "spattering" of scandal can never "splash" her, Brivet decides to take up with someone who would "undertake to produce the impression" of infidelity. This someone would, of course, have to be "exactly the right person—a special type" who can create a convincing appearance and who, as she "could easily be squared," "wouldn't mind" receiving a spattering in the "interest . . . of another person" (ST 177). And, although attractive enough to inflame the wife, this someone must also occupy a position on the social scale of a kind that would never threaten Mrs. Cavenham's peace of mind. With the aid of such a type, Brivet feels certain that the whole "affair" may be speedily and tidily "wound up." Following closely the logic of the scheme, the narrator asks after the fate of this someone who, having effected the desired end in the case, seems left at loose ends:

> "Then the other would be simply sacrificed?"
>
> "She would be," Brivet splendidly put it, "remunerated" . . . .
>
> "But suppose that, in spite of 'remuneration,' this secondary personage should perversely like you? She would have to be indeed, as you say, a special type, but even special types may have general feelings. Suppose she should like you too much?"
>
> It had pulled him up a little. "What do you mean by 'too much'?"

"Well, more than enough to leave the case quite as simple as you'd
require it."

"Oh, money always simplifies." (ST 178)

The "special type" Brivet employs to serve his "sacred purpose" is
Alice Dundene, the artist-narrator's model, who as a "professional" is
particularly adept in improvising "various subjects" for a price. She
does, inevitably, come to love Brivet, but she neatly stores those
feelings away so to avoid compromising the success of her appointed
task. As she explains to the narrator, once she understands that Brivet
"couldn't marry *me*," she dedicates herself to "want[ing] what he
wants" (ST 191). Her conduct is, on one level, so professional and, on
another, so deeply personal as to inspire the narrator to wax rhapsodic
on her "magnificent" and "wonderful" character. Indeed, he finds it
finally disturbing "that a woman like—yes, when all was said and
done—Alice Dundene should simply minister to the convenience of a
woman like Rose Cavenham" (ST 181). To the narrator, Mrs.
Cavenham seems "so smugly selfish . . . with so small a consciousness
of anything but her personal triumph that, while she had kept her skirts
clear, her name unuttered and her reputation untouched," Alice paid the
price with her skirt, name, reputation, and—most importantly, her
feelings (ST 186–7). Certainly, the conventional means of estimating
position and worth seems under attack, for when the narrator witnesses
Alice and Rose mirrored "face to face for some minutes," he marvels
that two women "of such almost equal beauty" should occupy "such
different places in the scale" of social value (ST 171). There is,
however, no adequate way to recognize a "special type" within the
social scale. Mrs. Cavenham, despite the use to which Alice has been
put on her behalf, persists in referring to her as "them," "by the
collective and promiscuous plural pronoun," regarding her not as an
individual but as an undifferentiated social class beneath her concern
(ST 185). Brivet, too, finds Alice easily dismissed, for he "ceased to see
her" as soon as his scheme had come to a successful conclusion, a
phrase which reminds us that he had not "seen" her during their very
public "relationship" as anything other than a means of securing a
much desired end. She disappears further when he stops "introducing
Mrs. Dundene by name into [his] talk" (ST 188), becoming
unindividuated in his speech as well. Wistfully Alice acknowledges her

"place" when she says to the narrator, "He [didn't] so much as *know* me" (ST 191), a remark with ironic resonance since Brivet never "knew" her in the biblical sense either, always careful of compromising Mrs. Cavenham or her sense of possessorship. Despite his discomfiture at seeing his model "devalued" as a viable social quantity, the narrator is every bit as guilty in his purchase of Alice as a "special type" who creates a variety of convincing appearances for his use, but never transcends that status. For the "payer" in such arrangements, money does indeed "simplify," proving the accuracy of Marx's observation that "everything that you are unable to do, your money does for you."[83] By acting as a buffer against authentic experience, money frees Brivet and his ilk from untidy emotional entanglements and guarantees that humane considerations need never interfere when contracted services—even of the most intimate kind—have been adequately remunerated.

When Maggie discovers the adulterous relation between her husband and her stepmother and resolves to do something about it, Charlotte—"great," "magnificent," "splendid" though she is—is but a "special type" who may be "squared," her personal quantity sacrificed to preserve a series of interdependent appearances: the appearance of the Prince's untarnished value as a "real thing," the appearance of Adam Verver's magisterial powers to "arrange," the appearance of the two marriages happily intact. Certainly, everyone "pays" an immense price to realign the couples so that Maggie might have her Prince restored, and all but Charlotte receive a handsome return on their payments. Maggie's loss of her father is converted into her gain of the Prince; the Prince's passionate affair with Charlotte becomes a fully realized marriage to Maggie; Adam's renewed control over his wife's attentions offsets the separation from his daughter. Only Charlotte's sacrifice remains unconverted to any benefit. Although she pays with "everything"—with the loss of the Prince, the freedom of her prior marital arrangement, and, in a sense, all of Europe—her contribution is devalued, her position and power utterly reduced.

Cut off from certain knowledge of her position and her fate, Charlotte seems like a caged bird "struggling" with secrets she no longer controls, whose "bruised wings" signify the "baffled consciousness" coming into repeated but fruitless contact with "the gilt wires . . . [of] the spacious but suspended cage" which encloses her (*GB* 465–66). As the newly "genial wife" at her husband's side, Charlotte no longer appears the brilliant, independent creature who led the way for the reticent and naive Ververs, but rather a creature subdued and mastered:

> Charlotte hung behind, with emphasised attention; she stopped when her husband stopped, but at the distance of a case or two, or of whatever other succession of objects; and the likeness of their connection would not have been wrongly figured if he had been thought of as holding in one of his pocketed hands the end of a long silken halter looped round her beautiful neck. He didn't twitch it, yet it was there; her didn't drag her, but she came. . . . (*GB* 508)

Both Maggie and the Prince sense Charlotte's distress in the extremity of her isolation, hearing in her voice "the shriek of a soul in pain" (*GB* 512) or "the sound . . . of a creature in anguish" (*GB* 514), but neither can afford to relieve her if they are to receive the full payback on their own sacrifices. Indeed, Maggie observes to the Prince, "it's as if her happiness had been necessary to us —as if we had need of her, *at her own cost*, to build us up and start us" (*GB* 550–51; emphasis added). Banished to Adam's "American City," Charlotte is "doomed" to act as an intermediary between her husband's collection of priceless but inanimate "real things" and the public, representing him to those who can neither comprehend her quality nor the collection's significance. Like Alice Dundene, Charlotte may be sacrificed to "use," sacrificed to the rather complacent appraisal that "she was not to be wasted in the application of [Adam's] plan" (*GB* 565).

Finally, however, it is not for Maggie or the Prince to redeem Charlotte from mere instrumentality, for as Carolyn Porter observes she "lives in a world presided over by the values of Adam Verver, whose influence is the product of the alienated power of money."[84] Only Adam has the power to amend the terms of her contractual/contracted use by acknowledging the full value of her "personal quantity" and take her as a full partner in marriage. To do so, however, would not only disrupt the market values which vouchsafe his power, it would also require him to abandon economic investment in favor of emotional engagement, to demonstrate a willingness to grapple with "the monster," marriage (*GB* 20). His failure to convert the basis of their relationship, to follow up on Charlotte's attempts to become a wife and partner to him, leaves them both abiding in marital chains. What readers find distressing in the sacrifice of Charlotte is not, as many critics have asserted, that it restores the two marriages to their conventional figuration, but that she cannot be saved, as the Prince will be, from marriage's "ghastly form" as absolute deadlock.

*

Not long before they are to be wed, Maggie suggests the "nice" future in store for the Prince within the Verver's realm of experience, where "the whole world, the beautiful world—or everything in it that *is* beautiful" lies at their disposal (*GB* 9). The Prince, however, gently undermines her enthusiastic assertion that this unique position enables them to "see so much" by countering, "you see too much . . . . when you don't, at least . . . see too little." The excess implied by "too much" is balanced by its opposite value "too little" in such a way as to make them seem virtually the same: indeed, the Verver's romantic tendency to over-invest what they "see" with qualities not actually present means they often fail to really see at all. Thus when Fanny Assingham tells her husband that it is Maggie "who'll see us through" (*GB* 205) the disaster that the discovered adultery would seem to portend, the reader is left to wonder what *Fanny* sees in "poor little Maggie" to be so reassured. In *The Golden Bowl* as in *The Portrait of a Lady*, one's relation to seeing functions as an index of relative innocence or experience. Isabel's seeing, we may recall, at first denotes her position poised on the threshold of potential knowledge—a position from which she might either retreat, passively accepting whatever "fate" deals her, or go forward, converting seeing into critical recognition and crucial action. Knowledge of her actual circumstances as well as of her blind complicity in constructing those circumstances marks her movement (which is a growth rather than a fall) from innocence into troubling experience. Vision—the power to penetrate the refractive surfaces of expertly contrived social appearances—proves the crux of Maggie's development as well, for the dawning recognition of the "funny form"(*GB* 316) her marriage has assumed galvanizes her into saving action—just as Fanny had foreseen it would.

The birth of Maggie's seeing dates from the evening when Charlotte and the Prince, after the house party at Matcham where they served as the family's emissaries, fail to arrive at Eaton Square for dinner at the expected hour. Something different in the accustomed pattern of her daily life startles Maggie into a partial recognition that her relationship with the Prince has somehow gone awry. Asked "what has opened her eyes?", Fanny—who witnesses Maggie's discomfiture—replies, "she misses him" (*GB* 280). Indeed, feeling an unanswered desire for her spouse, for his company—a desire which most certainly parallels that which the Prince felt when his wife's dutiful attendance upon her father made her constant absence a felt grievance—Maggie "decid[es] to do something . . . which would strike Amerigo as unusual" (*GB* 303) and so goes home without awaiting his return. She thus "administer[s] to her husband the first surprise" (*GB* 305) of their marriage and as a result sees flicker across his face the effect her act has had in making him "*visibly* uncertain" (*GB* 308). "Waking to the truth that she had never really had him" (*GB* 281), Maggie manages in that defining moment "to get nearer—nearer to something indeed that she couldn't, she wouldn't, even to herself, describe" (*GB* 304).

If Maggie's vision is yet piecemeal, her ability to articulate what she half-perceives yet unformed, she nevertheless resolves to act upon what she *can* see: that the "business of social representation" carried out by the Prince and Charlotte "in her service and her father's . . . was an affair of living always in harness" (*GB* 313). Recognizing her complicity in placing them in a position "so that the exertion was *all* theirs" (*GB* 315), she converts insight into action and jumps eagerly into the traces in order "to be *with* him again, quite with *them*, together" (*GB* 317). Maggie's desire to participate, to share "whatever the enjoyment, the interest, the experience" (*GB* 316) inspires her to "improvise" and "invent" so as "to bring about a difference" (*GB* 322) in their relations. The change for which Maggie aims suggests not only a realignment of husband and wife, father and daughter, but also a leveling of the hierarchy that unequally favors or burdens those who purchase and those who alienate labor. Unlike Adam, Maggie sees money cannot "do" for her; to allow money or contract to structure her relations would leave her life unlived, her marriage but an empty, "funny" form.

Despite her efforts, however, despite her offer of "the flower of participation" to her husband (*GB* 316), Maggie succeeds only in "divid[ing] them again . . . cut[ting] them up afresh into pairs and parties" (*GB* 336), creating an arrangement that leaves her still bereft of the Prince. "She regularly found that Amerigo had come either to sit with his father-in-law in the absence of the ladies, or to make, on his side, precisely some such display of the easy working of the family life as would represent the equivalent of her excursions with Charlotte" (*GB* 326). Thus the "business" of representation goes on for Charlotte and the Prince, albeit in a private "display" which, in its achievement of absolute balance and equilibrium, is calculated to reassure Maggie and her father that they are, indeed, the quantities they appear to be. Temporarily stymied by the stalemate her heroic efforts at rearrangement have wrought, Maggie's powers of perception nevertheless continue to develop. Indeed, the strange result of her improvisations itself becomes a vision for her to ponder, and as she scrutinizes it she at last recognizes that her "failure" to reunite with her husband is in fact due to the "success" of an orchestrated project of resistance to her idea:

> . . . how they must be working together for it [the appearance of contented family unity], and how my very success, my success in shifting our beautiful harmony to a new basis, comes round to being *their* success above all; their cleverness, their amiability, their power to hold out, their complete possession in short, of our life? (*GB* 352)

In thus understanding that the unsatisfying form of the marriages derives not only from her own complicity in "using" the pair, but from a corresponding complicity between Charlotte and the Prince, Maggie comes irresistibly to feel that there is "something" between them—a feeling that her serendipitous discovery of the antique golden bowl confirms.

There is an undeniable irony in the idea that Charlotte and the Prince, purchased for *their* use value, should turn the tables on Maggie and Adam and be in "complete possession" of their purchasers' "life." Certainly the old adage (neatly illustrated by Harriet Beecher Stowe's famous anti-consumerist parable of the parlor carpet)[85] that we may easily become slaves to our things echoes in Maggie's pained observation. It is more to the point, however, to note that the lovers' "possession" results from the secret knowledge they share and control. Once Maggie herself *sees* their coordinated flanking movements and *knows* of their adultery, they are divested of their power over and possession of her. Indeed, what fills Maggie with pity for Charlotte, who finally cannot see nor imagine the fact of her adversary's discovery, is the "looming vision" of the splendid creature "having gropingly to go on, always not knowing and not knowing!" (*GB* 448). This image of Charlotte so reduced, so unlike herself, suggests another construction that "possession" might bear in this context: self-possession, a confidence stemming from seeing and thus judging "where" you are in relation to others. "Seeing" does indeed transform Maggie, and from the first her critical recognitions of the nature of her circumstances charge her with "the sense of possession" (*GB* 312) so that she experiences the "enjoyment of confidence, from her knowing . . . what to do" (*GB* 315). By the time she confronts the Prince with the golden bowl and reads in *his* recognition of its containing, though broken, significant meaning, "she knew how hugely expert she had been made" (*GB* 448) in "judging," in converting what she sees into knowledge: "poor little Maggie" thus

> . . . was having . . . the time of her life—she knew it by the perpetual throb of this sense of possession, which was almost too violent either to recognize or to hide. It was as if she had come out—that was her most general consciousness; out of a dark tunnel, a dense wood, or even simply a smoky room . . . the change brought about almost by itself as great a difference of view as the shift of an inch in the position of a telescope. . . . (*GB* 449)

The image of Maggie emerging from dark, obfuscating spaces most certainly denotes her growing enlightenment, but the foregrounding of the phrase "she had come out" by deferring momentarily any reference to *what* indeed she had come out of, whether tunnel, wood or room suggests an emphasis on "she," on her fully realized nature coming forward and asserting itself. The timorous Maggie transformed by knowledge, she advances into a larger role, a deeper character: ". . . she felt not unlike some young woman of the theatre who, engaged for a minor part in the play . . . should find herself suddenly promoted to leading lady" (*GB* 449). This emergent sense of self-possession allows Maggie to cast off Adam's economy, for it provides her with all the capital required to redeem the Prince and renegotiate the terms of her marriage contract. Her "seeing," "knowing," and "judging" make possible conscious choices about what to pay and insures that, unlike Charlotte, she will not be victimized in her sacrifices.

Considering Maggie's position as a wronged spouse, it is strange that *she* need pay rather than exact payment to assuage the pain the marital transgression causes her. The conventional role as innocence outraged, however, with its demand for confession and abasement in return for forgiveness or, more radically, its resort to the divorce court to sever all ties suits Maggie not at all. Indeed, once Maggie "knows" of her own accord, she neither needs nor desires any explanations or confessions. When, in the days after the golden bowl has yielded up the lovers' secret, Fanny asks, "But didn't he explain?" to which Maggie emphatically replies, "Explain? Thank God, no!" (*GB* 455), for any further word on the subject would compromise "the decency of pride" necessary to regain their status as partners in marriage. Similarly, when Adam and Charlotte have at last departed for America, Maggie feels in the Prince's trying "clearly, to please her" an attempt to "repay" his debt for her sacrifice, but recoils when that repayment seems it might take on the form of reductive explanation:

> So far as seeing that she was 'paid' went, he might have been holding out the money-bag for her to come and take it. But what instantly rose, for her, between the act and her acceptance, was the sense that she must strike him as waiting for a confession. This, in turn, charged her with a new horror: if that was her proper payment she would go without money. (*GB* 566)

The plot which includes confession and retaliation as conventional elements would in fact exact a price Maggie is unwilling to pay, for the open rupture of divorce—whether in its figurative or literal sense—means that for the cold comfort gained by airing her grievance she would lose not only the Prince, but sacrifice her father and Charlotte as well. As she circles the grounds at Fawns one warm evening and catches a glimpse of this trio mutually engaged, Maggie knows that would be too much to bear:

> The sight, from the window, of the group so constituted, *told* her why, told her how, named to her, as with hard lips, named straight *at* her, so that she must take it full in the face, that other possible

relation to the whole fact which alone would bear upon her
irresistibly. It was extraordinary: they positively brought home to her
that to feel about them in any of the immediate, inevitable, assuaging
ways, the ways usually open to innocence outraged and generosity
betrayed, would have been to give them up, and that giving them up
was, marvelously, not to be thought of. (*GB* 471)

The price, then, of "the immediate, inevitable, assuaging way" in
divorce is indeed immense: the phrase "to give them up," in addition to
signifying Maggie's sacrifice of them, might also mean "to give up *on*
them," to lose faith *in* them and their inherent value, marking a
movement from innocence which bypasses experience for the refuge of
rank cynicism. Instead, to regain the Prince, to shelter her father and to
preserve Charlotte's security, Maggie pays what her new-found self-
possession affords her: the ability, if painful, to stand free of paternal
care and domination, to suffer apparent abasement at Charlotte's
instigation, but never to publicly reveal the depth of her resource or
reserve. Even this, though dear, is not too much when she realizes her
return; when Maggie looks upon the "beauty" of her husband and their
emergent new relation, "she str[ikes] herself as paying, if anything, all
too little" (*GB* 465).

   I would like to backtrack to the extraordinary passage in which
Maggie imagines a money-bag confession being proffered her so I
might suggest the manner in which she revises the terms of her
marriage contract. First, this passage recalls an earlier scene when the
Prince's sexual overture in the face of Maggie's "deeper need to know
where she 'really' was" seems an attempt to buy her off, to short-circuit
her intuition that something in their intimacy is missing. It is only by
"intensely resisting" him that Maggie maintains "her sense of
possessing . . . some advantage that . . . she might either give up or
keep," although she feels "her very bones register" that "her husband's
grasp really meant . . . she *should* give it up: it was exactly for this that
he had resorted to unfailing magic" (*GB* 339). The passage in question
also bears a marked similarity to a scene in which money, specifically
its quantified display, suggests another sexual payoff. While at
Brighton to purchase the rare oriental tiles from Mr. Gutterman-Suess,
Adam tenders Charlotte a marriage proposal that seems an attempt to
remedy the indecency of having "exposed" himself, via his "power of

purchase," to her:[86] "a man of decent feeling didn't thrust his money, a huge lump of it, in such a way, under a poor girl's nose . . . without seeing, logically, a responsibility attached" (*GB* 160). Having thus "compromised" Charlotte, Adam must do the right thing by her and make an offer of marriage. While the image of the "huge lump" being "thrust" before Charlotte is fraught with sexual innuendo, Adam is in fact impotent except through his money, a basis of "intercourse" which precludes humane feeling and demands in its stead a precise rendering of credit for debit per contract. Indeed, the passage in which a sexual overture takes on the appearance of a bribe that will cancel her vision does seem to suggest something of the ledger's exactitude, as if the tender(ed) offer of a confession could act as an offset equal in value to some deficit in Maggie's tally of things. However, Maggie seeks to base her marriage on a different system of exchange. Her rejection of the "money-bag" as compensation is not a rejection of sexuality *per se*, but rather the scuttling of an impotent economy dependent on such calculated equivalencies. Although critics such as Joseph A. Boone see Maggie as attempting "to wrest the form and content of married life into a non-threatening equilibrium"[87] she has in fact already registered her unease with the very stasis such balance implies. If at one point she believes "that their equilibrium was everything" (*GB* 310), she later realizes that "the equilibrium" works against her and "lasted in spite of [her] rearrangement; there had been a fresh distribution of the different weights, but the balance persisted and triumphed" over her best efforts (*GB* 351).

Maggie in fact resists such equilibrium by envisioning a marriage that will, for its very survival, substitute "need"—which recognizes an individual's multiple and shifting desire—for "use"—which depends upon inflexible, pre-defined performance—in a series of private rather than public exchanges. Indeed, almost as soon as the Prince is made aware that his infidelity is known, Maggie offers as the basis of their renewed relation a "prospect less contracted" (*GB* 438):

[there] was the possibility, richer with every lapsing moment, that her husband would have, on the whole question, a new need of her, a need which was in fact being born between them in these very seconds. It struck her truly as so new that he would indeed, absolutely . . . be *really* needing her for the first time in their whole

connection. No, he had used her, he had even exceedingly enjoyed her, before this, but there had been no precedent for that character of a proved necessity to him which she was rapidly taking on. (*GB* 435–36)

This "new need" requires that they work together to come out of the labyrinth Maggie imagines enclosing them and into a more nearly reciprocal union. This shared effort does not connote, however, a system of use and calculated balances, but rather relies on their mutual willingness to compensate for each others' deficiencies when either "comes up short" in their relations. Maggie's "helping him to help himself" allows the Prince "to help her," and thus answers his desire to *demonstrate* his inherent worth, his personal quantity. As a real thing, his value uncontested and untried, he was one of those people "so inordinately valued" that one let them off the hook, so to speak, and "didn't mind the so frequently marked absence in them of the purpose to really represent their price" (*GB* 196). Thus he could, " as a rule, take for granted" that there would always be, without effort on his part, "a balance in his favor" (*GB* 257). By demonstrating her need of his realized personal quantity "to save her from being the one . . . to pay all" (*GB* 477) for their union, she answers his own need to define himself outside the limits of his family's history and thus removes him from Adam's collection of priceless objects that he might himself be self-possessed.

With Maggie at last enfolded in the Prince's arms, the conclusion of *The Golden Bowl* would seem to achieve a sense of closure that *The Portrait of a Lady* does not. However, as Ruth Yeazell has noted, "no Jamesian novel has left readers themselves more *en l'air*"[88] in determining how this ending should be read. While some see this final embrace as indicative of Maggie's triumph in securing "full redeeming intimacy of intense passion" as well as "authentic commitment to the communion it affords and to the larger community of purpose it can make possible,"[89] others discount her achievement as merely conventional in that it "saves two marriages at the expense of two passionate relationships."[90] Others still see in the apparent comedic resolution "destabilizing ironies" which, like the gilded crack in the golden bowl, threaten to fracture the apparent wholeness of the moment.[91] Indeed, Maggie's burying her face in the Prince's breast in "pity and dread" (*GB* 567) does portend less a resolved fiction than "a character struggling to will such a fiction."[92] However, I would suggest one further reading—that Maggie's (re)visionary efforts have brought about not static wedlock, but the possibility of an unconventional plot within the conventional form. By risking engagement and (re)negotiating with the Prince the terms of their renewed union, Maggie acknowledges process—rather than static equilibrium—as the mode of marriage, thereby preempting divorce in either its literal or figurative form. Her revisionary tactics suggest the dynamic James describes as guiding his own process of textual revision; indeed, he specifically links "their [Maggie's and the Prince's] fortune with my method" as he discusses re-seeing elements of his work. These "renewals of vision" rely, James says, upon recognizing "the accumulated 'good stuff'" and responding with an effort of good faith to its appeal: "Actively believe in us and then you'll see."[93] Acting, then, in good faith that there is, indeed, "good stuff" to work with, James and Maggie alike find that within the "handsome wholeness" of the outward form, one might answer yet another appeal—"the appeal to variety, the appeal to incalculability."[94] In the New York edition preface to *The Wings of the Dove,* he similarly addresses the element of invention cultivated by prescription, the surprising freedom discovered with the limit of the form when one paradoxically finds "how many accommodations [the story-teller] can practice":

> Still, when not too blighting, they [prescription of form, conditions of publication] often operate as a tax on ingenuity—that ingenuity of the expert craftsman which likes to be taxed very much to the same tune to which a well-bred horse likes to be saddled. The best and finest ingenuities, nevertheless, with all respect to that truth, are apt to be, not one's compromises but one's fullest conformities. . . .[95]

If Maggie hides her eyes "in pity and dread," it is because her ingenuity has been thoroughly taxed, and will be—if the marriage is to thrive—over and over again.

NOTES

1. *The Complete Notebooks of Henry James.,* ed. Leon Edel and Lyall H. Powers (New York: Oxford University Press, 1987), 15. Subsequent quotations from this source are from this edition and are cited parenthetically in the text as *NB*.

2. According to Laurence B. Holland, "art or aesthetic reality was [for James] a process of creation to be engaged in, with a product—the union of form and vision which in the late Prefaces he came to call *marriage*—to be fashioned and enjoyed." *The Expense of Vision* (Baltimore: The Johns Hopkins University Press, 1964), xi.

3. James, *The Golden Bowl,* ed. with an introduction and notes by Virginia Llewellyn Smith (New York: Oxford University Press, 1983), 98. Subsequent quotations from this source are from this edition and are cited parenthetically in the text as *GB*.

4. E. L. Godkin, "Society and Marriage," quoted in Alfred Habegger, *Henry James and the Woman Business* (New York: Cambridge University Press: 1989), 29. Several scholars have provide excellent discussions on the conscious and unconscious influence of Henry James Sr. on his son's fiction, although they come to rather different conclusions than expressed here. See Annette Niemtzow, "Marriage and the New Woman in *The Portrait of a Lady,*" *American Literature* 47 (1975): 377–95; Robert White, "Love Marriage and Divorce: The Matter of Sexuality in *The Portrait of a Lady,*" *The Henry James Review* 7, no. 2–3 (1986): 59–71; and, for the most comprehensive treatment, Habegger, "The Lessons of the Father" in *Henry James and the Woman Business,* 27–62; and in his recent biography of Henry James, Sr., *The Father: A Life of Henry James, Sr.* (New York: Farrar, Straus and Giroux, 1994), 329–342 and 465–472.

5. Henry James Sr. defined promiscuity not in terms of a multiplicity of sexual partners, but as "intercourse which takes place between man and woman unsanctified by ties of the heart." Quoted in Habegger, *Henry James and the Woman Business,* 31.

6. Henry James Sr., *Love Marriage and Divorce , and the Sovereignty of the Individual: A Discussion Between Henry James Sr., Horace Greeley, and Stephen Pearl Andrews, ed.* Charles Shively (Weston, MA: M & S Press, 1975), 92.

7. Ibid., 24.

8. Ibid., 25–26.

9. In early 1874, when Beecher was named corespondent in the Tilton divorce suit and the daily news was filled with minutely detailed accounts of the proceedings, excerpts from James's letter were published in the *St. Paul Daily Press*. Shortly thereafter, on April 18, 1874, these excerpts were picked up and republished with commentary by the free-love advocate Stephen Pearl Andrews in *Woodhull & Clafin's Weekly*. For a full account of the Beecher-Tilton "scandal" and the renewed debate on marriage and divorce by Greeley, James and Andrews which it occasioned, see Habegger, *Henry James and the Woman Business*, 52–57; and Glenda Riley, *Divorce: An American Tradition*, 75–76.

10. *Love, Marriage and Divorce*, 94.

11. Ibid., 95.

12. Ironically, the word "wedlock" did at one time convey a spiritual meaning. According to Evelyn J. Hinz, it is "derived from the Old English *wed*, meaning a pledge, and *lac*, coming from the Germanic and Gothic *laiks*, meaning a dance. What wedlock once seems to have meant, then, is 'a pledge that is danced.' Since to archaic man dance was . . . the basis of ritual, we may assume that *once upon a time* wedlock *was* a ritual and marriage *was* sacred." See "Hierogamy versus Wedlock," 900–913.

13. Henry James, *The Portrait of A Lady*, ed. Leon Edel (Boston: Riverside Press, 1963), 482. Subsequent quotations from this source are from this edition and are cited parenthetically in the text as *PL*.

14. In *The Ordeal of Consciousness* (Cambridge, England: Cambridge University Press, 1967) Dorthea Krook concludes that Isabel, like James himself, harbored a "fear of, and revulsion from, sexual passion in its more violent, importunate forms" and thus flees Goodwood's final embrace (368); Alfred Habegger (*Henry James and the Woman Business*) suggests her "treacherous servility leads to a very conservative sort of responsibility, which finds freedom only in the acceptance of traditional forms" (159); for Annette Niemtzow ("Marriage and the New Woman"), Isabel returns to Osmond because "her sense of privacy . . . forces her to reject divorce . . . . The Countess Gemini, whose name suggests her false position . . . is transformed into an apparition of Isabel's own fears about what she herself may become" (382); finally, Millicent Bell [*Meaning in Henry James* (Cambridge, Mass.: Harvard University Press, 1991)] implies that Isabel isn't up to the challenge when she writes that divorce was "an alternative nearly unavailable to someone like Isabel when James wrote his novel. It was a recourse that upper-class women, in particular, were not supposed to reach for—not until the 1870s and

1880s did English law make provision for women as the injured party" (88). However difficult divorces were to obtain in England at the time, one needed only to look to Isabel's native country (why would she look for divorce in England when she lived in Italy and was a citizen of the United States?)—as Henrietta Stackpole suggests—to find relief from an untenable marriage relationship. Indeed, in *A Modern Instance*, published the year after James's *Portrait*, Howells demonstrates how easy it was to get a divorce. Further, Alfred Habegger argues that divorce was not only a familiar topic, but a "respectable enough option that Minnie [Temple] could comfortably bring it up" in writing to a lawyer friend about her chum Ella Dietz Clymber (163). To focus on the ease or difficulty of divorce as a remedy seems, however, to miss the significance of Isabel's return to Rome. If she is merely optionless—or the victim of her own personality flaws—what does the much touted "ado" amount to?

15. Habegger, *Henry James and the Woman Business*, 180.

16. Adeline Tintner, "The Centennial of 1876 and *The Portrait of a Lady*," *Markham Review* 10 (1980–81): 28.

17. Ibid.

18. Jay Fliegelman, *Prodigals and Pilgrims*, 267.

19. For a discussion of the modes of representing the split between England and America, see Gordon Wood, *The Creation of the American Republic, 1776–1787* (Chapel Hill: University of North Carolina Press, 1969); Eric Foner, *Tom Paine and Revolutionary America* (New York: Oxford University Press, 1976); and Edwin G. Burrows and Michael Wallace, "The American Revolution: The Ideology and Psychology of National Liberation," in *Perspectives in American History*, ed. Donald Flemming and Bernard Bailyn (Cambridge, Mass.: Harvard University Press, 1972). Like taxation, divorce itself became a revolutionary issue when, in 1773, England's Privy Council declared Pennsylvania's divorce act "disallowed, revoked and rendered null and void" and instructed the colonial governors to withhold consent from any provincial bill of divorce. See Thomas R. Meehan, "'Not Made Out of Levity': Evolution of Divorce in Early Pennsylvania," *Pennsylvania Magazine of History and Biography* 92 (1968): 441–464.

20. Riley, *Divorce: An American Tradition*, 32.

21. Quoted in Linda K. Kerber, *Women of the Republic: Intellect and Ideology in Revolutionary America* (Chapel Hill: University of North Carolina Press, 1980), 177.

22. Quoted in Frank Dewey, "Thomas Jefferson's Notes on Divorce," *William and Mary Quarterly* 39 (1982): 216–219. The case was never argued because of Blair's death.

23. Michael Grossberg, *Governing the Hearth,* 19.

24. Quoted in Kerber, *Women of the Republic:,* 180.

25. Quoted in Grossberg, *Governing the Hearth,* 19.

26. "The Marriage Contract in Seventeenth-Century English Political Thought," *Western Political Quarterly* 32.1 (1979): 79.

27. Nancy F. Cott, "Divorce and the Changing Status of Women in Eighteenth Century Massachusetts," *William and Mary Quarterly* 3, series xxxiii (1976): 593–94.

28. For an overview of the link between the War for Independence and the increase of divorce petitions, see Cott, "Divorce and the Changing Status of Women," 592; Kerber, *Women of the Republic,* 104 and 159; and Meehan, "'Not Made Out of Levity,'" 446.

29. Grossberg, *Governing the Hearth,* 10.

30. William O'Neill, *Divorce in the Progressive Era* (New Haven: Yale University Press, 1967), 89.

31. D. A. Gorton, "The Ethics of Marriage and Divorce," *The National Quarterly Review* 37 (July 1878): 48. The *National Quarterly Review* was established in New York in 1860 by Edward I. Sears, who was editor until 1876 when Dr. David A. Gorton assumed control. In proclaiming itself "American in the broadest and most legitimate acceptation of the term," it set itself in direct opposition to *The North American Review*, the only other general secular quarterly of the period, which was distinctly Bostonian in tenor. According to Frank Luther Mott, "the *National* was a quarterly review of classic form, frankly modeled on the famous English reviews. Its articles had weight and substance." Although its circulation was modest, it occupied a position of esteem; *The London Spectator* voted it "at once the most learned, most brilliant, and most attractive of all [America's] periodicals." See Mott, *A History of American Magazines*, vol. 3, 530–533.

32. Gorton, "The Ethics of Marriage and Divorce," 31.

33. As I have indicated in note 4, Niemtzow, White and Habegger have argued that Henry James Sr.'s views on marriage and divorce are validated in *Portrait* when Isabel renounces Goodwood in favor of "the straight path" back to Rome and Osmond. However, the fact that Henry James Jr. endorsed his father's views in several letters written in the 1870s—a fact upon which these

arguments rely—does not by itself mean that he maintained this position some ten years later while writing *Portrait.*

34. Gorton, "The Ethics of Marriage and Divorce," 38.

35. Ibid., 41–42.

36. Ibid., 45–46.

37. Isabel says to herself, "When a woman made such a mistake, there was only one way to repair it—just immensely (oh, with the highest grandeur!) accept it" (*PL* 334). Later she tells Henrietta, "One must accept one's deeds. I married him before all the world; I was perfectly free; it was impossible to do anything more deliberate" (*PL* 400).

38. In "The Marriages of Henry James and Henrietta Stackpole," Elise Miller reads this dismissal of Henrietta's position as James's "refusal to view Isabel's future in terms of marriage and as an abandonment of marriage/divorce as the defining context of Isabel's struggle for identity" [*The Henry James Review* (Winter 1989): 26]. However, while I agree that James does work against the conventional marriage plot (as Millicent Bell has so ably argued), he checks Henrietta because divorce is no remedy for what stymies Isabel: the inevitable struggle between husband and wife arising both from the institutionalized inequalities of marriage as well as from the individual personalities yoked intimately together. Isabel's "change" must come from (re)negotiating her status *within* her marriage, a step that presupposes an internal change. Similarly, in *The Golden Bowl*—in which divorce is once again rejected as a remedy for marital difficulty—marriage ("a fearful thing at best") is represented as something one must face. As Fanny Assingham enjoins Amerigo, "don't run away from it." Henrietta's habit of always looking for solutions in the future, of endorsing the break with the past that both divorce and the West suggest, works against the idea of negotiating a workable relationship with the past and tradition, an idea that both Isabel's and Christopher Newman's movements *back* to Europe imply.

39. Wells begins her article by asking a question that seems directed to James's *Portrait*: "What is this curious product of today, the American girl or woman? Does the heroine of any American novel fitly stand as a type of what she is? and, furthermore, is it possible for any novel, within the next fifty years, truly to depict her as a finality, when she is still emerging from new conditions in a comparatively old civilization, when she does not yet understand herself, and when her actions are often the awkward results of motives, complex in their character, unconscious to herself?" (817–23).

40. The liberality with which the West granted divorce has been attributed to many causes, among them being the legislative willingness to free settlers from the bonds of their old lives so that they might begin afresh as citizens in fledgling states and as contributors to developing economies. See Mary Sommerville Jones, *An Historical Geography of Changing Divorce Laws in the United States* (Ann Arbor: University Microfilms, 1980), 31; and Val Nolan, "Indiana: Birthplace of Migratory Divorce," *Indiana Law Journal* 26 (Summer 1951): 517–520.

41. *Henry James: Letters,* ed. Leon Edel, vol. 2 (Cambridge, Mass.: Harvard University Press, 1975), 57. Subsequent quotations from this source are from this edition and volume and are cited parenthetically in the text as *HJL.*

42. Martha Banta provides a detailed account of Henry James's attempt to define "the American character" at the time of the United States Centennial in her "Introduction" to *New Essays on The American,* ed. Martha Banta (New York: Cambridge University Press, 1987): 1–42.

43. V. S.. Ingram, *The Centennial Exposition* (Philadelphia: Hubbard Brothers, 1876), 98.

44. Ibid.

45. "In and About the Fair," *Scribner's Monthly* 12 (1876): 745.

46. "A Sennight of the Centennial," *Atlantic Monthly* 38 (1876): 101.

47. Quoted in *Elizabeth Cady Stanton, as Revealed in her Letters, Diaries and Reminiscences,* ed. by Theodore Stanton and Harriet Stanton Blatch (New York: Harper's, 1922), 266.

48. Mrs. E. D. Gillespie, *A Book of Remembrance* (Philadelphia: J. B. Lippincott, 1901), 270.

49. Quoted in Gillespie, 311–12.

50. Quoted in *A History of Woman Suffrage,* ed. by Elizabeth Cady Stanton, Susan B. Anthony and Mathilda Joslyn Gage, vol. 3 (Salem, New Hampshire: Ayer, 1969), 28.

51. General Joseph R. Hawley, quoted in *History of Woman Suffrage,* 28.

52. Mrs. Sarah Langdon Williams, quoted in *History of Woman Suffrage,* 52.

53. James D. McCabe, *The Illustrated History of the Centennial Exhibition* (Philadelphia: National Publishing Co., 1876), 213.

54. *History of Woman Suffrage,* 31–34.

55. In a letter of June 26, 1876 addressed to Susan B. Anthony, Mrs. C. I. H. Nichols made explicit the relation between the equitable arrangement of the

domestic sphere and the state of the union. She wrote "that the sequestration of rights in the homes of the republic makes them baneful nurseries of the monopolies, rings and fraudulent practices that are threatening the national integrity; and that so long as the fathers sequester the rights of the mothers and train their sons to exercise, and the daughters to submit, to the exactions of usurped powers, our government offices will be dens of thieves and the national honor trail in the dust. . . ." Quoted in *History of Woman Suffrage*, 50.

56. "An International Episode," in *The New York Henry James*, vol. 14 (Fairfield, New Jersey: Augustus Kelley, 1976), 305. Subsequent quotations from this source are from this edition and are cited parenthetically in the text as *IE*.

57. *The American Scene* (New York: St. Martins, 1987), 250.

58. Although Mrs. Touchett seems cold and indifferent in her conduct of a life so deliberately separate from her husband and son, there is at least the hint that all-consuming business may have been the cause which, "at an early stage in their community," sends her to take up a Florence residence while Mr. Touchett remains behind "to take care of the English branch of his bank" (*PL* 30–31).

59. Habegger, *Henry James and the Woman Question*, 39.

60. "The Construction of Privacy in and around *The Bostonians,*" *American Literature* 64 (December 1992): 725.

61. *The Real Thing: Imitation and Authenticity in American Culture, 1880–1940* (Chapel Hill: University of North Carolina Press, 1989), xv, 141.

62. Ibid., xvii.

63. Ibid.

64. This number was arrived at because the ballroom in Mrs. Astor's Fifth Avenue brownstone could comfortably accommodate 400 guests. As McAllister explained, "if you go outside that number you strike people who are either not at ease in a ballroom or else make other people not at ease," concluding that New York society was after all but "twenty score of well-bred persons, called the world." Quoted by Arthur T. Vanderbilt II in *Fortune's Children: The Fall of the House of Vanderbilt* (New York: William Morrow, 1989), 98. Seeking to define ever more exclusive distinctions, the Rev. Charles Wilbur de Lyon Nichols—once dubbed "Ward McAllister's first Apostle on the Philosophy of Society"—published *The Ultra-Fashionable Peerage of America, with a few appended essays on Ultra-Smartness* (New York: George Harjes, 1904). He selects 150 "ultra-fashionables" (at once restricted to and defined by their presence in New York) and, in "descending degrees of

fashionable precedence," the "400," "supplemented by a limited few Ultra-fashionable folk of the provincial cities and towns; the outer fringe of the '400,' the Colonial and Knickerbocker families; and the wealthy upper middle class in American society—society in the crude" (3).

65. In "Pecuniary Canons of Taste," Veblen discusses the invidious distinction telegraphed by consumption of man-made articles (whose value resides in the "honorific waste" incurred in production) rather than machine-made articles manufactured for the same purpose: "The point of material difference between machine-made goods and the hand-wrought goods which serve the same purposes is, ordinarily, that the former serve their primary purpose more adequately. They are a more perfect product—show a more perfect adaptation of means to an end. This does not save them from disesteem and depreciation, for they fall short under the test of honorific waste. Hand labour is a more wasteful method of production; hence the goods turned out by this method are more serviceable for the purpose of pecuniary reputability . . . . Commonly, if not invariably, the honorific marks of hand labour are certain imperfections and irregularities . . . . The ground of superiority of hand-wrought goods, therefore, is a certain margin of crudeness . . . .

"The appreciation of those evidences of honorific crudeness to which hand-wrought goods owe their superior worth and charm in the eyes of well-bred people is a matter of nice discrimination. It requires training and the formation of right habits of thought with respect to what may be called the physiognomy of goods. Machine made goods of daily use are often admired and preferred on account of their excessive perfection by the vulgar and the underbred who have not given due thought to the punctilios of elegant consumption." *The Theory of the Leisure Class*, with an introduction by Robert Lekachman (New York: Penguin, 1979), 159–60.

66. For a discussion of the magazine's early attacks on James and realism, see Martha Banta, "From 'Harry Jim' to "St. James' in *Life Magazine* (1883–1916): Twitting the Author; Prompting the Public," *Henry James Review* 14 (1993): 237–56.

67. *Life*, 4, no. 100 (Nov. 27, 1884); 20, no. 511 (Oct. 13, 1892); 13, no. 319 (Feb. 7, 1889).

68. *The Art of the Novel: Critical Prefaces by Henry James*, foreword by R. W. B. Lewis, with an introduction by R. P. Blackmur (Boston: Northeastern University Press, 1984), 203–4. Lady Barbarina, however, swims against this tide of Eastward migration and marries an American.

69. *Life*, 25, no. 635 (Feb. 28, 1895): 132.

70. *Life*, 17, no. 423 (Feb. 5, 1891). The mere instrumentality of the American Girl in these foreign marriages is echoed later by Conseulo Vanderbilt, who remarked that in her marriage to the Duke of Marlborough, she went from being "a pawn in my mother's game" of status-mongering to providing what her husband called "a link in the chain" of generations. Quoted in Vanderbilt, *Fortune's Children*, 172.

71. *Life* 15, no. 377 (March 6, 1890).

72. *Life*, 17, no. 423: 157. A *Life* cartoon which appeared just after the Vanderbilt-Marlborough wedding (26, no. 673 [Nov. 21, 1895]) does issue just such a warning in its caption: beneath the illustration of a woman driving a buckboard loaded with money drawn by four rank horses reads the inscription, "Many imported Thoroughbred sires reach this market yearly from all parts of Europe. It would be advisable, perhaps, to require before investing—besides the pedigrees—all possible guarantees to soundness, confirmation, action, gait, Etc., Etc., Etc."

73. Caption to the cover illustration for *Life* 17, no. 421 (Jan. 22, 1891) in which an elderly member of the aristocracy is presented with a youthful American bride crowned with a sack of money.

74. *Life* 16, no. 415 (Dec. 4, 1890).

75. *Life* 26, no. 658 (Aug. 8, 1895).

76. *Life* 26, no. 667 (Oct. 10, 1895): 228. The idea that America derived some benefit from this exportation of cash is conveyed when *Life* concluded that "[o]ne particularly redeeming feature is that some of this money may be spent on Blenheim, and good Americans who pass their vacations in England may have the chance to gaze on the results."

77. Vanderbilt, *Fortune's Children*, 149. Rutherfurd was of "Old" New York stock, his mother a direct descendant of Peter Stuyvesant, the last Dutch governor of New York. Gail MacColl and Carol McD. Wallace, *To Marry and English Lord* (New York: Workman, 1989), 152.

78. This contract, dated November 6, 1895, stated that "[w]hereas, a marriage is intended between the said Duke of Marlborough and the said Consuelo Vanderbilt, and whereas pursuant to an agreement made upon the treaty for the said intended marriage, the sum of $2,500,000 in 50,000 shares of the capital stock of the Beech Creek Railway Company, on which an annual payment of 4 per cent is guaranteed by the New York Central Railroad Company, is transferred this day to the trustees. And shall during the joint lives of the said Duke of Marlborough, [and] Consuelo Vanderbilt, pay the income of the said sum of $2,500,000 . . . unto the Duke of Marlborough for his life." In

addition, William K. Vanderbilt signed a separate agreement to pay the Duke and Duchess $100,000 every year for life. Quoted in Vanderbilt, *Fortune's Children,* 173–174.

79. Ibid., 175.

80. *Life* 25, no. 635 (Feb. 28, 1895): 132. This savvy advice perhaps struck a chord, for in 1895 alone, eight other American heiresses married titled Englishmen; many others found Continental bridegrooms. See McColl and Wallace, *English Lord,* 165.

81. Such a position might be compared to the concept of "specific performance" in contract law, an action to compel enactment of a provision of an agreement rather to accept remuneration for damages incurred by the failure to perform: "The doctrine of specific performance is that, where damage would be inadequate compensation for the breach of an agreement, the contractor will be compelled to perform specifically which he has agreed to do. As the exact fulfillment of an agreement is not always practicable, the phrase may mean, in a given case, not literal, but substantial performance." Henry Campbell Black, M.A., Black's *Law Dictionary,* (St. Paul, Minn.: West Publishing Co., 1968, Rev. 4th ed.), 1295. Carolyn Porter [*Seeing and Being: The Plight of Participant Observers in Emerson, James, Adams and Faulkner* (Middletown, Conn.: Wesleyan University Press, 1981)] argues that the Prince has only "exchange value" because he is held above the flow of commodities on the marriage market. He doesn't become an appreciated "use value" until Charlotte, in renewing their former bond, creates a demand for him (see pages 145–147). However, the social demand for the Prince's presence, which fulfills the Ververs' social requirement, means his use value comes into play with the signing of the marriage contract.

82. "The Special Type," *The Complete Tales of Henry James.,* ed. Leon Edel, vol. 10 (Philadelphia: Lippincott, 1964), 171. Subsequent quotations from this source are from this edition and are cited parenthetically in the text as ST. Regarding the Vanderbilt divorce, James wrote in his notebooks: "the thing [the subject for "The Special Type"] suggested by what was told me the other day of the W. K. Vanderbilt divorce: his engaging the *demi-mondaine,* in Paris, to *s'afficher* with him in order to force his virago of a wife to divorce him" (NB 145). The *pro forma* adultery was carried out with *demi-mondaine* Nellie Nuestretter of Nevada. MacColl and Wallace, *English Lord,* 156.

83. Quoted in Porter, *Seeing and Being,* 134.

84. Ibid.

85. "The Ravages of a Carpet," *Household Papers and Stories* (Boston: houghton-Mifflin, 1896), 1–22.

86. In *The Expense of Vision,* Holland discusses the connection between the purchase of the tiles and the "purchase" of Charlotte, noting the transaction, solemnized with wine and cake, "is one of the most complex events in the novel since it founds the proposal of marriage on an act which is both commercial and a ceremony" (360). However, he does not discuss the imagery's sexual dimension.

87. "Modernist Maneuverings in the Marriage Plot: Breaking Ideologies of Gender and Genre in James's *The Golden Bowl,*" *PMLA* 101 (May 1986): 379.

88. *Language and Knowledge in the Late Novels of Henry James* (Chicago: University of Chicago Press, 1976), 100.

89. Holland, The *Expense of Vision,* 50.

90. Porter, *Seeing and Being,* 133.

91. Boone, "Modernist Maneuverings," 384.

92. Yeazell, *Language and Knowledge,* 125.

93. *The Art of the Novel,* 341.

94. Ibid., 329.

95. Ibid., 296.

CHAPTER THREE

New Wives for Old: Divorce and the Leisure-Class Marriage Market in Edith Wharton's *The Custom of the Country*

" . . . why does the obsolete institution of marriage survive with you?"

"Oh, it still has its uses. One couldn't be divorced without it."

—Charles Bowen replying to Raymond de Chelles, *The Custom of the Country*

I

In 1913, divorce was most certainly on Edith Wharton's mind. January saw the serial publication begin for *The Custom of the Country*,[1] a novel which expands the portrait of the "marriage market" so incisively developed in *The House of Mirth* to include the crucial role of the turn-of-the-century divorce industry within that economy. Building on the observation Lawrence Selden makes to Lily Bart that marriage is the "vocation" women of her social class are "brought up for,"[2] Wharton's deeply ironic novel proves that divorce is the logical mechanism for market expansion, providing women with the means to forge nuptial careers based not on a single liaison, but on successive—and ever more successful—unions. Indeed, from the outset it is evident that Undine Spragg—the market-savvy heroine of *The Custom of the Country*—is acutely aware of the benefits divorce might afford a "disappointed" wife. Husbands who aren't "in the right set" and thereby hinder a wife's ability to "really get anywhere" can be got "rid of," and all to the wife's "credit" for wanting change.[3] Guided by this ledger sheet of social credits and liabilities, Undine capitalizes on a series of advantageous marriages and timely divorces, ostensibly improving her social position with each calculated move she makes.[4]

The year *The Custom of the Country* was published, Edith Wharton was herself divorced from her husband of nearly twenty-eight years, Edward "Teddy" Wharton. Wharton's divorce petition, granted from a French "divorce mill" on the grounds of Teddy's embarrassingly public adulteries, freed her from a truly untenable union.[5] Unlike Undine Spragg, Wharton sought divorce not to "trade up" in the marriage market, but because she found, after agonizing self-reflection, her definition of marriage as "a living together, a sharing of all" impossibly compromised by life with Teddy.[6] The decision to divorce, as necessary as it had become, nevertheless must have cost Wharton dearly. Her biographers—R.W.B. Lewis, Cynthia Griffin Wolff and, most recently, Shari Benstock—all suggest that she feared her divorce would, by force of convention, take on a melodramatic tone, with Teddy cast as the abused and helpless victim of her frivolous whim.[7] Wolff notes that Wharton went so far as to prepare for her future biographer a bundle of papers composed of letters and doctors' reports detailing Teddy's unstable mental condition—papers that serve as a brief of sorts, arguing in defense of her actions against those who, like the rigid matrons of *The Age of Innocence*, inevitably believe "that when 'such things happened' it was undoubtedly foolish of the man, but somehow always criminal of the woman."[8]

Such concerns on Wharton's part were not without justification. Although New York society had moderated its views on divorce since the Gilded Age setting represented in *The Age of Innocence*, it was by no means tolerant of the fact in the early years of this century. The idea that women, driven by frivolous if no longer criminal desires, were particularly culpable when marriages ended by court decree continued to dominate the popular conception of the "divorce problem." Literature of the period often reinforced this view, and works by two of Wharton's friends are of particular interest. *The Orchid* (1905), by Robert Grant, follows the progress of a selfish, head strong young woman who marries for money and amusement, but divorces for love, "selling" her infant daughter back to her husband in order to secure a two million dollar settlement. The scenario, of course, foreshadows Undine Spragg's own custody negotiations with Ralph; in fact, it was from Wharton that Grant had heard of the New York divorcée who had received millions for just such an arrangement.[9] In a comic vein, Langdon Mitchell's 1906 hit play *The New York Idea* relates the story of a discontented socialite who, having broken up her marriage on a whim, returns to her husband when it becomes evident that he intends to exercise his new-found freedom by remarrying. One character's observation seems to capture what Wharton will portray as the emerging marital custom of the country: "The modern American marriage is like a wire fence—the woman's the wire—the posts are the husbands. One—two—three! And if you cast your eye over the future, you can count them, post after post, up hill, down dale, all the way to Dakota."[10]

Wharton herself populated the fringes of her fiction with sketches of upwardly mobile divorcées; indeed, *The House of Mirth* is liberally punctuated with socialites' wry observations about the common, frequently dangerous, but not fatal social illness in their midst: "Some one said the other day that there was a divorce and a case of appendicitis in every family one knows" (*HM* 43). Characters like Mrs. Welly Bry, "a lady of obscure origin and indomitable social ambitions" who "had already sacrificed one husband, and sundry minor considerations, to her determination to get on" (*HM* 117–118), and Mrs. Norma Hatch, "whose reversion to her Christian name was explained as the result of her latest divorce" (*HM* 287), represent the class of social climbers that Wharton will later label "the invaders," their calculated successes on the marriage market providing the ironic accents which highlight Lily Bart's inability to see to fruition any of her several nuptial opportunities. In *The Custom of the Country*, Wharton moves these invaders and their antics from the margins to the center of her tale, combining them to form the character and career of Undine Spragg, "a monstrously perfect result of the system"(*CC* 208) which destroys Lily Bart. Never touched by an emotion larger than the desire for position or possession, Undine—her name invokes the popular period image of the soulless, shape-shifting sea creature—embodies the new social class threatening to level the values and traditions of the old

New York order.[11] Yet Wharton's most acerbic criticism centers not on Undine and her ilk, but on "the system" and its productions—like the profitable and increasingly notorious migratory divorce industry—that aided their progress. The divorce industry, from Wharton's personal perspective, must have seemed particularly galling, for its reputation for encouraging "rotary marriage" along the lines of the period's pervasive "rotary consumerism" had so contaminated a necessary legal remedy as to bring even the most legitimate case under suspicion.

II

When, in *The Custom of the Country*, the newly remarried Indiana Rolliver (formerly Binch, née Frusk) admonishes the recently divorced but not yet recycled Undine Spragg Moffatt Marvell with the savvy market wisdom that "a divorce is always a good thing to have" (*CC* 346), she expresses a contemporary trend in American advertising which emphasized the benefits derived from consumption of a product rather than the inherent qualities of the product itself.[12] The benefits most often marketed, whether the product in question were a new car, a new washing machine, a new dress, or a new bread flour, were increased amusement, mobility, freedom and status, the very benefits Undine would have enjoyed had she held a divorce in ready reserve, a trump card played to secure through Peter Van Degen the desired position among "the showy and the promiscuous" who embodied "the future" (*CC* 193). Yet the aim of such advertising was not to satisfy but to stimulate desire by providing a vision of the good life forever unrealizable because it was constructed on an ever-receding horizon of grand, illimitable abstractions. Indeed, the only future seemingly ensured by such advertising promises was that of the market economy itself, for the focus on benefit over product subtly redefined perception of what constituted the "necessities of life" by shifting attention from "commodities which are indispensably necessary for the support of life" to "whatever the custom of the country renders it indecent for creditable people . . . to be without."[13] The ambiguity generated around the concept of needs and what was required to satisfy those needs was crucial in conditioning the high-intensity consumption which characterized Undine Spragg's America: as consumers lost a secure sense of what was necessary to life and seized upon products which promised a life consistent with abstract notions of "creditability" or "respectability," the process of consumption became equated with social survival.

Advertising, relying upon mass produced images which "brought the beautiful within the reach of all"[14] to condition consumption, spurred the market to unprecedented expansion in the decades of most concern in Wharton's fiction. What had been a verbal medium exerting an appeal to a buyer's reasoned needs by providing unembellished product information gave way to compelling visual dramas centered around the image of a product. By placing products in settings evocative of leisure and privilege, advertisers addressed non-rational yearnings, encouraging consumers to project themselves into the constructed frame and savor thereby a richer, fuller life. The marketing strategists who dictated the change to pictorial formats attracted further attention to their products by increasing both the number and frequency of their advertisements, so that by 1910 advertising comprised more than 50% of daily newspaper copy. Retail establishments became the most prominent advertiser during this period, prompting one journalist to remark that the newspaper had become "an appendage of the department store."[15] The advertising saturation suggested by this remark meant the daily newspaper brought the store to the consumer, making its goods constantly available for visual inspection and, thus, stimulating such a boom in sales that shopping emerged as a major leisure activity in America.[16] Merchants and advertisers evidently recognized the truth at the heart of Thorstein Veblen's arch portrayal of marriage relations described in *The Theory of the Leisure Class*: since women, especially of the moneyed class, function to display their husbands' wealth and power through the conspicuous consumption of goods, advertisements were increasingly directed at the female audience.

Consumer desire had not only to be created, however; its satisfaction had also to be legitimized, and in this several of the period's intellectuals reinforced advertising's primary message. While Veblen launched his ironic attack on the leisure class pursuit of "conspicuous decency," prominent economists were advancing theories which linked increased consumption with advanced civilization. In 1895, George Gunton celebrated the completion of the 125,000 acre, 250 room Biltmore estate, claiming that such ostentatious display would lead "to a new direction of devoting American wealth to the uplifting of [the] American standard of taste and social cultivation."[17] Professor Simon N. Patten, of the University of Pennsylvania's Wharton School of Economics, spent nearly thirty years arguing that social and individual development depended upon the pleasures of continuous and varied consumption. Based on his second law of consumption, which held that "[t]he change from one commodity to another . . . revives and increases the satisfaction of consumption," Patten asserted that "[t]he progress of society consists, not in increasing the consumption of the articles in use, but in substituting new articles with a large sum of pleasure" to stimulate the consumer as well as the market.[18] With this emphasis on variety, the notion of consumer "creditability" shifted from an individual's fixed possession of a few luxury items to a continuous renewal of goods, so that "[t]he standard of life is determined, not so much by what a man has to enjoy, as by the rapidity with which he tires of the pleasure. To have a high standard means to enjoy a pleasure intensely and to tire of it quickly."[19] Time-honored values of frugality and self-restraint were further challenged and the culture of consumption sanctioned with Patten's claim in *The New Basis of Civilization* (1907) that "[c]haracter is acquired . . . by the activities and amusements in the shop and street, not by restraints of church and home. The new morality does not consist in saving, but in expanding consumption . . . not in the thought of the future, but in the utilization and expansion of the present."[20]

Theories like Patten's also helped to overcome the troubling aspect of waste inherent in the logic of an expanding capitalist market, reassuring consumers who were conditioned both to abandon products that ultimately failed to satisfy a perceived need and to spend more money on new products and promises. To ensure internalization of this profitable mode of consumption, advertising in newspapers and women's magazines encouraged the habits by which buying supplanted the economy of domestic production, carefully masking the problematic connotations of waste, exhaustion and destruction contained in the concept of consumption. Often, advertising copy semantically transformed consumption into production to assure women they had not lost their power to contribute to the economy. Buying was portrayed as a "productive act" because it could "multiply manifold the satisfactions from a given income," or, as a Macy's ad promised, shopping "would yield you more" than ever thought possible.[21] Other ads suggested that "buying" was more creative than "making," for in buying women exercised the freedom to choose from a vast array of goods on the market.[22] Indeed, the very mode of pictorial advertising, with its reliance upon mass-produced "copies" of an "original" (whether that original was the product or a work of art used as a backdrop for the product image) facilitated this message of cyclic consumption and disposal. As Walter Benjamin observed, the mechanical reproduction of images, because it emphasizes plurality over uniqueness and transitoriness over permanence, creates a "sense of the universal equality of things" *qua* things—things that are because of their infinite reproducibility easily replaceable. Even the viewer participation evoked by such advertising representations conditioned such consumer behavior. "Concentration," or the state of being absorbed, is replaced with "distraction," or the state of absorbing, when the unique original gives way to a multiplicity of copies, creating thereby what might be termed a state of consumer amnesia: having consummated the perceiver-object relation by "absorbing" the representation, the consumer-spectator is freed to move on to the next consumable image, the next "distraction." [23]

Americans internalized the model of continuous consumption and, significantly, carried it beyond the purchase and disposal habits associated with clothing, appliances and furniture. In *The American Scene* (1907), Henry James noted that this "rotary system" of consumption affected even family dwellings and public buildings: in Boston and New York, the wholesale destruction of old buildings and their replacement with the new bespoke "a perpetual repudiation of the past" to satisfy not an aesthetic, but an economic idea of taste.[24] As artifacts constructed for an economy that canonized waste as a social good, the new structures seemed to trumpet their temporary status as virtue that ensured continuation of the cycle: "We are only installments, symbols, stop-gaps . . . expensive as we are, we have nothing to do with continuity, responsibility, transmission, and don't in the least care what becomes of us after we have served our present purpose."[25] Deprived of the settings in which public rituals and private histories were enacted, memory—and the attendant sense of self—suffers dislocation; as the "restless analyst" witnessed the "unmaking" of the buildings which encoded his past, he felt "as if the bottom had fallen out of one's own biography, and one plunged backward into space without meeting anything."[26]

If James reads in the obliteration of familiar settings and structures an emblem of the new social dislocation—a divorce of sorts between present and past selves, Wharton adopts a slightly different tack in *The Custom of the Country*, arguing that the logic of consumption and disposal urged in contemporary advertising schemes extended most insidiously into the home, where familial relations conveying identity, continuity and tradition were similarly at risk of being "unmade." To her already potent critique of the marriage market, Wharton adds the role that the booming migratory divorce industry plays by creating a product, marketed in terms of the increased freedom, mobility and status it can provide, that keeps the marriage economy expanding because spouses and even families become one more disposable item in the rotary system of consumption. Yet, like so many product promises, the benefits seemingly secured by a quick trip to a western divorce mill proved illusory, for this legal remedy was neither a means of liberating women from the marriage economy nor of advancing their fortunes within it. Rather, as Wharton perceives, the migratory divorce industry functioned as an extension of that economy by recycling women back onto the marriage market after exacting from them both their time and money.

III

The western states' migratory divorce industry arose because, like any other business, it responded to consumer demand for a particular product; the divorce industry flourished in the late nineteenth and early twentieth centuries because it became increasingly adept in modifying its product to meet new consumer requirements and in diversifying its offerings to capture an ever greater market share.[27] Almost from the nation's inception, liberalized divorce laws and the consequent increase in divorces granted were associated with westward growth. Dissatisfied spouses, particularly from conservative states such as New York or New Jersey (which granted absolute divorce decrees only in cases of adultery), looked west to Pennsylvania as early as 1815 for laws that recognized, in addition to adultery, a range of complaints as legitimate grounds for ending a marriage. Though lunacy (in 1843) and conviction of a felony (in 1854) were added to Pennsylvania's divorce statutes, the "divorce haven" reputation—and business—passed westward to Ohio in the 1840s, to Indiana in the 1850s and 1860s, to Illinois in the 1870s and 1880s, to the Dakotas from 1880–1907 and finally to Nevada, which held divorce dominion well into the twentieth century. The product incentives which swelled the westward progress of those seeking marital freedom included an incompatibility clause in Indiana, railroad accessibility in Chicago, short residency requirements in the Dakotas, and provision for private hearings and immediate remarriage in Nevada. Between 1880 and 1900, the number of divorces granted in the United States doubled, and by 1920 had more than doubled again.[28] While the so-called divorce havens were not in themselves responsible for this tremendous increase, they nevertheless provided those who could afford it an attractive site for severing the marriage bond: fully seventy percent of the Dakota divorce trade was comprised of out-of-state traffic.[29] During this time and in accord with the general market trend, women supplanted men as the largest consumers of divorce decrees in the liberalized west.[30]

The liberality with which the western states granted divorce has been variously attributed to progressive attitudes in championing women's rights, public sympathy engendered by the plight of wives deserted by men drawn westward by the prospect of gold or adventure, or to legislative willingness to free a settler from the bonds of the old life so he—or she—might begin afresh.[31] However, neither progressive nor altruistic motives truly account for the liberal divorce statues in these territories; indeed, the provisions in the law were not intended to facilitate divorce for the future benefit of women, but to swell the rolls of registered voters and thereby hasten the move toward statehood and, more significantly, to respond to a growing consumer demand that would enhance a state's economy.[32] The lucrative divorce business afforded by liberal and often broadly interpreted statutes and the competition which emerged between certain western states to attract that business was taken up in the satiric short story "Divorce" (1856).[33] It concerns the professional career of a young lawyer who moves to Michigan in 1847 to find and exploit whatever "course of proceeding promised the greatest pecuniary award in the future" (D 630). Surveying the legal field, he is discouraged to discover each branch of the law well covered, until one day a "Yankee" strides into his office and demands, "set yourself right about it and get me a divorce!" (D 631). Vague memories of the scriptural injunctions against divorce and faint ethical concerns at first hold the young attorney back from accepting this charge; however, once he researches the liberal codes afforded by Michigan law, he knows he has found his niche:

> Here was a broad and rich field for a legal harvest for anyone who would step in and cultivate it. Here were seven modes of egress from the state of matrimony; and, if those who bore the conjugal yoke uneasily had but some guide to teach them the ease with which it might be cast off, honors and wealth would soon pour in upon him from their abundant gratitude. (D 631)[34]

When the Yankee returns, the lawyer has acceded to his demand and prepared a brief that, by skillfully twisting the case facts, meets the letter of the law concerning desertion. Presented with the bill for divorce, the court orders the Yankee's absent wife to respond to the suit pending against her within ninety days—an order published in a village newspaper that "she was morally certain not to see" (D 632). At the next session of the court, the divorce is finalized.

As the supplier of a service much in demand, the lawyer soon has a thriving business accommodating the usually shady facts of a marital dispute to meet the requirements of the liberal law. Indeed, as the lawyer boasts, it would be a "fortunate" and "remarkably circumspect" couple against whom he could not dig up some "*prima facie* [evidence for] . . . the existence of at least one of the causes for divorce." Thus "scarcely a person, who thought a chance for improving his or her conjugal relations offered, applied for my aid in vain," and the young lawyer becomes both wealthy and famous for "improving" marriages by dissolving them (D 633).

However, a cloud appears on the his sunny financial horizon when he hears of a local man who, rather than appealing to our lawyer for marital improvement, heads to Indiana where the laws and residency requirements create an even more attractive environment for divorce. Seeing his lucrative trade heading south, as it were, in the "mania for Indiana divorces," the disgruntled lawyer acknowledges superior facilities are to be found:

> From my knowledge of the parties who have since obtained divorces
> in that state, and the ease with which they got them, I judge it to be
> only necessary that they should present themselves in court, make
> oath that they are citizens (having slept one night in the state six
> weeks before), and that they want a divorce—and thereupon it is
> granted. (D 633)

But not only does our young lawyer worry about an impending
financial calamity; domestic disaster seems imminent as well. With
Indiana's divorce procedure so enviably easy and railroad access so
efficient, he finds he must keep careful watch over his own wife lest
she slip over the border and file her own petition. However, if she
should succeed in filing for marital dissolution, the righteously
indignant lawyer-husband "shall insist at least upon [his] protest being
entered . . . as a permanent record of his abhorrence for the Hoosier
state, its laws, and the tribunals which administer them" (D 634).

Both those who deplored the divorce "industry" in South Dakota—
Undine Spragg's destination in seeking divorce from Ralph Marvell—
and those who championed it agreed that economic factors governed
the state's legislation. Episcopal Bishop William Hare, who led the
protest against South Dakota's divorce trade, charged that the people of
the state closed their eyes to the "morally enervating" situation
"because the divorce mills are profitable":

> Divorce litigation has brought large money, it is said, into our needy
> state. The business of the florists and jewelers has increased ten and
> twenty fold. Hotel proprietors are growing rich. Thus, unconsciously,
> those who reap the harvest are led to throw an attractive guise over
> what, but for their self-interest, would wear a hideous form.[35]

Such charges from those on the moral high road did not place the
industry's supporters on the defensive. When, in 1892, legislation was
introduced to lengthen the residency requirement from six months to
one year—a change that would have seriously affected the economic
boom divorce had created—industry advocates argued, "Why should
the legislature, on merely sentimental grounds, drive out of South
Dakota and into North Dakota and Nebraska a business which brings to
Sioux Falls over $100,000 a year?"[36] Recognizing that the state

"owe[d] its prosperity to the ease with which the stranger [could] become a citizen of South Dakota and thus make use of its laws," the legislature defeated the bill.[37]

The prosperity the divorce industry generated in towns with convenient railroad access was considerable. Because divorces obtained by migration were especially costly—both in terms of legal fees and in setting up a second household within the state to meet residency requirements—the industry attracted an affluent clientele. The approximately one hundred divorce-seeking men and women who populated the Sioux Falls "colony" at any given time might spend as much as $5,000 each beyond court and legal fees during their stay, generating annual revenues estimated between $150,000 and $500,000 in that city alone. According to a 1908 feature article in the Minneapolis *Journal*, town merchants, "prepared for the demands of the divorce contingent's patronage," laid in a stock of "high-grade goods," while landlords, hotel owners, physicians, dentists, jewelers, florists, and livery stable owners all "found the divorce colony a source of considerable profit." In an area dubbed "Divorce Row" by local residents, attractive furnished cottages were held ready to rent to South Dakota's notorious "six month residents" at rates ranging from $75 to $100—at a time when apartments in New York City rented for $35–50 per month.[38] Lawyers were the special beneficiaries of the Sioux Falls divorce trade, reportedly paying conductors on trains arriving from Chicago to direct "coveted" divorce cases to their offices or to divorce colony hotels they owned.[39] Members of the legal profession were also suspected of charging variable fees based on the size of a client's bank account or the potential notoriety of a suit:[40]

> Heaven help the unfortunate applicant for divorce who goes to [South]Dakota thinking that his or her case will cost the exact amount the attorney demands for a fee . . . . A divorce lawyer usually charges two hundred and fifty dollars. If he happens to be an ex-judge he demands five hundred dollars or more; in fact, a client can never tell what his expenses will be, because there are so many extras; such as the taking of depositions, etc., etc. Sometimes the applicant for divorce is surprised by having an extra fee demanded; if he demur, the attorney tells the judge not to sign the decree, or, if it has been

signed, the attorney takes possession until the unfortunate client complies with his demand.

Any person who attempts to fight a Dakota divorce must have a large balance at his banker's, because the legal fraternity are all united on one point: that is, to bleed their victims.[41]

The *Life* cartoon "Two Souls with but a Single Thought" (Fig. 3.1) refers not, as one might first believe, to the couple intent upon procuring a divorce, but rather to the law partners whose aim to "Cheatem & Soakem" unites them in the lucrative business of dissolving matrimonial bonds.

The Sioux Falls divorce mill was credited with stimulating such a boom among lawyers, hotel owners and tradespeople that other cities actively sought to capture a share of its market. A Chicago newspaper ran a series of articles aimed at providing the Sioux Falls colony with adverse publicity because business people were "jealous" of South Dakota's encroachment on what had been a Chicago "specialty."[42] Yankton, a rival South Dakota divorce town, attempted to attract some of the Sioux Falls trade by building a new hotel "designed especially to gain the patronage of divorce colonists," and opening it with a gala "society" ball, while a Fargo, North Dakota, hotel owner organized the South Dakota lobby to lengthen the residency requirements and thus "kill the business there [so] it will all come to us."[43] Clearly, the mercenary motive outweighed any progressive or altruistic urge to free women and men from unhappy or undesirable unions.

Advertising, a prominent feature of the migratory divorce trade, was employed to sustain this economic boom. By focusing on the attendant benefits of consumption rather than on the divorce product itself—a marketing strategy already familiar in the larger consumer economy—the industry fashioned itself as an unexceptional parallel to more traditional businesses. Although such marketing was considered unethical by most state bar associations, lawyers nevertheless placed advertisements in eastern newspapers for a clientele who would appreciate the benefits of a divorce obtained "without publicity or exposure" that was "legal everywhere."[44] As the trade moved westward, this straightforward offering of goods and services was joined by a marketing strategy of indirect inducement, concealing behind a veneer of adjunct benefits an appeal for divorce business. The Yankton hotel proprietor prepared a "beautifully printed" circular that noted the advantages of his establishment and sent it by the hundreds for distribution among "society" in New York, Boston and Philadelphia. Not to be outdone, the owner of the principle Sioux Falls hotel, upon refurbishing his building, sent out similar circulars which guaranteed the additional inducement of privacy from intrusive newspaper men. To calm the fears of women who did not relish the prospect of publicly putting forward the details of their suits, an article about a young but "learned" Sioux Falls judge whose treatment of "the fair sex" was "marked by the tenderest sympathy and the most delicate solicitude for their interests" was planted in a Chicago newspaper.[45]

Society page publicity, by providing beautiful images of affluence for consumption and emulation, worked in concert with the marketing strategies employed to generate divorce commerce, becoming itself a form of divorce advertising. As scandalous as divorce continued to be in some social circles, the society columns of the major Philadelphia, New York and Washington papers and gossip sheets such as *Town Topics* provided lengthy accounts of "name" cases. Alva Vanderbilt, a woman who *knew* the value of being first to risk the latest trend or fashion, boasted of her divorce "from one of the richest men in America":

> I always do everything first. I blaze the trail for the rest to walk in. I was the first girl in my "set" to marry a Vanderbilt. Then I was the first society woman to ask for a divorce, and within a year ever so many others had followed my example. They . . . had not dared to do it until I showed them the way.[46]

The New York papers, accustomed to printing the details of Alva's lavish society entertainments, likewise commented upon her sumptuous divorce settlement from William K. Vanderbilt.[47] In addition to the details of a petitioner's suit and settlement, these columns offered a view of the good life—accommodations, fashions and amusements—enjoyed by the likes of socialites Mrs. William Rhinelander Stewart, Florence Bigelow Dodge and Marquise Margaret Laura de Stuers as they awaited their Dakota divorce decrees.[48] The *Life* illustration "In the Lobby of the Court" (Fig. 3.2) confirms that the divorce court—and

TWO SOULS WITH BUT A SINGLE THOUGHT

Fig. 3.1 "Two Souls" [*Life* 60, no. 1435 (April 28, 1910)]

IN THE LOBBY OF THE COURT

THE CONTINUOUS DIVORCE PERFORMANCE

Fig. 3.2 "In the Lobby of the Court" [*Life* 55, no. 1430 (March 24, 1910)]

Fig. 3.3 "Divorce Frieze" [*Life* 70, no. 1818 (Aug. 30, 1917)]

Fig. 3.4 "Mapping Matrimony" [*Puck* (Jan. 22, 1879)]

HER DIVORCE SUIT

Fig. 3.5 "Her Divorce Suit" [*Life* 49, no. 1270 (Feb. 28, 1907)]

THE EMBARRASSMENTS OF DIVORCE.

He: WE MET LAST IN EIGHTY-TWO.
She: AH, YES! LET ME SEE. WHO WAS I IN EIGHTY-TWO ?

Fig. 3.6 "The Embarrassments of Divorce" [*Life* 26, no. 675 (Dec. 5, 1895)]

thus the society pages which reported upon them—had become a public stage on which women effected performative acts of self-transformation and thus advertised their changed marital, social and economic stature. However, one had to know the public taste of the moment. In the 1889 *Life* cartoon "The Emptiness of Life," one divorce "performer" laments to a friend her loss of audience interest, a sure sign of her diminishing social "creditability": "I feel terribly discouraged. When I obtained my first divorce it was the sensation of the day; the second attracted some attention; but yesterday there were not half a dozen people in the courtroom."[49] On the other hand, an *Arena* article calculated to counter the negative press the Sioux Falls divorce community had received featured another image of the divorcée, and asserted the dignified behavior, "moral courage," "unusual grace, or beauty, or mental gift" possessed by "the women of the colony." Adorning the text which publicizes their womanly virtues are photographs of several attractive divorce petitioners.[50]

Certainly, this last example of indirect advertising of colony "benefits" suggests not only the sobriety and respectability of the Sioux Falls enterprise, but also subtly reveals that divorce was not the only product available on the market. Indeed, like Undine's friend and roommate Mabel Lipscomb in the unnamed South Dakota divorce town, many colonists found themselves "unpairing and pairing again . . . with ease and rapidity" (*CC* 287) in a pattern which matched the rotary system of consumption.[51] A Sioux Falls *Daily Press* headline proclaimed, "Weds the woman he shadowed: Detective employed in divorce case gets Wife from the Proceedings," and but three days later reported that a Mrs. Peck, wife of Columbia University Latin Professor Harry Thurston Peck, secured her divorce with "a light touch and a quick getaway" in the company of her husband-to-be.[52] *Life's* representation of rotary marriage and divorce (Fig. 3.3) proved the simplicity and logic of the whole procedure: marital ties snipped by divorce free spouses to move on to forge new bonds.[53] Indeed, Wharton's fictional clipping from a society gossip column announcing the "quick work untying and tying" (*CC* 584) characteristic of Undine's Reno divorce ironically echoes both text and subtext of these contemporary accounts. According to the authors of *The Divorce Mill*, such practices were routine: "a number of women come to Sioux Falls under the escort of their future husbands, and these gentlemen make all the arrangements for the temporary comfort of their fair yet hopeful companions."[54] The language of contemporary news and feature articles reveals that such rotation achieved by the "separation and *rearrangement* of married couples" was understood to be part of the business: "Wives bearing famous names come *to trade* them for names not so famous, but borne by more attractive men."[55] The matrimonial history inscribed upon the curvaceous posterior of the prospective bride in Fig. 3.4 not only displays her sequential matrimonial adventures, it also suggests how her past (and quite possibly her future) has been determined by the names she has bargained for and traded. Indeed, the only way for a woman to "make a name" for herself and "belong" is to take a man's.[56] "Her Divorce Suit" (Fig. 3.5) demonstrates how a woman's marital history—even thirty years later—defines her; however, in 1907 it's no longer *who* (or whose) she's been, but *where* she's been to exchange identities.

Metaphors of farming and manufacture, structured as they are around notions of cycle, product and profit, governed many of the period's representations of divorce. A *Nation* columnist forecast a bumper harvest of divorcées, noting that the year's especially promising "divorce crop" ensured that "the product [would] fully equal if not surpass that of any previous season" in Sioux Falls.[57] Another journalist, bemoaning Sioux Falls' reputation as a "divorce mill," claimed that the "noxious atmosphere" generated by the "wholesale divorce business" had "crushed out" legitimate interests—the packing plant, the canning factory, the linen and lumber mills—from the city's economy. "All industries are dead but one, and on that the whole town gets its sustenance."[58] However, the process represented by such analogies between the migratory divorce trade and industry or agriculture confuses the logic of production in which raw materials are converted into usable commodities; the "divorce mill" was unique in its ability to reclaim "used goods" for the marriage market by transforming "old" wives into new brides. Adopted as a function of the leisure class marriage economy, divorce seemed to provide the necessary mechanism for market expansion, liberating women from unprofitable unions and supplying—as the transformation from one status to another was effected—the marketable image of a "new" self to be (re)circulated and consumed.

IV

In *The Custom of the Country*, Wharton links the prevalence of divorce with modern consumer behavior, suggesting that "the system," in its codification of women's dual function as consumer-spectators and as spectacles for consumption, predisposes them to end their marriages and jettison their spouses when the quest for "conspicuous decency" is frustrated. Divorce in fact proves less an embarrassment than a lack of social "creditability" when market rather than moral values are at stake: as consumers, women were freed to "trade up" to a husband-backer of respectable means; as consumables, they were reconstituted as desirable, eligible objects by legal decree and recycled back onto the marriage market, their changed status advertised in court documents and society columns alike.[59]

As "a monstrously perfect result of the system" (*CC* 208), Undine Spragg both exemplifies and exploits the intimate bond between her consumable and consumer status. From the moment of her christening, it seems, she is conditioned to consider herself much like the "hairwaver [her] father put on the market the week she was born" (*CC* 80). Yet, her value as a product on the marriage market is determined, not by any stable intrinsic value she might possess, but by her ability to generate a series of pleasing appearances—advertising "copies" based on "originals" seen in fashionable society—and thus stimulate consumer desire. Like Claude Popple, who scoffs at realism as a mode for society portraits by questioning "how [such] portraits *look* in a drawing room" (*CC* 195, emphasis added), Undine is an artist who presents idealized—and thus marketable—images that will "look" well in the various social spaces she aspires to fill. Her first glimpse of Ralph's "blurred and puzzling" milieu sends her off to a Fifth Avenue gallery to study up, as it were, for her next foray into that new world. In every gallery patron's dress and mannerism Undine notes "the 'look' which signified social consecration"; she therefore flings herself into a series of skillfully imitated "rapt attitudes before the canvases, scribbling notes in the catalogue" (*CC* 48) so as to appear among the initiated. Ever "doubling and twisting on herself" (*CC* 6) to produce such effects, Undine learns to strike the right note in all the spectacles she (re)presents and thereby ensures her continued marketability. With her future in-laws, "she found that to seem very much in love and a little confused and subdued by the newness and intensity of the sentiment, was, to the Dagonet mind, the becoming attitude for a young lady in her situation" (*CC* 91); with Peter Van Degen she profitably adopts the stance of "the type of heroine who scorns to love clandestinely, and proclaims the sanctity of passion and the moral duty of obeying its call" (*CC* 365); with deChelles, she twists back again to reproduce an image of "the incorruptible but fearless American woman, who cannot even conceive of love outside of marriage" (*CC* 404). Undine is indeed a lovely, "undoolaying" form that simultaneously suggests the meaningful associations of the "original" and acquires meaning according to her viewer's desires.[60] As Mrs. Spragg proudly asserts, "my daughter's only got to show herself" (*CC* 88) to be successful on the marriage market.

While displaying her own version of "the look" in the Fifth Avenue gallery, Undine's attention is captured, her "floating desires" momentarily focused, by a bejeweled tortoise shell eyeglass worn by a female patron. She is "struck by the opportunities which this toy presented for graceful wrist movements and supercilious turns of the head. It seemed suddenly plebeian and promiscuous to look at the world with a naked eye" (*CC* 48). It is significant that Undine should seize upon the extravagant eyeglass as a prop to enhance her own display, for the sights she composes for consumption rely upon her own seeing, upon "her quickness in noting external differences" (*CC* 91) in the social canvas and turning them to her own use. For although Undine is "fiercely independent" in the tradition of her native west, she is "passionately imitative" (*CC* 19) as well, incorporating into her own repertoire of effects all that her discriminating eye recognizes as "smart" or "original." She first glimpses the "feats and gestures of Fifth Avenue" by "poring over the daily press" (*CC* 28) while yet in Apex; once in New York, she emulates the beautiful images of society that are retailed in "Boudoir Chat," purchasing a stock of pigeon-blood note paper used by the "smartest women" (*CC* 18) or having her morning chocolate abed, "after the manner described in the articles on 'A Society Woman's Day'"(*CC* 41).[61] She responds to her culture by what she sees "advertised" as leisure class respectability in the Sunday supplements or Mrs. Heeny's endless supply of newspaper clippings, so that "all life seem[ed] stale and unprofitable outside the magic ring of the Society Column" (*CC* 50). Undine makes the desired transition from seeing to being seen, from a "consumer" constantly peering in the "shop windows" of society to a social commodity in her own right; once she has fashioned her own leisure class liaison with "exclusive" Ralph Marvell, she experiences "the delicious sense of being 'in all the papers'" (*CC* 97), her increased status as a "creditable" social entity advertised for all to see. Later, anticipating the sensation Popple's portrait of her will generate "thron[ed] in a central panel in the spring exhibition, with a crowd pushing about the picture, repeating her name" (*CC* 198), she savors the potent boost such an exclusive form of publicity will lend her image. Whether in the newspaper descriptions of her elegant exploits or in the portrait publicly displayed, Undine finds herself represented to the world as the "newest" of the beautiful images offered for emulation and consumption.

To maintain her viability as an object of the public gaze, however, Undine requires newer and newer expressions of distinctiveness. Throughout the novel, she establishes her identity and value by "absorbing" the latest fashionable necessity: dresses that look "too lovely," colored note paper that establishes her as "smart," a parterre box at the opera that places her among the "stylish." Whatever fails in the immediate moment to augment a creditable, marketable "self," Undine discards like the offending dinner dresses grown too old-fashioned in the cut of their sleeves. Each time she believes herself "in conscious possession of the 'real thing'"(*CC* 98), it is her fate to have that momentary confidence "spoiled by a peep through another door" which reveals "something still better beyond . . . more luxurious, more exciting, more worthy of her" (*CC* 54).[62] Just when she secures a match that will guarantee her long-awaited access to New York's aristocratic inner circle, she also discovers the powerful attraction exerted by the "showy and promiscuous"; once in the "smart set," she glimpses the "brilliant existence" maintained by those practicing "the art of living" in "the impregnable quarter beyond the Seine" (*CC* 193, 285, 385). Undine cannot long remain satisfied with any of the many situations into which she negotiates her way, for as John Berger suggests, one who adopts the idiom of fashion as a means of self-expression depends on the envy of others to define success: it is an issue of "social relations, not objects . . . not of pleasure, but of happiness: happiness as judged from the outside by others." [63] To be an object of envy drives up one's value as an object of desire: Undine finds nothing "more delightful than to feel that, while all the women envied her dress, the men did not so much as look at it" (*CC* 228); however, "[t]o know that others were indifferent to what she had thought important was to cheapen all present pleasure and turn the whole force of her desires in a new direction" (*CC* 286).

Thus Undine's ceaseless search both *for* and *to be* "the best" the market has to offer conditions her to seek divorce when marriage fails to provide what she believed "should subsist together in any well-ordered life: amusement and respectability" (*CC* 354). Throughout the novel, the rotary system of consumption spills into her personal relations, for she values people—as she does things—for their style and brilliance, qualities which accrue to her benefit by virtue of her association with them. Hence she is alive to the substantial "value" of refined Raymond deChelles' "power of exciting Van Degen's jealousy" (*CC* 287) and recognizes "what an acquisition"(*CC* 478) her son, Paul, would prove in securing de Chelles' affection, but dismisses Harriet Ray for wearing "last year's model" (*CC* 33). Divorce proves the necessary mechanism to maintain leisure-class respectability, and Undine picks up and discards husbands almost as soon as they fail to please her. When Ralph "disappoints" Undine's expectations, he devalues her, and she characterizes her situation as a "waste." With her balance-sheet mentality, she tallies the "benefits" and "drawbacks" of her marriage to Ralph and decides her fortunes would be better served by divorcing him and placing herself back on the marriage market. Certainly, divorce and remarriage would seem to lead to profitable advancement: her friend Indiana "gain[s] her end" easily with Rolliver (*CC* 271), and Mabel's "future was assured" by her "venture" in the South Dakota divorce town (*CC* 367–8). But Undine finds that, however necessary such a venture might be if she is to trade up and regain her value, divorce actually proves "a blunder" (*CC* 352)[64] which "diminish[es her] trading capacity," her calling card but a "debased currency" when stripped of the status Ralph's name supplied (*CC* 361) or unsecured by a new, more prestigious liaison and name.[65] For women of Undine's class who lack a society pedigree or sufficient wealth to do without one, speculation on the market requires a man's name or money: such women are but vessels that may be filled with or emptied of value depending on their marital status or prospects.

Although she suffers devaluation, Undine is able again to trade up on the market; backed by the money gained from the sale of Van Degen's pearls (with which he had bought her services as a mistress—a bargain for him considering what it would "cost" to secure her as his wife), she has the means to refashion and recycle herself as a desirable object. By the time she remarries Elmer Moffatt, she would seem to have come full circle in her quest for creditability, yet the habit of distraction, of absorbing the "real thing" of the moment *for* the moment, haunts her: "she still felt, at times, that there were other things she might want if she knew about them" (*CC* 591). Possessing enough wealth to satisfy even her titanic appetite, Undine settles upon something money can't buy as the last "real thing" she desires, and the cycle begins anew. Although Undine's narrative would seem to describe a trajectory of success as she parlays pigeon-blood note paper into a tiara of pigeon-blood rubies during the course of her career speculation, Wharton makes it clear that for women, driven by market imperatives to consume and be consumed, the circle is in fact a spiral requiring ceaseless renegotiation for survival.

*

In characterizing divorce as "the home-made article" (*CC* 575), manufactured in America and superior to any French-Catholic annulment with which it might compete, Elmer Moffatt tacitly acknowledges its commodified aspect as a product codified, regulated and sold by interests that profit from its consumption. A selling point well known to divorce seekers of the type Undine represents are grounds capacious enough to fit almost any grievance. Like the cagey consumer she is, Undine explains to old Mr. Dagonet the product convenience such grounds afford the "disappointed" woman in converting a "trivial pretext" to use: "Oh, that wouldn't be the reason *given*, of course. Any lawyer could fix it up for them. Don't they generally call it desertion?"(*CC* 95). Desertion is the reason she uses in suing Ralph for divorce, recognizing that its catch-all nature in some way sanitizes the proceedings. As Mr. Spragg tells Ralph, "[t]here wasn't any other plea she could think of. She presumed this would be the most agreeable to your family" (*CC* 333). Divorces involving the names of the social elite profit newspapers as well as lawyers, and so Undine makes use of the opportunity to retell and retail the story of her own disappointment "on the first page of [a] heavily headlined paper":

"Society Leader Gets Decree . . . . Says Husband Too Absorbed In Business To Make Home Happy" (*CC* 343). Recycled with variations that reduce the human and personal aspects of the breakup to the general, impersonal and absurd, the story—in the form of a typical modern day problem—finally makes its way to an advice column which promises its subscribers "a Gramophone, a Straight-front Corset, and a Vanity box among the prizes offered for its solution" (*CC* 344). Other businesses that spring up under the divorce umbrella include dress makers who were beginning to provide outfits that were "not quite mourning, but something decently regretful" (*CC* 487) to observe the deaths of ex-spouses, and stationers who know the correct form to use on a divorcée's visiting cards.[66]

Many of course have commented that Undine's self-bartering leads to her social advancement, but it is important to note that Moffatt, too, profits by her career speculations. Indeed, he manages his interest in her like a stock investment, guarding the secret of their previous marriage so Undine isn't compromised as "used goods" before she secures the Marvell name, and outlining the plan by which she can leverage her son to gain the financial backing required for an annulment and, thereby, accession to a new, even more prestigious name. To ensure her success, he even invests Ralph's stake in a risky venture that promises a return sufficient to buy back his son. The woman Moffatt rediscovers at Saint Désert has improved her social fortunes considerably, and with the appraising eye of the speculator-collector he weighs Undine's value as the girl he married in Apex against that of the woman who has two society marriages to her credit. He pronounces her "a lot more fetching" (*CC* 568) than before and, having vastly increased his own worth, desires that she might be added as his wife to his collection of "unmatched specimens" that represent "the best" the market has to offer (*CC* 538). Although Undine adopts the "French view" of her marriage to deChelles and offers to become Moffatt's mistress, he is adamant about the terms of her return, insisting "you were my wife once, and you were my wife first—and if you want to come back you've got to come that way: not slink through the back way when there's no one watching, but walk in by the front door, with your head up, and your Main Street look" (*CC* 572). This is the reverse of the bargain Van Degen strikes with Undine, and reveals the two men's different notions of "cost" and "gain" grounded in their respective social positions. Moffatt not only understands the value of a specimen like Undine, but also recognizes that it is only as his wife that he can display her and realize to his own social credit her appreciated worth. The publicity surrounding their remarriage, particularly as it focuses upon the priceless and pricey gifts he showers upon Undine, advertises his pecuniary prowess and establishes for those who might wish to compete the new standard of "creditability."

While divorce most certainly secures the interests of social climbers and profits those who capitalize upon its business opportunities, it also has its uses among the old guard of New York society. As the "invaders" with their newly minted fortunes break down the barriers restricting entry into the exclusive circles, divorce becomes a marker used to distinguish—as money and leisure no longer can—the aristocracy from the upwardly mobile middle class. Although there "was no provision for such emergencies in the moral order of Washington Square" (*CC* 336), the incidence of divorce within New York society nevertheless enables members of the old order to indulge in coded demonstrations of their superiority. The "black cashmere and two veils" that Ralph's mother dons to visit her "misguided" divorced friend is, of course, as much a costume of mourning as it is of concealment. Yet its double-veiled excess must certainly have been more conspicuous than concealing, drawing attention to her secretive "errand of mercy" and providing a display of social distinction that bespeaks largess even as it signifies removal from the "contaminated." Similarly, when Bowen (who has himself never married) holds forth on "the whole problem of American marriages" (*CC* 205) and "the key to our easy divorces" (*CC* 207), it is from a position of superior perspective. As he says, "I want to look down on them impartially from the heights of pure speculation" (*CC* 205)—heights which are defined by class as well as gender privilege. Thus distanced, Bowen can condescend to sympathize with "the poor deluded dears" who seek release from marriages "where all romantic values are reversed" (*CC* 207–8). Clare Van Degen can afford to adopt the attitude that divorce is "awfully vulgar" (*CC* 347)[67] and Harriet Ray resolve "never to receive a divorced woman" (*CC* 78), for neither needs to enhance the value that her inherited name automatically confers. Divorce thus serves to determine a woman's worth and class: those like Undine who must use the courts to renegotiate themselves in the marriage market are likened

to currency whose value is dictated by extrinsic forces; women like
Clare are akin to real property whose value is based on intrinsic
qualities and therefore less vulnerable to fluctuation. While upward
mobility and social creditability seem the benefits divorce promises to
deliver, it in fact proves the ultimate barrier to Undine's aspirations,
barring her from "the one part she was really made for" (*CC* 594)—that
of Ambassador's wife.[68]

*

Wharton's 1904 story "The Other Two" is in some respects the
precursor to *The Custom of the Country*, providing a comic slice of life
from turn-of-the-century polite society in which manners and feeling
have been outpaced by changes in the laws of marriage and divorce.
Waythorn, a New Yorker of some means and reputation, marries the
twice-divorced Alice Haskett Varick despite his friends' counsel
against such a liaison and the innuendo circulating around her.
Progressive in his attitudes, he believes that "society has not yet
adapted itself to the consequences of divorce, and that till the
adaptation takes place every woman who uses the freedom the law
accords her must be her own social justification."[69] By his own
reckoning, the circumstances of Alice's previous marriages fully justify
use of the courts: her first divorce was "the natural result of a runaway
match at seventeen" (OT 83) with a man who "had wrought havoc
among her young illusions" (OT 91); her second decree was based on
"grievances . . . of a nature to bear the inspection of the New York
courts" and, therefore, a veritable "diploma of virtue" (OT 83).[70]

Chance encounters with Alice's ex-husbands shake Waythorn's
sang froid, however. Haskett gains regular admittance into the
household to visit his seriously ill daughter, and Waythorn discovers to
his discomfiture that he is not the "brute" his wife had allowed him to
infer, but rather a mild, slightly shabby man with a genuine concern for
his daughter's well-being. Alice's second husband is similarly pushed
to the fore of Waythorn's consciousness when, after meeting
accidentally on the train, Varick asks his successor to handle a delicate
business negotiation. Regular contact with these men prompts
Waythorn to ponder their strange relation—a relation constructed by
the fact each has called Alice "wife" in his turn—and he begins to feel
as if he were "a member of a syndicate. He held so many shares in his
wife's personality and his predecessors were partners in the business. If

there had been any element of passion in the transaction he would have felt less deteriorated by it. The fact that Alice took her change of husbands like a change of weather reduced the situation to mediocrity." Indeed, Alice's imperturbable calm in the presence of her former mates provokes Waythorn to question, "[h]ad she . . . no theory about her relation to these men?" (OT 95).

The theory by which Alice operates is of course the same one which governs Undine Spragg's actions: women find "success" in commodified self-display, ever adapting themselves as desirable objects for men with the means to provide the perfect setting for their talents. Like Undine, Alice also begins in modest circumstances, "chafing at her life, and secretly feeling that she belonged in a bigger place." But with her handsome looks and the "hints of a New York fashion paper"(OT 91), she lands something better: her first divorce and subsequent remarriage to Varick provides the "passport to the set whose recognition she coveted"(OT 83); a second divorce delivers her into Waythorn's possessorship where his part of the "business" is to advance her social fortunes a bit further.

If ambition is the cause of Alice Waythorn's several marriages, then forgetfulness is the mode she adopts to manage the ramifications of those dissolved unions, and in this she seems to have "discovered the solution of the newest social problem" (OT 95). Indeed, Waythorn marvels "at the way in which she had shed the phase of her existence which her marriage with Haskett implied. It was as if her whole aspect, every gesture, every inflection, every allusion, were a studied negation of that period of her life" (OT 91). Like a snake that seasonally renews itself by shedding its skin, Alice—in discarding her husbands—also jettisons traces of the past she has shared with them. Her memory of those men as separate personalities has become so indistinct that she sometimes confuses or conflates them, as when she pours a measure of brandy into the coffee of a surprised Waythorn, who has just that afternoon observed Varick in this very practice:

> Waythorn uttered a sudden exclamation.
> "What's the matter?" she said, startled.
> "Nothing; only—I don't take cognac in my coffee."
> "Oh, how stupid of me," she cried.
> Their eyes met, and she blushed a sudden agonized red. (OT 88)

In the story's comic climax, all trace of memory—and the embarrassment it may lend a situation—seems effaced when circumstance unexpectedly unites Waythorn, Alice and her former husbands around the afternoon tea-table. Although "three men stood awkwardly before her" (OT 98), Alice adopts her "way of surmounting obstacles without seeming to be aware of them" (OT 83) and carries out her duties as hostess without ado. "Serene," "unruffled," "imperturbable," she forgets the bond which once linked her to "the other two" and thereby expunges any meaning that would compromise her position or disturb her composure. Just as the divorcée whose confusion over who *she* was "in eighty-two" (Fig. 3.6) leads to some confusion over the identity of an acquaintance from that period of her life, so Alice meets nothing from her past in the present, but suffers no sense of dislocation or angst; her biography is renewed as easily as this year's fashions.[71]

A memory purged of inconvenient or distressing details proves the ideal "solution" to managing Undine's several divorces as well, for her consumer amnesia facilitates the "rotary" consumption of husbands. Like products which promise to satisfy Undine's shifting desires, these men each in their turn capture her attention, but then fade from consciousness after they fail really to be "the best" or "the real thing" she longs for. As part of a discarded and increasingly indistinct past, Undine's husbands lose their individuating features, "gradually becoming merged in her memory" (*CC* 591) as a single type and experience. The capacity ever to "[blot] out another memory" (*CC* 107) as the situation demands also allows her to maintain the image of herself as unconsumed goods on the marriage market. Because it is imperative that she appear the virginal ingenue to effect a society wedding, Undine in essence "forgets" Elmer Moffatt's identity, cutting him at the opera the night of her engagement to Ralph. When they meet secretly the next day, Undine is eager to gain Moffatt's assurance "that nothing shall be known" (*CC* 113) about their former connection, and anxiously seeks to erase—even from their private words together—any reference to that fact. Each time he recollects a part of their shared Apex history, she silences him, asking at one point, "What's the use of raking up things that are over?" (*CC* 111). For Undine, what is "over" is as if it had never been, her earlier experiences "frankly forgotten"; indeed, "her sentimental memories went back no farther than the beginning of her New York career" (*CC* 481) and cannot, therefore, hinder her social climb.

Constantly unmaking her memory so as to update her identity, Undine cannot understand the significance of the past, whether invested in persons or their things, nor can she comprehend a notion of value existing beyond that of conspicuous and temporary display. Hence she has no scruples in "renewing" the jewels given to her for her engagement and wedding and which betoken her entry into the Marvel family history. By resetting the "family relics, kept unchanged through several generations," Undine "destroy[s] the identity of the jewels" (*CC* 213–14) and their link, as "sentimental possessions" rather than market commodities, with the past. Such possessions bespeak an intimacy, a congruence, with their possessor that transform them into media of the possessor's essence; as Gillian Brown has argued, these transformed (and transforming) possessions "so closely correspond to the wills and feelings of their owners that they appear to be them rather than to be serving them."[72] Thus, by "lay[ing] hands on things which are sacred" (*CC* 545) and removing the jewels—or the ancient Saint Désert tapestries—from their associative settings, Undine inflicts a very personal "wound" (*CC* 214) upon family tradition and continuity. She then carries forward these objects, qua objects, into each new marital setting as emblems of the new social dislocation, the "divorce" of the present from the past.[73]

As a child of these several divorces, Paul Marvel stands as Wharton's equivalent of the "restless analyst" who meets nothing recognizable or self-confirming in what should be familiar surroundings. Paul's world, fashioned as it is amid the upheavals caused by Undine's constant comings and goings, is a bewildering one in which people—like "the father he had been most used to, and liked best" (*CC* 577)—"too often disappeared and were replaced by others" (*CC* 580). His toys and books, the "dear battered relics" of childhood, suffer a similar fate, for in the ever-shifting scene of Undine's operations, "none of the new servants—they were always new—could find his things, or think where they had been put" (*CC* 577). In this rootless milieu, the most ephemeral of artifacts—Mrs. Heeny's newspaper clippings—become for Paul a substitute for memory, the only source from which to discover a narrative that will explain his past or provide a link to the woman who is nominally his mother. From earliest childhood, a "new batch of clippings" retrieved from among face creams and sweets at the bottom of Mrs. Heeny's enormous bag supply his most memorable contacts with "the fascinating Mrs. Ralph Marvell" (*CC* 314–6), and in this Paul ironically duplicates the young Undine's own study of the society pages for a glimpse into the world of the "smart set." However, unlike his mother, who creates from these accounts a self commensurate with her social aspirations, Paul is in search of an authentic personal history, and hopes that the clippings "might furnish him the clue to many things he didn't understand, and that nobody had ever had time to explain to him. His mother's marriages, for instance: he was sure there was a great deal to find out about them" (*CC* 582). In the clipping which proclaims the "[q]uick work untying and tying" (*CC* 584) of Undine's latest nuptial venture, Paul does indeed find the "key to her transitions"—and his own (*CC* 583). As the text plunges forward, seeming to outpace the claims of the past with its staccato cadence mimicking the report of the proceedings' record-breaking speed, it reveals the one fact which most matters to Paul: in giving evidence of deChelles' "brutality," Undine "had said things that weren't true of his French father. Something he had half-guessed in her, and averted his frightened thoughts from, took his heart in an iron grasp. She said things that weren't true . . . That was what he had always feared to find out . . ." (*CC* 586). The discovery is doubly threatening for Paul, for the authority of the newspaper's account unmakes that part of his history he can remember, challenging the boy's power to claim his own recollection of deChelles as real and meaningful. He also learns that words may be separated—divorced if you will—from the truth to satisfy a personal and immediate need. Thus confronting a world in which language has disposed of its referentiality to be of "use," Paul reads between the lines of the newspaper clipping how tenuous his own hold in Undine's present can be, and the probable account of his own future.

*

Although by the end of *The Custom of the Country* one may be inclined to invert Charles Bowen's estimate of Undine as a "monstrously perfect result of the system" and gauge her a perfect monster, Wharton surely intended that her "heroine" be greeted—at least initially—with some measure of sympathy. As R. W. B. Lewis notes, Wharton endowed Undine with several of her own most individuating attributes: her love of dressing up and playing "great lady" in front of a mirror, her impatience with "fossilized" conventions, her bustling energy, and even her own childhood nickname, "Puss."[74] Significantly, both Wharton and Undine seem united by a desire for renewal; yet in Undine, this drive becomes identified with mere replacability and recycling—a denial of the earlier American legacy of the national Adam in which "rebirth" was neither mechanical nor cheap.

Thus the social initiate who puzzles over the hieroglyphic New York scene soon disappears from the text to be replaced with the monster "capable of anything" (*CC* 546) to advance her social fortunes, including the degradation of marriage from personal communion to business contract. Unlike Undine, Wharton resisted the idea that the most fundamental of human rituals—giving oneself in marriage—could be construed as a mercantile exchange. Certainly the publicity generated around Undine's several divorces as a necessary feature of her social climb was conspicuously absent in Wharton's own divorce. Her sense that her domestic problems were—and should remain—a private rather than public matter suggests her continued adherence to the "old" values, a fact evident in a letter written to her former lover Morton Fullerton several months after her divorce decree had been pronounced:

> I want to send you a line at once to thank you for your letter, & to say that you did *absolutely right* in telling the reporters that you knew nothing of my divorce.— I have told all my friends of it, & that is sufficient. I obtained it on the ground of adultery in Boston, London & France, with documents *à l'appui*, duly recorded by the court; & you are [at] liberty to say this to any friend of mine who speaks to you about the matter. In case of other enquiries, please simply say what you have already said: *"I know nothing."* As you know, the public can't get at the register of the French courts, & the reporters will soon tire of their vain researches.[75]

One could well read the production of *The Custom of the Country*— especially in light of Wharton's fear that scandal might attach itself to her divorce—as an attempt to proclaim through Undine's despicable career her own alienation from "the system" that produced—and even profited by—such monsters. Yet as a public document that in some way replicates the appeal contained in the private bundle of papers left to her biographer, *The Custom of the Country* itself participates in the process Wharton rejected, becoming an advertisement—renewed in her subsequent divorce novels *The Age of Innocence, The Mother's Recompense*, and *The Children*, which announced her fundamental difference from "the invaders" and asserted her place in the old order from which she had seemed divorced. Although she proclaims an alliance with the "real" of the old guard, the "real" is presented in the commercial form of a book and with a character whose self-bartering figures what Wharton and her publishers will attempt to do with that book.[76] Affirming the old pieties, Wharton cannot avoid implying her enclosure in the new—or deny her own ties to self-advertisement even as she eschews publication of her private acts.

NOTES

1.   Work on *The Custom of the Country* began as early as the winter of 1907 or spring of 1908, but with Wharton's love affair with Morton Fullerton and increasing difficulties with her husband, Edward "Teddy" Wharton— complications which undoubtedly forced Wharton to re-evaluate her conservative notions of marriage—work on a text which satirized society marriage and divorce was perhaps too fraught with personal anxiety to continue. Once she had more or less resolved her relations with these men, work proceeded apace and she finished the novel's final chapter in August, 1913. *The Custom of the Country* was published in a single volume by Scribner's in October 1913. See in particular R. W. B. Lewis, *Edith Wharton: A Biography* (New York: Fromm International, 1985), 345–348.

2.   Edith Wharton, *The House of Mirth* (New York: Scribner's, 1905); rpt. with an introduction by Mary Gordon (New York: Library of America, 1985), 9. Subsequent quotations from *The House of Mirth* are from this edition and are cited parenthetically in the text as *HM*.

3.   Edith Wharton, *The Custom of the Country* (New York: Scribner's, 1913) 94–96. Subsequent quotations from *The Custom of the Country* are from this edition and are cited parenthetically in the text as *CC*.

4.   The critical discussion of *The Custom of the Country* has encompassed several issues that are of significance to this study—the twilight of old New York values in the face of the aggressive egoism and energy of the *nouveaux riches*, the question of "success" in Undine's ability to manipulate and control

her environment, and the economics of the marriage market. Geoffrey Walton [*Edith Wharton: A Critical Interpretation* (Rutherford, N. J.: Farleigh Dickinson University Press, 1970)] sees the marriage of Undine and Ralph as expressive in microcosm of the "social comedy" which pits the New York aristocracy against the "invaders" of the rising middle class. Walton does not treat the role divorce plays in this "comedy" to define contesting classes, nor does he conceive of Wharton's condemnation as having a broader target than the bustling *nouveaux riches*. Other critics have placed an economic spin on the demarcation of old and new values; in comments which instantly call to mind Thorstein Veblen's description of leisure class marriage, Blake Nevius [*Edith Wharton: A Study of her Fiction* (Berkeley and Los Angeles: University of California Press, 1953)] notes that *The Custom of the Country* depicts the alteration of the moral landscape characteristic of the old order at the hands of a middle class in which wives are oppressed by too much leisure and husbands distracted by too much business. Gary H. Lindberg [*Edith Wharton and the Novel of Manners* (Charlottesville: University Press of Virginia, 1975)] argues at greater length that money is the solvent loosening and ultimately destroying standards of conduct, value and meaning associated with the New York aristocracy in "the most dizzying age of American capitalism" (121). G. S. Rahi [*Edith Wharton: A Study of Her Ethos and Art* (Amritsar: Guru Nanak Dev University Press, 1983)] follows a similar trajectory, finding that relentless pursuit of wealth, power and pleasure "delinks" (117) social behavior from its moral and ethical foundation; Rahi's language would suggest he is describing something akin to "divorce," but he does not capitalize on the metaphoric potential of this significant term.

In pondering the oft quoted observation that Undine was "a monstrously perfect result of the system," a range of critics, from Nevius to Allen F. Stein [*After the Vows Were Spoken: Marriage in American Literary Realism* (Columbus: Ohio State University Press, 1984)], emphasize Undine's role as victimizer (she "holds all the cards" says Nevius [149]) rather than victim. Of most critical significance among these arguments is Elizabeth Ammons' "The Business of Marriage" in *Edith Wharton's Argument with America* (Athens: University of Georgia Press, 1980) in which she asserts that Undine "controls her own life" (98) by exploiting the mechanism of the marriage market. She finally concedes, however, that this control is effectively contained by the system, for women "still live through men" (112). Others seem more sensitive to the fact that "the system" produces Undine: they portray her, as does R. W. B. Lewis in his superb biography of Wharton, "as much a victim as an aggressor," her marriages tokens of imprisonment by, rather than triumph over, the system (349–50). Lindberg points out that "the system" is larger than the institution of marriage itself; to be a viable product on the marriage market, Undine becomes "the hapless prey of every new fashion and every social objective she encounters" (118). Cynthia Griffin Wolff [*A Feast of Words: The Triumph of Edith Wharton* (New York: Oxford University Press, 1977)] shifts the argument to emphasize Undine's role as a consumable product, and views her "as the perfectly commercial item, able to simulate anything the purchaser desires" (149). Carol Wershoven [*The Female Intruder in the Novels of Edith Wharton* (Rutherford, N. J: Farleigh Dickinson University Press, 1982)], making effective implicit use of Veblen's theory, links these arguments by describing Undine's quest as one to become the "supreme consumer-ornament." She argues that a woman's position in the marriage economy necessarily blurs consumption and production: Undine's "chameleon-like nature" allows her to become the perfect product so she might, by marriage, be made into a "respectable consumer" (60). Judith Fryer's 1986 study *Felicitous Space: The Imaginative Structures of Edith Wharton and Willa Cather* (Chapel Hill: University of North Carolina Press) similarly provides an engaging discussion of Undine as a product and consumer. Undine's endless ability to compose and place before an audience pleasing pictures allows her to accede to the role of consumer. This power is finally mutilating, however, for it dooms Undine to consider herself in relation to how she is seen by others (104). One of the most compelling of the studies on the various economies enacted in the novel is Ellen Dupree's "Jamming the Machinery: Mimesis in *The Custom of the Country (American Literary Realism* 22.2[Winter 1990]: 5–16); Dupree asserts that Wharton's discourse enacts the feminist strategy described by Irigaray in that Undine Spragg's character and career "mimics patriarchal discourse for the purpose of escaping its power to define her," exposing its values in the process (5).

Several critics of *The Custom of the Country* see it in terms of the domestic novel, and of the conventionally separate masculine/feminine, market/domestic, public/private spheres problematized, particularly in Undine's similarity to both her father and Elmer Moffatt, Wall Street operators. Beverly R. Voloshin ("Exchange in Edith Wharton's *The Custom of the Country*," *Pacific Coast Philology* 22 [1987]: 98–104) characterizes Undine as a "female capitalist" whose self-promotion, limited as it is to the marriage market, causes "home and market, private and public, self and commodity [to be] thoroughly and shockingly interfused" (101). In "'Grave Endearing Traditions': Edith

Wharton and the Domestic Novel" [in *Faith of a (Woman) Writer*, ed. Alice Kessler-Harris and William McBrien (New York: Greenwood Press, 1988): 31–40], Jeanne Boydston argues that the domestic novel is implicated in the ideologies it attempts to critique, a fact Wharton capitalizes upon in her work so that the "career of Undine Spragg is but another expression of Wharton's perception that the chief tragedy of industrial wealth was its capacity to invade the well-ordered values of the home" (35).

The studies by Wolff and Ammons still, I think, provide the best analysis of the target of Wharton's attack in their discussions of the leisure class marriage economy. Neither, however, looks at the role divorce plays in keeping the marriage economy expanding, nor do they link the divorce industry with advertising's role in conditioning consumption. Ammons in fact states "it was marriage, not divorce, that roused [Wharton's] cynicism" (124) in telling Undine's story, an assertion I modify in this chapter.

5. For years she had agonized over the persistent problem of Teddy who, diagnosed as "neurasthenic," had become increasingly irresponsible, unpredictable and even violent. Wharton's friends counseled her to leave him (Henry James urged, "... you must insist on saving your life by a separate existence. You must *trancher* at all costs"), but she continued to seek remedies of various sorts to restore Teddy to his former self until her energy and patience were quite exhausted. See Lewis, particularly pp. 300–308, 316–318, 330–336; and *Henry James and Edith Wharton: Letters 1900–1915*, ed. Lyall H. Powers (New York: Scribner's, 1990), 182. On the subject of civil divorce decrees granted in France, see Lindell Bates, "The Divorce of Americans in France," *Law and Contemporary Problems* 2 (June 1935): 322–328.

6. Quoted in Lewis, *Edith Wharton: A Life*, 318.

7. In addition to the pages already cited in Lewis' biography, see also Cynthia Griffin Wolff, *A Feast of Words:*, 226–227; and Shari Benstock, *No Gifts from Chance: A Biography of Edith Wharton* (New York: Scribner's, 1994), 278–279.

8. Wharton, *The Age of Innocence* (New York: Appleton, 1920); rpt. with an introduction by R. W. B. Lewis (New York: Collier Books, 1968), 96.

9. See Frank Bergman, *Robert Grant* (Boston: Twayne, 1982), 89. Grant, appalled by the nation's divorce situation, worked for uniform marriage and divorce laws that would make migratory divorce obsolete. He also was Wharton's confidant and advisor as she made the decision to divorce. The divorcee who received two million dollars for the "sale" of her son was prominent New York socialite Rita Lydig; she used the money "to groom

herself for the next marriage." See Veronique Vienne, "In a Class by Themselves," *Town and Country* (Nov. 1994): 175.

10. *The New York Idea* (Boston: Walter H. Baker & Co., 1907), 121.

11. For a discussion of the symbolic power of Undine's name and her role as a harbinger of doom for the old order and, in particular, its art, see Candace Waid, "The Devouring Muse," in *Edith Wharton's Letters from the Underworld: Fictions of Women and Writing* (Chapel Hill: University of North Carolina Press, 1991), 135–155.

12. The necessarily compressed history of advertising's role in conditioning consumption and the role of women as consumers in this section is indebted to the following sources: Stuart Ewen and Elizabeth Ewen, "Americanization of Consumption," *Telos* 37 (Fall 1978): 42–51, and *Channels of Desire: Mass Images and the Shaping of American Consciousness* (New York: McGraw Hill, 1982); Daniel Horowitz, *The Morality of Spending: Attitudes toward the Consumer Society in America, 1875–1940* (Baltimore: Johns Hopkins University Press, 1985); William Leach, *Land of Desire: Merchants, Power and the Rise of a New American Culture* (New York: Pantheon Books, 1993); T. Jackson Lears, "From Salvation to Self-Realization: Advertising and the Therapeutic Roots of the Consumer Culture, 1880–1930," in *The Culture of Consumption: Critical Essays in American History, 1880–1980*, ed. Richard Wightman Fox and T. Jackson Lears (New York: Pantheon Books, 1983); Roland Marchand, *Advertising and the American Dream: Making Way for Modernity, 1920–1940* (Berkeley and Los Angeles: University of California Press, 1985); Victor Margolin, Ira Brichta and Vivian Brichta, *The Promise and the Product: Two Hundred Years of American Advertising Posters* (New York: Macmillan, 1979); Elaine Tyler May, *Great Expectations: Marriage and Divorce in Post Victorian America* (Chicago: University of Chicago Press, 1980); James D. Norris, *Advertising and the Transformation of American Society, 1865–1920* (New York: Greenwood Press, 1990); Miles Orvell, *The Real Thing: Imitation and Authenticity in American Culture, 1880–1940* (Chapel Hill: University of North Carolina Press, 1989); and Michael Shudson, *Advertising, the Uneasy Persuasion: Its Dubious Impact on American Society* (New York: Basic Books, 1984).

13. Adam Smith, *An Introduction into the Nature and Causes of the Wealth of Nations,* ed. Edwin Cannan (New York: Modern Library, 1937), 821.

14. Simon N. Patten, *The Consumption of Wealth* (Philadelphia: University of Pennsylvania, 1901), 34.

15. Charles Edward Russell, *These Shifting Scenes* (New York: George H. Doran, 1914); quoted in Shudson, 152.

16. As one indicator of the boom in consumption, the number of people involved in the distribution of goods rose from 850,000 in 1870 to 2, 870,000 in 1900, and claimed 31.5% of the U. S. labor force. See May, *Great Expectations,* 138; Norris, *Advertising,* 96.

17. "The Opening of Biltmore," *Gunton's Magazine* 10 (January 1896), quoted in Horowitz, *The Morality of Spending,* 45. Social arbiter Ward McAllister similarly claimed that the lavish expenditures of the fashionable "400" was both economically beneficial and culturally uplifting to society as a whole: "The mistake made by the world at large is that fashionable people are selfish, frivolous and indifferent to the welfare of their fellow-creatures; all of which is popular error, arising simply from a want of knowledge of the true state of things. The elegancies of fashionable life nourish and benefit art and artists; they cause the expenditure of money and it distribution; and they really prevent our people and country from settling down into a humdrum rut and becoming merely a money-making and a money-saving people, with nothing to brighten or enliven life; they foster all the fine arts; but for fashion what would become of them? They bring to the front merit of every kind; seek it in the remotest corners, where it modestly shrinks from observation, and force it into notice; adorn their houses with works of art, and themselves with all the taste and novelty they can find in any quarter of the globe, calling forth talent and ingenuity. Fashionable people cultivate and refine themselves, for fashion demands this of them. Progress is fashion's watchword; it never stands still; it always advances, it values and appreciates beauty in a woman and talent and genius in a man. It is certainly always most charitable; it surrounds itself with the elegancies of life; it soars, it never crawls." *Society as I Have Found It* New York: Cassell Publishing, 1890), 160–161.

18. Patten, *The Theory of Dynamic Economics* (Philadelphia: University of Pennsylvania Press, 1892), 41, 44. Like Veblen, Patten noted the satisfaction derived from invidious consumption of goods: "To the pleasure of consuming an article is added another pleasure, arising from the social position which the possession of this article gives to its owner. This second pleasure has much greater force than the first . . . . Without this exclusive spirit, the growth of higher pleasures would have been greatly retarded. Music and literature could not have had their present influence with men, but for the patronage of wealthy families seeking some exclusive mark by which they could be distinguished from the common people." *The Consumption of Wealth,* 32.

19. Patten, *The Consumption of Wealth*, 51.

20. Patten, *The New Basis of Civilization* (New York: Macmillan, 1907), 215.

21. Quoted in Ewen, *Channels of Desire*, 70.

22. Maxine L. Margolis, *Mothers and Such: Views of American Women and Why They Changed* (Berkeley and Los Angeles: University of California Press, 1984), 156.

23. Benjamin, "The Work of Art in the Age of Mechanical Reproduction," *Illuminations*, ed. and with an introduction by Hannah Arendt (New York: Schocken Books, 1968), 221–223, 239.

24. Henry James, *The American Scene* (New York: St. Martin's Press, 1987), 182, 38. Certainly Raymond de Chelles' heated assertion that Americans, "as proud of changing as we are of holding to what we have," characteristically "come . . . from towns as flimsy as paper, where the streets haven't had time to be named, and the buildings are demolished before they're dry" (*CC* 545) echoes James's concern.

25. James, *American Scene*, 8.

26. Ibid., 164–5.

27. For a detailed account of the development of the migratory divorce industry here summarized, see Blake, *The Road to Reno,* 116–172; Jones, *An Historical Geography of Changing Divorce Laws in the United States*, 21–41; and Riley, *Divorce: An American Tradition*, 85–107.

28. The divorce rate increased from 0.4 per 1000 persons in 1880 to 0.8 in 1900 and to 1.75 per 1000 in 1920. See Blake, *The Road to Reno,* 228.

29. See Jones, *An Historical Geography of Changing Divorce Laws in the United States*, 48; Riley, *Divorce: An American Tradition*, 67. The common perception (or misperception), informed by hundreds of newspaper and magazine articles, gossip columns and witty literary references of the type referred to above in *The New York Idea* about Dakota divorces, was that divorce colonies precipitated the rise in marital breakups and the general moral decay of civilization. These sources do indeed make the "divorce problem" seem far more prevalent than it in fact was.

For instance, Margaret Lee's 1883 novel *Divorce; or, Faithful and Unfaithful* (New York: Frank Lovell & Co.) was successful enough in its representation of the injustice done by the migratory divorce statutes to be reprinted again in 1889 with an introduction by W. E. Gladstone which argued for uniform national divorce laws. Like Marcia Hubbard in Howells' *A Modern Instance*, Constance Travers discovers all too late that she has been sued on the grounds of "incompatibility of temper." She protests, "How could it be legal? she had transgressed no law. . . . A woman could not be divorced when she had done nothing to deserve it—and without her knowing anything about it" (394). Her uncle explains that her husband ". . . has taken advantage of what is a disgrace to the United States, its want of uniform divorce laws. He has lived for over a year in Connecticut, and he has complied with all that the law there demands" (397).

30. The *Indianapolis Daily Journal* of December 3, 1858 noted that among divorce seekers, "women outnumber men two to one." By 1880, statistics revealed that the female to male ratio had increased to 2.7 to 1, although by 1900 it had fallen again to about 2 to 1. See Alfred Cahen, *Statistical Analysis of American Divorce* (New York: Columbia University Press, 1932) and O'Neill, *Divorce in the Progressive Era* (New Haven: Yale University Press, 1967), 20–26. In 1909, George Elliot Howard reported that one third of all divorces granted to women were on the grounds of desertion as a "righteous solution of an economic problem." See "Divorce and Public Welfare," *McLure's Magazine* 34 (December 1909): 240.

31. See Nolan, "Indiana: Birthplace of Migratory Divorce," 515–527; Jones, *An Historical Geography of Changing Divorce Laws in the United States*, 30.

32. See Blake, *The Road to Reno,* 122; Jones, *An Historical Geography of Changing Divorce Laws in the United States*, 31. In *Reno Reveries: Impressions of Local Life* (Reno: Charles E. Week, 1912), divorcée Leslie Curtis asserts that "Contrary to General Opinion," "Nevada's six-months residence requirement was not made to favor matrimonial misfits, but to give citizenship to prospectors and miners who wander about and seldom remain a year in one place. Consequently, Nevada, being a young and thinly settled State, secured voters by shortening the residence requirement" (55). For a general discussion of the economic motives beneath the West's liberal treatment of woman, see Mari J. Matsuda, "The West and the Legal Status of Women: Explanations of Frontier Feminism," *Journal of the West* 24 (Jan. 1985): 47–56. See also Ernest Groves, "Migratory Divorce," *Law and Contemporary Problems* 2.3 (June 1935): 296; and Frank Ingraham and G. A. Ballard, "The Business of Migratory Divorce in Nevada," *Law and Contemporary Problems* 2.3 (June 1935): 302–309.

33. "Divorce," *Putnam's Monthly* 8 (Dec. 1856): 630–634. Subsequent quotations are from this source and will be cited parenthetically in the text as D.

34. The seven causes adjudicated to be sufficient for divorce in Michigan were: 1) adultery; 2) physical incompetency; 3) the sentence of either party to imprisonment for three years or more, in any prison, jail or house of correction; 4) desertion by either party of the other for at least two years; 5) habitual drunkenness in either party; 6) extreme cruelty, whether practiced using personal violence, or by any other means; 7) gross and wanton neglect, on the part of the husband, to provide a suitable maintenance for the wife, when of sufficient ability to do so.

35. Quoted in M. A. DeWolfe Howe, *The Life and Labors of Bishop Hare, Apostle to the Sioux* (New York: Sturgis & Walton, 1911), 360.

36. *Sioux Falls Argus Leader*, 26 January 1893.

37. George Fitch, "Shuffling Families in Sioux Falls," *The American Magazine* 66 (Sept. 1908): 442. Leslie Curtis similarly asked what the citizens of Reno owed to "the little fad, divorce" in a verse entitled "The Colony":

> If you legislate against the Reno Colony,
> To other fields the fair ones you will drive.
>> For ill-advised propriety
>> Brings poverty with piety
> And some of us would much prefer to thrive.
> Does Reno really know how much the Colony
> Contributes to the cafes and the stores?
>> Hotels would soon be closing,
>> The population dozing,
> If broken hearts should favor other shores.

38. "Must We Wait a Year for Divorce? The Question that Threatens to Reduce South Dakota's Popularity," *The Minneapolis Journal* 5 (July 1908). For a further discussion of the business boom supported by the Sioux Falls divorce colony, see Connie De Velder Schaffer, "Money versus Morality: The Divorce Industry of Sioux Falls," *South Dakota History* 20.3 (Fall 1990): 207–227.

39. "A Study of Sioux Falls, South Dakota," in an unidentified newspaper dated December 16, 1894 (Old Courthouse Museum Collection, Sioux Falls, South Dakota).

40. Wealthy socialite Margaret Laura deStuers, niece of John Jacob Astor, was reported by the New York *Times* of December 24, 1892, to have paid her Sioux Falls attorney $25,000 for a divorce, while William Du Pont paid

$32,000 for a decree in South Dakota. Quoted in Schaffer, "Money Vs. Morality," 215.

41. Harry Hazel and S. L. Lewis, *The Divorce Mill: Realistic Sketches of the South Dakota Divorce Colony* (New York: Mascot Publishing, 1895), 7–8.

42. "Divorce in South Dakota," *The Nation* , 26 January 1896.

43. "Divorce as a State Industry," *The Nation*, 5 May 1892; *Sioux Falls Argus Leader*, 14 January 1893 and 2 March 1895.

44. New York *Herald*, 18 September 1870. See also Doane Robinson, "Divorce in Dakota," *South Dakota Historical Collection* 12 (1924): 273.

45. *The Nation*, 5 May 1892.

46. Quoted in Vanderbilt, *Fortune's Children,* 150.

47. *The New York Times* of March 6, 1895 reported that Mrs. Vanderbilt was to receive "suitable provision": "the fine city house at Fifth Avenue and Fifty-second Street, the marble palace at Newport, the country place at Islip, L. I., and a cash settlement of between $3,000,000 and $10,000,000."

48. Robinson, "Divorce in Dakota," 274. From accounts such as these, Wharton no doubt constructed the fictional clipping reporting Undine's progress from Reno which notes the "copper velvet and sables" she wore to court and dangles the tantalizing material circumstances of her marriage to "one of the six wealthiest men east of the Rockies" (*CC* 585–6).

49. *Life* 13, no. 323 (Feb. 29, 1889).

50. James Realf, "The Sioux Falls Divorce Colony and Some Noted Colonists," *Arena* 4 (November 1891): 699, 701.

51. In "Shuffling Families," Fitch writes that "[a] dozen or more Sioux Fall business men have picked wives from the divorce colony . . . [b]ut most of the romance of the colony comes from the exiles who manage to fall in love with one another during their stay and who celebrate their respective releases with a wedding"(450).

52. Sioux Falls *Daily Press*, 2 September 1908 and 5 September 1908. Mrs. Peck most certainly violated the ideal of woman-wife Professor Peck had articulated in his conservative appraisal of marriage, "For Maids and Mothers" [*Cosmopolitan* 21 (June 1899): 149–162]. Peck argues than a man "does not yearn for a new type of wifehood; *for he does not wish the sort of wife who would be a species of domestic comet*"; rather, he desires a woman who will, from the precincts of "the perfect home," exercise "the gifts God has given her as will insure the greatest service to society, to the state, and to humanity." Quoted in Martha Banta, *Imaging American Women: Idea and Ideals in Cultural History* (New York: Columbia University Press, 1987), 678.

53. A series of cartoons entitled "Our Great American Sport: Divorce Ranks First Among Out National Pastimes" with the text by Dorothy Parker [*Vanity Fair* 13 (Jan. 1920): 62–3] also noted this rotary system. For the "Endless Chain," the caption reads: "As soon as divorce mercifully looses one set of shackles, a change of partners is rapidly effected, new bonds are formed—and there they are, right back at the beginning again." Or, as another illustration in the series proclaimed, "divorce simply gets one into the right frame of mind for a fresh start in matrimony."

54. Hazel, *The Divorce Mill*, 4.

55. Fitch, "Shuffling Families," 443–444; emphasis added.

56. Mrs. B, a pretty young thing already three times married, laments to her newest spouse, "Oh, if I were a man *I* would make a name for myself." Tom replies, "Strikes me you've done pretty well as it is. This is the third you have made" [*Life* 9, no. 211 (1887)]. In another *Life* illustration, two confer about the social identity of a fashionable lady: "She belongs to the 400, doesn't she?" "Well, she ought to by this time. She's married three of them" [*Life* 41, no. 1054 (Jan. 8, 1903)].

57. *The Nation*, 5 May 1892.

58. "A Study of Sioux Falls, South Dakota," 16 December 1894.

59. According to Alfred McLung Lee, in 1870 the New York *Sun*, in response to the changing mores and interests of its female readership, added to its customary announcements of marriages and deaths the categories "Born" and "Divorced." *The Daily Newspaper in America: the evolution of a social instrument* (New York: Macmillan, 1947): 326–327. The publicity accorded divorce was depicted in a *Life* cartoon in which a father notes to his daughter, "This is a new book-list of the marriages of the divorcées, you know." She replies, "It must be the new "Who's Whose" [*Life* 63, no. 1639 (March 26, 1914)].

60. This merely expands on Wolff's observation that Undine becomes "the perfectly commercial item: able to simulate anything the purchaser desires." *Feast of Words*, 249.

61. While manners books tended to recommend plain white or ivory note paper for a lady's correspondence, conduct guides published in women's magazines and daily society columns tended to advertise stylish trends for emulation and consumption. As Undine discovers, a woman's stationery is her emissary into the world, and must be fashionably correct; hence this "hint" on "The New Note Paper" in the June, 1910 *Good Housekeeping*: "Letters from Europe in this past few months have been noticeable for dainty, new ideas in

stationery, particularly the delicate tints of the paper, resembling certain dress goods. A result has been the adoption by American women of fashion of writing paper to match their favorite costume or their boudoir, in tint. Invitations are often issues on paper corresponding with the color scheme of the luncheon decorations. A gold bevel on the edge of the paper is much in vogue; so is the monogram or die."

62. Although Wershoven has argued that Undine's "self" is composed of "layers of mannerisms, of style, of continental or New York chic" (*The Female Intruder*, 72), I would suggest that, as a rotary consumer, Undine in fact disposes of such things as soon as they have ceased to be of use and moves on to the next mannerism or style. The only continuity of self for Undine is in her titanic, shifting desire.

63. *Ways of Seeing* (New York: Viking-Penguin, 1977), 132.

64. In characterizing her premature divorce from Ralph "a blunder," Undine reveals the "logic" which grounds the New York view of marriage and divorce: "Since she had not been 'sure' of Van Degen, why in the world, [her New York friends] asked, had she thrown away a position she *was* sure of?" (*CC* 352). This is the rationale recorded by Jane Burr in her *Letters of a Dakota Divorcée* (Boston: Roxburgh Publishing, 1909) when she writes home to a friend: "Surprising that a girl as young as Alice Noah . . . should just take out legal separation papers in New York. How can the *modus vivendi* suit her better than divorce? Perhaps she wants to cinch her alimony until she finds another affinity. Then Alice for Dakota. It is foolish to cut your financial string when you might just as well dangle, especially until you find something worth dropping for" (70–71).

Besides committing an economic blunder, Undine seems also to have blundered socially, choosing South Dakota as the destination for severing her marriage vows rather than fashionable Rhode Island: "Dakota divorces are still a good deal frowned on in the *beau monde*. Try to remember that only Rhode Island divorces are *comme il faut.* (The Newport Variety is far smarter than the Providence or Bristol brand.) Dakota divorces are a trifle cheaper and more expeditious, but it should be borne in mind that the climate of Sioux Falls is very variable and that the hotels and theaters are, to say the least, indifferent." Francis W. Crowninshield, *Manners for the Metropolis: An Entrance Key to the Fantastic Life of the 400* (New York: Appleton, 1908), 104.

65. *The American Code of Manners* (New York: W. R. Andrews, 1880) first linked the social calling card to the language of accounting, noting that it served as the index of one's "social credit": ". . . a fashionable woman, on

coming in from her afternoon drive, reads the cards on her hall table as a merchant reads his day-book or ledger. It is her debit and credit account. It is a record of her social bankruptcy or her soundness. . . . For all, the little white messenger, engraved with a name, is the ready money of society" (186–7). For the etiquette governing the form of a divorced woman's calling card, see note 66 below.

66. At least as early as 1903, conduct manuals devoted space to insure the proper forms were followed in accurately encoding a divorced woman's marital status on her calling cards: "A divorced woman usually settles, in or out of court, at the time of her legal separation, whether or not she shall resign the surname of the man who was once her husband. If she retains his surname she nevertheless omits the use, on her visiting cards, of his Christian and middle names, and substitutes her own, or revives the use of her own surname, thus: Mrs. Maynard Carrington. This arrangement, to the initiated, implies that Mrs. Carrington was before her marriage a Miss Maynard. On the other hand, if a divorced woman wholly resigns the name of the man who was once her husband, she is not privileged to reclaim her maiden title as well as name, by having her cards engraved, for example, thus: Miss Emily Althea Maynard; the Emily Althea Maynard must be prefixed by the title of Mrs." Quoted from *Correct Social Usage: A Course in Good Form, Style and Deportment* (New York: The New York Society of Self Culture, 1903), 211. See also Helen L. Roberts, *Putnam's Handbook of Etiquette: A Cyclopaedia of Social Usage, Giving the Manners and Customs of the Twentieth Century* (New York: G. P. Putnam's Sons, 1913), 90.

67. For all the "vulgarity" of divorce, Clare seems to know a great deal about it. She is amazingly adept at decoding Undine's strategy to use her custody rights over Paul as a means—not toward an "appearance of respectability," as Ralph believes—but to raise money to purchase an annulment. As she says to Ralph, "She's much too clever to burden herself with the child merely to annoy you. What she wants is to make you buy him back from her" (*CC* 446).

68. It is worthy of note that Wharton (probably gleefully) chooses as Undine's "final" desire the position of Ambassador's wife—a post which is traditionally "bought" by political support and which often proves but a "rotary sale" as political parties win and lose power.

69. Edith Wharton, "The Other Two," *The Selected Short Stories of Edith Wharton*, ed. R. W. B. Lewis (New York: Scribner's, 1991), 83. Subsequent

quotations from this story are from this edition and are cited parenthetically in the text as OT.

70. The single ground for an absolute decree of divorce in New York was adultery, and until 1919, only the "innocent" party could remarry in the state without waiting a probationary five years. In 1919, the law was relaxed, and the probationary period reduced from five to three years. The stringency of New York law, which had one time denied remarriage to either party to a divorce, makes it unlikely that Alice's first divorce was secured in New York. She, like hundreds of others, probably headed west for a divorce colony "mill."

71. *Life* ran many cartoons which capitalized on the confusion and embarrassment of family relationships generated by multiple marriages, divorces and remarriages. "In Chicago" depicts the meeting, after several years, of an older man and a perambulator-pushing young friend. He hails the young man with, "Eh—how's this, Tom? Congratulations, old boy!" Tom reddens and replies, "H'm. Well, the-er-fact is it's about three months now since my wife got a divorce from the gentleman who should be congratulated for *this*" [*Life* 13, no. 381 (Jan. 31, 1889)]. At the opera, a fashionable couple comments on the marital status of a statuesque beauty who enters on the arm of an acquaintance: "Is she is first wife?" "Well, as he married her again after divorcing her, she is what you might call his first wife once removed" [*Life* 32, no. 837 (Dec. 15, 1898)].

72. Brown, *Domestic Individualism: Imagining Self in Nineteenth-Century America* (Berkeley and Los Angeles: University of California Press, 1990), 52. Benjamin also discusses the trend in "the age of mechanical reproduction" of removing originals from their associative settings and the consequent destruction of their "auras." See *Illuminations*, 221–223.

73. Candace Waid makes a similar observation about the severing of certain items from their original setting, although her point is to suggest the mythic force of the wound Undine inflicts rather than to see such dislocations as the result of consumer marketplace logic in which everything is reduced to object status. See "The Devouring Muse," 169.

74. Lewis, *Edith Wharton: A Life,* 350.

75. *The Letters of Edith Wharton*, 300–301.

76. See Lewis, *Edith Wharton: A Life,* 311–12 and 345–6, for a discussion of Wharton's oft expressed concern that her books were not well promoted and the resulting negotiations with her publishers.

CHAPTER FOUR

(Pre)Occupations Worldly and Domestic: Working Wives and the Specter of Divorce, 1910–1920

At the turn of the century, the rapid growth of cities, increased industrialization and developing technologies demanded an extended labor force, and women in unprecedented numbers responded by entering the American workplace as factory workers, shop girls, and office clerks. If the dramatic influx of women—especially of the previously untapped reserve represented by the white middle class—into the ranks of the employed could be termed "the most significant event in the modern history of women,"[1] it nevertheless was an event that failed to win unalloyed acceptance for their extra-domestic labor. The image of the independent New Woman carving out a space for herself in the public sphere of business was clearly in conflict with the lingering Victorian imperatives that restricted respectable female activity to the home. By the 1910s, however, it was clear that women wage earners were in the workplace to stay, and Americans faced that fact with reactions ranging from anxiety to resignation to guarded optimism. The decade is a particularly compelling one for gauging these reactions, for the strengthening suffragist movement foregrounded the issue of a woman's right as well as her capacity to assume the full burden of citizenship, and events of the period, the most dramatic of which was the Great War, provided the opportunities to prove the legitimacy of her claim. As the need arose to fill thousands of new jobs, a culture centered on male values was forced to re-evaluate the meaning and significance of women's labor. At issue was the way in which "women's work" would be defined: by essentialized qualities, or by abilities? by cultural imperatives, or by individual desire? by precedent, or by economic expediency?

Three distinct modes of cultural expression helped to shape the middle class woman's attitude in the decade's re-evaluation of feminine labor: the vocational advice book, the mass circulation woman's magazine, and the popular novel. Surprisingly, given the divergent aims of each of these sources and the differing values generally assumed to inhere in certain generic forms, these socio-cultural documents prove simultaneously progressive and regressive in their representation of women's work, encouraging women into the job market even as they attempt to salvage older home-sphere values. A consensus emerges from these texts that seems oddly resistant to the changing times: although a job could fill the interim period between school and marriage and even prepare a girl to be a wife, it must never become a career. For the "real woman," domesticity still reigned supreme. For those who weren't so circumspect and tried to combine marriage and extra-domestic work, the period's popular literature raised the specter of depraved femininity: the woman who usurps the role of breadwinner "unmans' her husband, "unsexes" her self and heads inevitably for the divorce court.

I

The 1913 advice book *Vocations for Girls* enjoined "every woman and girl in this twentieth century [to] congratulate herself on the numerous means open to her for self-support and, if need be, for helping to fill the family exchequer,—means which are not only remunerative from a money point of view, but which are pleasant, respectable, and capable of widening the outlook of the worker."[2] Indeed, during the century's first decades, the opportunities available to women workers seemed limited only by individual choice.[3] Marion Harland exhorted her readers to "Choose Something to Do *and do it*! Thirty years back this injunction would have meant to a young woman in moderate circumstances 'prepare yourself to become a governess or a principal of a school!' Now—what may it not signify and include? If we would know how times have changed, and we with them . . . survey the fallen and disintegrating boundary walls." Suffragist Frances Willard agreed:

"Nowadays a girl may be anything, from a college president down to a seamstress or a cash girl. It depends only upon the girl what rank she shall take in her individual calling."[4] Despite the tone of optimism and invincibility these sentiments convey, a female worker was far more likely *to be* a cash girl than a college president—or a doctor, a lawyer, or a member of any other "learned" profession.[5] Among the factors shaping employment profiles, advice books like *Vocations for Girls* played at least a minor role. By describing the job market as it already existed rather than by prescribing new career paths for women, these manuals tended to reinforce the status quo. To this end, most such reference sources published between 1880 and 1900—the years leading up to the twentieth-century explosion in female employment—more closely resemble conduct books than vocational guides.[6] As Sarah Eisenstein asserts, "a major motif of this literature is the attempt to reconcile the experience of work and the world of the lady,"[7] to ensure that the Victorian "angel in the house" was not compromised by her extra-domestic labor. The advice books' focus upon dress, deportment, degrees of collegiality appropriate to the workplace and the moral consequences of the publicity inherent in wage labor aimed to stem the threat women's employment represented as "an insidious assault upon the home . . . the knife of the assassin aimed at the family circle."[8]

Indeed, the domestic sphere seemed under a double threat, for wage work carried women—civilization's potential wives and mothers—away from the home. Just at the time when young women should have been preparing themselves to take husbands, the independence and adventure work promised seduced them into delaying marriage and the acquisition of skills necessary for homemaking:

> [The working girl] does not look upon housekeeping as a trade to be learned, but expects to blossom into domestic competence after the marriage ceremony . . . the interest of the girl is divided between present wage earning and future housekeeping. She has to look over a period of years before taking up her life career, and is meanwhile distracted by a largely or wholly unrelated wage-earning occupation.[9]

Work also seemed liable to deliver the young innocent into the clutches of sexual adventurers rather than into successful or legitimate marriages. Because women workers were in the dependent and metaphorically charged position of "selling" their time and efforts to predominantly male bosses, labor investigators and reformers alike expressed concern that women would be unable to resist their employer's sexual advances. The department store saleswoman seemed particularly prone to this danger. A Retail Clerks Union representative reported, "we know of [sales] girls who must submit to buyers if they want to hold their positions."[10] Progressive reformers worried that low wages and long hours resulted in a "starvation in pleasure" which left them particularly susceptible to temptation.[11] As Susan Porter-Benson notes, quoting the Vice Commissioner of Chicago, the transition from the sales counter to the brothel—and thus forever away from sanctioned relations—was all too easy: "some of the girls who are most tempted, and enter lives of prostitution, work in the big department stores, surrounded by luxuries, which all of them crave, and sell large quantities of those luxuries for a wage compensation of about $7.00 or $8.00 a week, or even less."[12]

As grave as such workplace pitfalls were in making single women unsuitable for marriage, the dangers stemming from a married woman's employment loomed even larger, for on her shoulders rested the ideals of society in her role as wife and mother. According to the Academy of Political Science's 1910 *Proceedings*, "childless working wives are a permanently demoralizing influence on their husbands. If these are inclined to idleness they can idle the more because the wives work."[13] Demoralized because of their wives' independence, these husbands often sought remedy in divorce; equally, armed with "ideas" and a means of self-support, wives in ever increasing numbers found divorce a relief from marital burdens.[14] Working wives seemed also to represent a threat to the future, for with their participation in the labor force "comes an increase in the number of children who are never born" and peril for those who are:

> Whether the wage-earning mother leaves home, or brings her work into the home, her children pay the penalty. If she is away, they are upon the street or locked into their rooms. From the street to the court is but a short step. From the locked room to the grave has been for unknown thousands of children a step almost as short, many having

been burned and others reduced by long intervals between feedings to that exhaustion in which any disease is fatal.[15]

With such dire images in the public eye, it is small wonder that the massive nineteen-volume report on *Women and Children Wage Earners* (1910) posed as central questions: "Is the trend of modern industry dangerous to women? . . . Are her moral qualities also affected, and if so, in what manner?"[16]

To counter the assault on femininity, hearth and home, vocational advice books well into the 1910s adopted the tactic of reinforcing traditional, often essentialized, views of women and their proper roles. Since "the maintenance of the home is woman's major vocation," asserted the Dean of a Boston women's college, the choice of a "minor vocation"—the work done outside the home before becoming a wife and mother—must "always be linked" to performance of that primary role: "no work for women can be urged or defended which tends to lessen her efficiency in her major occupation."[17] The strategy of another vocational manual was to recoup the appeal homemaking had lost: "The picturesque and dramatic aspects of housekeeping should be emphasized; constant insistence should be laid on the dignity of woman's tasks in the home; housework should be made a fine art linked with all that is best in life."[18] Even *Vocations for Girls*, which had applauded the modern marketplace for providing opportunities "capable of widening the outlook of the [woman] worker," abruptly shifts gears—in the very next paragraph: "But granted that congenial, remunerative work is open to every woman and girl *who is obliged* to go out into the world as a worker, fortunate indeed is the girl who is not called upon to do this, but who finds her work in her own home. It seems strange that any girl should prefer office work and the business life to work in her own home."[19] The idea that women's employment beyond the domestic sphere resulted from undeniable obligations (being "called upon" rather than responding to a "calling") returned to the earlier image of novelist Laura Jean Libbey's diminutive heroines who braved the workplace in order to support a beloved dependent.[20] Such models reinforced the view that "the woman who worked. . . worked temporarily, and because of unforeseen and exceptional circumstances, not as a member of a group who expected to work as a part of the normal course of their lives, in response to foreseeable exigencies of their circumstances."[21] By the end of the decade, more progressive vocational guides might assert a value beyond financial compensation in women's careers by insisting that "in order to bring up children to be intelligent citizens and workers, both parents must be intelligent citizens and workers themselves,"[22] but work was still subordinated and placed in the service of mothering. And the range of careers remained narrow. Although the advice books *Careers for Women* (1920) and *Women Professional Workers* (1921) emphasize training and aptitude over conduct and describe opportunities for female aspirants in the sciences, law and government, these categories are far overbalanced by descriptions of jobs that merely shift the site of domesticity by transferring traditional housekeeping skills into the marketplace.[23]

II

The evident tension between a woman's family and self, between her "own home" and her "widening . . . outlook" beyond the home marks not only these vocational guides, but also characterizes the pages of what was in many ways their periodical equivalent, *Good Housekeeping*, in the decade spanning the years 1910–1920. From its inception in 1885, *Good Housekeeping* was—as asserted in its subtitle—"Conducted in the Interests of the Higher Life of the Household," yet from its primarily urban, white, middle class female readership came the most dramatic influx of women swelling the ranks of the employed.[24] To acknowledge the importance of work in these women's lives, both the feature articles and the fiction in *Good Housekeeping* provided information about the range of employment available, the education or skills necessary to obtain various jobs, and the strategy of maintaining a position or advancing a career. Coupled with this vocational information, however—often in the very pieces that provided the employment tips—was an ideology which vigorously upheld marriage, home and family as a woman's chief concern and "crowning glory." By providing assurances that "normally constituted" female workers were and would always be primarily concerned with "womanly" duties,[25] the magazine was able to construct a view of the marketplace as something which could, under certain circumstances, contribute to rather than undermine domesticity.

One way to ensure the primacy of the domestic sphere was to create new business activities or glamorize traditional ones which would keep women centered in the home. Early in the decade, *Good Housekeeping* advocated schemes which would allow women to earn money without leaving the family circle. "Writing for Household Magazines" (Nov. 1910) not only allowed the "open-minded," "observant," and "energetically interested" woman, married or single, to earn an income "without neglect of her family," it kept her attentions properly and profitably fixed on domestic concerns. Similarly, "The Order of the Golden Bee" and its later incarnation "Fortuna's Daughters" were "secret" sororities under the auspices of *Good Housekeeping* which promised to make a housewife's "idle house pay handsomely." Other feature articles sought to prove "how easy it was for the family woman with her eyes open" to reap the benefits of already established domestic skills. By selling baked goods from her own kitchen, eggs from her own henhouse or opening a tea house in her own dining room, the family woman could make a respectable income.[26] "The Wooing of Julia Earle" (Nov. 1915) explores one of several possible options for generating income from the home. Confronted with the need to support her family after a fire destroys her father's business, the heroine—a recent high school graduate—goes out into the world of work only to find she is unqualified to be a secretary-stenographer, a governess or a boarding-house manager. Julia turns her attention back to the domestic scene and, with the help of her younger sister, opens a day-care center run from their own kitchen and backyard. After two years of business ups and downs, Julia assesses her accomplishment:

> Apart from the money in the bank, there have been incalculable advantages. For instance, we've both been at home . . . Keeping books and regular hours and sending out bills has been good for us both. And then Sally and I have helped out with the household expenses regularly. If she and I hadn't paid the taxes and interest last year, I really think we'd have lost the house.[27]

While the story trumpets the girls' resourcefulness in creating a business opportunity on a shoestring, it also subtly asserts the traditional view of women as the conservative center of household values. The sisters' work within the home quite literally "saves" the house and thus preserves the family structure sheltered within it.

To complement the income-generating tasks carried on within the home came a business terminology that was increasingly used in *Good Housekeeping* articles to describe the traditional unpaid functions a woman carried out as a wife and homemaker. This language had the effect of transporting the home into the modern age of scientific efficiency, transforming "housework" into "home economics." The linking of domestic and public spheres by means of a business vocabulary also assured the homemaker that she contributed significantly to the world's work and missed none of the challenge or excitement of the office or department store. A series of articles such as "The New Profession of Matrimony" (Feb.-April 1913) and "The Business of Being a Bride" (May 1914) likened marriage to a "matrimonial firm" in "the business of producing citizens." Like any product, children were "valuable assets" to the firm which must be intelligently managed if civilization is to realize a "profit." As a homemaker—or "shop boss"—a woman was urged to incorporate scientific management principles into her domestic labors. In order to assess what would "lead to more and better product from her matrimonial firm," she must "budget" her attention so as to determine efficiently the needs of the physical plant and its product. It is not surprising to discover that, as in the life of her business counterpart, "The Housewife's Vacation" (Aug. 1914) was a necessary "cost" of efficient household management.[28]

In recasting the home as a business to be run, the issue of compensation for domestic services also arose. The short story "The Head of the Department" (Oct. 1910) provides a literal treatment of the domestic scene as a business and is unique in its insistence on the real value of a wife's homemaking skills to her husband-employer. Mr. Walters, a widower and prominent business executive, places an advertisement for a housekeeper to run his household's "manifold and complex machinery." Although Walters had never considered his wife's work "of any particular money value," he soon realizes he had "grossly and stupidly undervalued" his wife's contribution to the "firm" when a Mrs. Wilbur insists that a housekeeper must be valued just as any competent "head of a department." She demands—and gets— $5,000 per year for her services. Mr. Walters ups her salary to $7,000 to retain her for a second year, but loses her after she receives a "tempting offer" from a "competitor" who offers "superior inducements": love, marriage and, in effect, her own "business."[29] Even as the story asserts the real worth of a woman's domestic skills, its subtext suggests that the value of a traditional domestic situation exceeds that of autonomy and an excellent wage. Thus, while the business terminology created the semantic illusion that the modern housewife participated in a production economy, she was afforded—at best—"psychic pay" for her labor.

This trend was seemingly countermanded with the advent of the Great War and the consequent demand for "compete mobilization of the women of the country" into the jobs left vacant by men going off to fight. *Good Housekeeping* ran feature articles each month urging women out of their homes and into war service. In a potent sense, women war workers became the "angels" in a house the size of a nation and, in traditionally feminine "self-forgetting service," promised to "save the world in crisis" much as they preserved the home and family in times of peace.[30] "Women's work" suddenly became anything from traditional domestic chores expanded to a community scale—soup kitchens, food processing, clothing and uniform manufacture—to yeoman's labor in the fields, factories and offices as crop harvesters, blacksmiths, telephone lines(wo)men, munitions workers and linotype operators.[31] Accomplishment in the workplace was frequently attributed to essentialized female characteristics: a woman's "feminine desire to beautify" made her a better painter of battleships, her love of "listen[ing] in on the world" made her a better wireless operator, and her "devotion" (to her job? her man? her country?) made her a better shell inspector. Although the opportunities in the wide-open job market promised women a chance to "prove themselves" at "man's work," the market was subtly transformed into an extension of the domestic world that women maintained while their men were away from home doing the "real" war work of fighting. Like wives sending their husbands to the office, women "furnish[ed] the necessaries" and "increase[d] the store of provisions" for the men at the front. *Life*, in an issue devoted to "Women in the War," proudly acclaimed "the army of women at home" whose work as "house managers" put them "In the Ranks" (Fig. 4.1) beside the fighting men.[32]

As quickly as the definition of "women's work" had expanded to meet the needs of a nation at war, so it constricted again when those needs were met. At least in part because their labor was figured in terms of domestic service, women were expected to "willingly take [their] place at the hearthstone again" in a "renaissance of domesticity after the war."[33] Hence, when the men began to come home from Europe, *Good Housekeeping* returned to articles which promoted "Housework for Health" (Sept. 1919) or again advocated finding financial opportunity within the home.[34] Such articles made their appeals to the "new" New Woman whose self-perception and desire for independence had been forever affected by the War, but who nevertheless wished to retire from a world which had become "aggressive . . . shoppy [and] commercial."[35]

Although in service to the "higher life of the household," the pages of *Good Housekeeping* nevertheless exude support and encouragement for the business woman—in marked contrast to the earlier tactics of other periodicals with similar views on the primacy of domesticity. Whereas women workers had been excoriated as "irresponsible and troublesome" in hopes of shaming them back into the home,[36] *Good Housekeeping* provided them an overview of the wide range of employment opportunities in which they might serve. Besides the anticipated sales or clerical positions (found, interestingly, primarily in the magazine's fiction), serialized articles such as "Your Daughter's Career" (July-Dec. 1915) presented images of women working in non-traditional jobs as architects, elevator engineers, art appraisers and horse trainers, and detailed the demands and rewards of being a doctor, lawyer, journalist and nurse.[37] In each of these articles, however, it is clear that a woman's extra-domestic career must respond to the imperatives of her "natural" calling and be "conditioned by the home." If work had its compensations, "a real woman" nevertheless discovered her greatest reward in tending home and family.[38]

Good Housekeeping fiction reinforced this message: story after story finds a young woman who achieves success in the workplace, flourishes as a result of her efforts, and then leaves the site of her achievement for marriage and home. Marion Eastman, the one heroine in *Good Housekeeping* fiction who opts for career over marriage, is an aberration, as the story's concluding comment makes clear:

> Are you disappointed that this was not a love story? All girls don't care for love and marriage, you know; some of them are satisfied with careers that forever close to them the doors to homes of their own. But that isn't the way of the normal girl; to her business is an occupation for the years between school and marriage.[39]

While women faced an either/or proposition where work and marriage were concerned, the options—and the women who choose between them—are by no means valued equally. This brief editorial assessment discounts the career woman, smugly hinting she is somehow lazy or remiss in settling for (being "satisfied with") work rather than striving for marriage; there is even a tinge of anxiety that, in her deviation from the norm, her sexual orientation is suspect. On the other hand, the choice made by the "normal girl"—tomorrow's "real woman"—confirms the view that women need occupy but a temporary place in the workforce, passing the otherwise empty time between the ending of one stage of life and the beginning of another in an easily jettisoned job. Even with the expanding job opportunities for women in the "amazing twentieth century," marriage and career were represented as mutually exclusive options, at least in part because marriage was itself a career:

> But whether it presents itself as a matter of economic necessity or a matter of personal choice, as surely as you have a daughter, you have to face the question of her career. A generation ago it was only a son's career that excited question. A daughter's was foregone—in marriage. But there is no girl born within the last two decades . . . that does not face a problematic future. The amazing twentieth century has brought uncertainty to her prospects. She may marry—or she may become a civil engineer, a diplomat or a blacksmith.[40]

Another article touting the college woman's skill in business promotes the distinctly modern advantage that the business woman, having astutely built up her firm, "may sell out [her] well-run establishment with dignity and profit—not simply shut up shop" when embarking upon marriage. The option to continue operations never arises because "business wears a temporary aspect to most girls."[41]

Life, too, presented the situation faced by the modern woman in terms of a choice to be made between mutually exclusive options—the domestic *or* the public sphere. In a Gibson illustration captioned "Tragic Moments: which shall be her sphere?" the fact that a home is but an indistinct backdrop behind a self-assured young woman as she firmly grasps the world (in the form of a globe) while gazing beyond the illustration's frame (and away from her beau's imploring eyes) suggests her choice has already been made—a choice which accounts for some "tragic moments."[42] In "Two Sisters of the Future" (Fig. 4.2), the tragedy wrought by such choices becomes clearer: the woman who pursues her "natural" instincts in nurturing domestic service will be counted the "failure" by modern standards, while the public woman—masculine in her dress, her habits and her abstracted scowl—will be the so-called success.

Extra-domestic careers clearly were regarded as marriage's poor relation, holding value only insofar as they served to provide a woman with something useful to do when she wasn't engaged at home:

> [There are] four essential reasons why any twentieth century girl's immediate problem is best solved by preparing for a career: (1) If she marries, she is able to marry from choice, instead of necessity; (2) If she does not marry, she has her means of livelihood and her work-interest and, through them, the chance for a happy useful life; (3) If she marries happily, the work-interest can be easily subordinated to domestic interest for as long as the latter shall endure; (4) If she marries unhappily, she has something to fall back on in loneliness and disappointment.[43]

A woman's reasons for having a career are all contingent upon her prospects for marriage. A career may help her find a better mate and a more successful union, or it may provide a safety net if marriage fails or fails to materialize.

Perhaps to dispel the notion that domesticity could be undermined by the single working woman, *Good Housekeeping* offered a variety of reassurances that she maintained a healthy interest in "normal" feminine pursuits and appearances. Feature articles such as "Delia's Flat"(Nov. 1910) and "A Business Woman's Home" (Jan. 1912) supply ample photographic evidence of working girls' interest in homemaking

IN THE RANKS

Fig. 4.1 "In the Ranks" [*Life* 70, no. 1820 (Sept. 13, 1917)

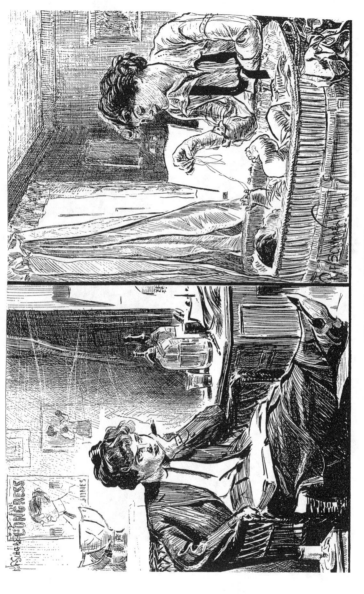

THE SUCCESS   TWO SISTERS OF THE FUTURE   THE FAILURE

Fig. 4.2 "Two Sisters" [*Life* 65, no. 1701 (June 3, 1915)]

RECTORETTE CHAUFFEURINE FEMAIL CARRIER FIREWOMAN PULLMAN PORTRESS COLLEGIENNE

SOME COMING FASHIONS

Fig. 4.3 "Some Coming Fashions" [*Life* 63, no. 1643 (April 23, 1914)]

Fig. 4.4 "The Feminization of Labor" [*Life* 64, no. 1673 (Nov. 19, 1914)]

ADVICE TO HUSBANDS OF FEMINISTS
BEWARE OF YOUNG AND HANDSOME STENOGRAPHERS

Fig. 4.5 "Advice to Husbands of Feminists" [*Life* 64, no. 1661 (Aug. 27, 1914)]

THE HUSBANDETTE

"MY GOODNESS, BUT I'LL BE GLAD WHEN ELECTION IS OVER."

Fig. 4.6 "The Husbandette" [*Life* 55, no. 1429 (March 17, 1910)]

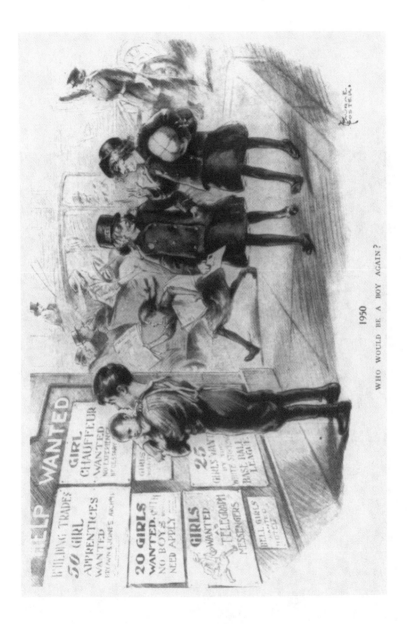

Fig. 4.7 "1950" [*Life* 64, no. 1676 (Dec. 10, 1914)]

Fig. 4.8 "Extinct" [*Life* 63, no. 1652 (June 25, 1914)]

and the therapeutic effect derived from such pursuits: "the business woman needs and craves domesticity as a balance wheel." The monthly fashion columns were periodically devoted to grooming advice and the latest apparel for the business woman, recognizing that in business, as in courtship, "clothes play the important role in the first 'sizing up.'" The emphasis on "becoming" colors, "daintiness," and "freshness" in "making the business woman attractive in the world of trade" suggests she need not subdue her femininity as she enters a man's world—or, as *Life* ironically suggests, as she takes up traditionally male occupations (Fig. 4.3).[44] Indeed, having been told that "the work of the home [has] been taken from a woman's hands and that she must follow it into the world," female workers were encouraged to bring their feminine charms and domestic skills into the marketplace and do their "special work": restore order, harmony and beauty to the often chaotic world of work.[45] If *Life* could image only the possible disruptions to occupations wrought by stereotypical feminine *pre*occupations (Fig. 4.4), *Good Housekeeping* touted the positive feminine influence: by bringing "sunshine and sympathetic interest," adeptness at subtle negotiation, and the desire for "efficiency and attractiveness" into the workspace, women transformed the office or store into a more comfortable, homelike environment. Ideally, clients were to feel as guests while female employees acted as hostesses.[46] "The courtesy of a gracious hostess," according to the article "Fifteen Minutes Plus" (Nov. 1913), "is at home in any region, it is applicable to any transaction, in the Land of Self-Support; and whenever it is practised, it eliminates from the business day the oft recurring 'bad quarter of an hour.'" Part of a woman's duty, then, whether in the home or office, was to "take the time and trouble to study the disposition, and try to understand the attitude, of someone who is close . . . in office hours" and respond to (inevitably) his needs.[47] One fictional heroine embarking upon her career took just such advice to heart. Sizing up her harassed potential employer, she "felt a desire, half maternal and half executive, to help him." Not surprisingly, the sympathetic and enterprising young woman becomes a valuable asset in this and subsequently larger firms.[48] Feminine manners and appearance, converted from "aesthetic pleasures" into necessary "duties," were thus established as commodities to be traded for position in the marketplace, so that "the very business of being a woman" was understood to provide "experience that can be routed to real value economically."[49]

As traditionally "female" functions moved from the home and into the public sphere, the workplace became a highly visible site of domesticity and *Good Housekeeping* began to portray the job market as a fruitful extension of the marriage market. Job performance demonstrating management skills as well as womanly charm became a potential mode of self advertisement. Certainly, the notion of women as commodities to be bargained for was a *Good Housekeeping* staple. In a survey taken of bachelors on the subject of matrimony, one man saw a wife as his "one best investment" who would "pay big dividends from the start." A female reader insisted that adequate training in housekeeping "was worth money, and commanded the best husband in town."[50] Nowhere is the idea of women as items of exchange more clearly presented than in "January Sales" (Jan. 1912), a verse by Carolyn Wells offering "sundry warnings and wise counsel whereby young ladies may escape the bargain counter." The illustrations accompanying the text show a series of young women in beguiling poses under the appraising eyes of young men in the market for

> Dainty goods, all fresh and nice,
> [That] may be bought at special price. . .

> This Department Store of Life
> Offers many a Bargain Wife.
> But, of course, one can't expect
> Absolutely *no* defect.

> He who takes a wife for his,
> Must accept one marked "as is."
> Other traits he may prefer,
> But "as is" he marries her.

As a practical matter, then, the workplace could prove a useful "display window" to showcase a woman's qualifications for marriage because it increased her contacts with men who, due to class or geographical constraints, would not otherwise enter her world. "The working girl has a better chance to marry than the society girl," one reader asserted, "because the former has chances to meet men day after day and so establish the tie of propinquity."[51] "The Tale of Melissa Clarissa DeLisle" bears out this observation perfectly. A typist with "her living to earn," Miss DeLisle is an attractive, trim and vivacious self-promoter who gains the attention of Percy McRae, the son of the firm's owner. Marriage follows a glamorous courtship, and Melissa's "days at the office are over and done."[52] However, the popular perception that going into business was the strategic career move woman made to get a permanent position in marriage bore a bit too much of the stamp of cunning for *Good Housekeeping*. The often ridiculed stereotype of the office girl, as a sexual adventuress who "menaces the happiness of multitudes of homes" had no place in the magazine's pages.[53] Hence, Melissa's façade of trim elegance degenerates into slovenliness and she loses, "by stupid and silly neglect/[Her] husband's esteem and [her] own self-respect." But it is the conscious angling for a husband and the cynical view of romantic love implied that was objectionable, for there are a score of fictional characters who do indeed find love and marriage as a result of being in the marketplace as workers.

Good Housekeeping portrayed a number of girls transformed into women (and eventually wives) when they take on careers. As one mother notes as she gazes upon a group of her daughter's working friends, "the vagueness of girlhood had faded. It was as if life had taken a sharp pencil and drawn a distinct outline around each personality."[54] The development of one fictional heroine, Julia Earle, typifies this development:

> Two hard and busy years had not taken away the laughter from Julia's eyes, nor the unconquerable childishness from the curve of her little chin, but in other ways she was changed. The untidy glory of her hair was neatly bound and snugly pinned now, and she wore a trim gown of dark gray linen, relieved only by a prim little embroidered collar, and white cuffs. Something in her expression was altered, too. There had come a certain new directness in her look, and a certain firmness in her mouth that bespoke changes of character as well as of appearance.[55]

Significantly, rather than encouraging recklessness or bohemian independence, this portrait's emphasis on bound hair and wrists reassures the *Good Housekeeping* reader that work is a stabilizing, taming influence for young women. Yet it is also an empowering experience as Julia's "direct" gaze and "firm" mouth testify, for work helps to distill a girl's real talents, values and desires and leads her to make "womanly" choices for home and marriage over workplace and career. As the transition from "vague" girlhood to capable womanhood is effected, the job market is itself transformed into a marriage market providing a public space to display one's suitability for wife- and motherhood.[56]

Throughout the decade, then, *Good Housekeeping* maintained the position that employment before marriage could operate in the service of domestic interests by preparing women to become legitimate helpmates. Work seemed to teach young women the necessary lesson of subordinating individual (and individuating?) desires to the service of an external entity or goal and thereby reinforced traditional female and marital roles. As one *Good Housekeeping* contributor wrote, "if I were making laws for women, I should make a law—two years in business before marriage. Marriage would be happier for it. In business a woman learns, if not to conquer, at least to conceal her petty impatiences. In business a woman learns to spur her laziness with perseverance."[57] Thus Julia Earle reassures her beau that work has not made her independent of him, but rather has taught her "to be a help, instead of a burden to—anyone I should happen to marry."

To ensure its readership understood that the business world was but an intermediary step in the transition to married life, *Good Housekeeping* offered many examples why the true woman must forsake her job if domestic harmony was to be maintained. Marriage, as a formalized arrangement of reciprocity between husband and wife, must balance useful efforts exerted within and without the home to be successful. One woman reader placed herself in the role of husband and offered this view of the relationship:

> Generally speaking, I should feel that, in marrying me, my wife took obligations on herself other than those expressed in the marriage service. If I provided her with a home, freed her from the slavery of wresting a living from a world always reluctant to grant it to average abilities; if I took from her the responsibility of a provision for sickness and old age, lifted from her shoulders the awful responsibility of the future: if I assumed those duties in her stead, I

should feel she owed me a comfortable, attractive, sweet-smelling home.[58]

Questions about this balance naturally arise: What happens to this exchange if the wife earns a living outside the home? Indeed, what becomes of the husband's role if a wife can provide for herself? The anxiety over marital roles, particularly over a wife's traditional dependency, is evident from this statement from another *Good Housekeeping* reader survey: "Since I have been working and purchasing for myself, I have more and better things. I fear, however, that they are at the expense of respect and confidence in my husband. I realize we are drifting apart, and the outcome I cannot see."[59] The Veblenesque model of marital roles in which the husband as "money maker" provided the means for his "money spender" wife to "carry to successful issue the business" of the union was coming under siege by the consumer imperative that had once driven it.[60] The ever-increasing need to demonstrate social credibility by the acquisition of goods assured that some women would enter the workforce to pay for such goods.[61] As one working wife confessed, "I went into business because I wanted a parlor carpet."[62] Indeed, as the advice books warned, a woman's ability to provide for herself seemed to threaten the institution of marriage itself. One career woman asked: "Why should I get married? There isn't one married friend of mine who has anything like the money for dressing that I do. . . . Today it's only the exceptional man that is worth the while of the competent business woman."[63]

"The Homemaker" (Feb. 1910) demonstrates how the working wife threatens the stability of her marriage because she devalues her husband's masculine role as provider. Sally Andrews, a wife of six months, works secretly as a stenographer in order to afford a maid and other small luxuries that will make a rented flat seem a home. Tom Andrews, believing his good domestic fortune stems from his wife's extraordinary management of his small salary, discovers one day that Sally is not in the home managing but in an office earning the means to engage a housekeeper. Initially he casts himself as the deceived husband, but eventually succumbs to Sally's logic that her job provides a better (if not happier) home for them:

They are paying me twenty a week now, and are going to raise me in January. Of course, I'll give it up if you say. But that twenty dollars pays for Mary; it helps pay for the rent. How would you like to live he way the Joneses do? And I have to buy some new clothes—my trousseau is giving out! [64]

Andrews calculates "how many years must elapse before he could reasonably expect to give Sally what it appeared she was providing for herself" and reconciles himself to the situation. A sequel-reply appeared in the April 1910 number which emphasized Sally's hardness and Tom's complete demoralization:

> I've lost my real man-hood. I'm a drone and cast aside now as useless. I'm no real use to Sally. She is a self-supporting, self-contained, self-sufficient young woman who has a right, I suppose, to make certain demands of life. If I cannot meet those demands why should she limit herself—her experience of life—to me? I'm not a success. Let her find her mate—I'll make room for him. [65]

By disrupting marriage's time-honored balance between husbandly and wifely duties and erasing the barrier between the public and private spheres, the working wife not only unmans her husband, she also unsexes herself. Self-contained and self-sufficient, she doubly offends the feminine ideal which, paradoxically, requires both selfless service and dependency.

But if a husband was "inclined to idleness," did a wife still risk unhappiness by working to meet her financial obligations? "How I Dealt with Jack—A Wife's Story" (July 1913) bears out the findings reported in the Academy of Political Science's 1910 *Proceedings:* a wife's failure to align with socially encoded gender roles "demoralizes" her spouse and "unsexes" them both. After an "insane engagement" and a "hasty marriage," a wife finds that her husband is "a helpless, incapable, irresponsible creature" who loves to spend money but has no intention of making it himself. Although time after time she puts him on notice "to brace up and get a position," the wife remains the sole source of support for the couple. At last realizing that her husband is constitutionally incapable of holding down a conventional job, she gives him one last chance before divorcing him: while she went to work each day, "he should keep the house; he should be the woman and I the man." Jack is fortunate; the discipline of housework reclaims him and "by degrees the man he had been intended for began to crop out in various ways." As a successful writer, he *still* works at home, but so does his wife. These "chances" the generous hearted wife offers, however, unman husbands according to an apparently successful hotel entrepreneur, Mrs. Radner ("Did She Wrong Her Husband?" Jan. 1914). Having earned prominence and respect as a business woman, she nevertheless asks, "Have I achieved success? . . . I've made money. I've done good work. I've won for myself a position of respect among those who know me; but I've failed in the biggest thing in my life. I have failed as a wife." Rather than make her husband struggle to succeed, Mrs. Radner allowed him to become dependent on her achievements and, in so doing, "robbed him of his manhood." Thus she asserts "most of us women who achieve professional success fail as wives. The wives who really help their husbands are the weak, dependent women who force out of men the best that is in them."

Life similarly addressed "the problem" of the independent woman from her oppressed husband's point of view. Distinctly masculine in her goals and her demeanor, the modern working woman is likely to reinscribe the power relationship which already existed in the workplace between the male employer and "his" female employee. If a wife might be jealous of her husband's pretty stenographer, the reverse might also be warranted when the "feminists" take over business and men are relegated to positions of clerical worker *or* house husband (Fig. 4.5). One illustration looking forward to 1920 forecasts that the successful woman of business would be able to humor "the little man" by offering him an office job and a (false) sense of his worth to her.[66] Or, she may convert him to a diminutive "husbandette" (Fig. 4.6) while she carries on with the more important matters in the world. Diminished, unmanned, and left to the bewildering "feminine" chores of housework and child-rearing, the modern American male and his hapless charges in a cartoon entitled "Les Miserables" fall victim to working women's pursuit of an extra-domestic career. Given not only the attention lavished upon the female worker in the modern age, but also the terrible price paid by men for her advancement, who indeed "would be a boy again?" (Fig. 4.7). Like the entrepreneur Mrs. Radner whose successful career ruined her husband's self-esteem and their

marriage, the working wives and feminists presented in the pages of
Life were "unnatural," "perverted half-women" who exacerbated "the
divorce evil" and, thus, undermined the institution of marriage for all
(Fig. 4.8).[67]

Certainly one of the most glaring absences in the pages of *Good
Housekeeping* is the lack of systematic or serious discussion of the so-
called "divorce evil" or the effect of the rising divorce rate on
American women and their families. Although statistics reveal that
between 1910 and 1919 the national divorce rate hovered around 20 per
cent, the magazine's editorial and fiction features rarely explored the
marital relationship beyond the romance of discovering one's soulmate.
If marital discord was broached, the difficulties between spouses were
resolved before divorce was examined as a real option. Even the
mention of the word divorce seemed taboo.[68] The single notable
exception to this silence occurred in Dorothy Dix's "Mirandy" columns
in which black "folk" gave voice to a whole spectrum of anxieties
plaguing the American family. According to those in Mirandy's circle,
"divorshe" was either a rich man's pastime or a poor man's comic
emulation of upper class antics and was the inevitable result of
regarding wives as commodities to be traded in when they failed to
provide an adequate return on their husband's "interest":

> . . . why dese heah rich folks is always a-gittin divorshes—hit's to
> pass de time away. A millionaire gits a house, or a horse, or an
> autimobile dat he gits tired of, an' he thinks dat he'll amuse hisself by
> gwine out an' tradin' hit off wid somebody else, but dere ain't no
> excitment 'bout dat, becaze dere ain't no difficulties in de way. All
> dat he's got to do is to put his hands in his pockets an' pay de
> difference, an' dere he is wid anodder house, or horse, or autimobile
> dat he don't lak no better dan he did de fust one.
>
> Hit sholy does git on his nerves, an' make him pevish, ontel one day a
> good idee strikes him, an' dat is dat he'll trade off his wife for a new
> one, an dat takes a lot of trouble, an' makes a lot of scandal, an' costs
> him a lot of alermony, an' hit's full of excitement, an' sort of gives
> him a run for his money, an' dat's why he does hit.[69]

"Mirandy on Old Wives for New" shows how the aspiring underclass model their behavior on the example set by the rich. As Sam Pigget explains to Mirandy,

> I's jes follerin' de fashions of de rich an' great. I's gwine to do lak dem millionaires does whut started out po' an' humble, an' married dat way, an' den when dey got rich and pros'pous, dey traded off deir ole wives for new wives to match deir plush furniture. . . .Whut I'm gwine to divorshe [my wife] for is whut dey calls in de law de incomparability of temper, which signifies dats she's got ole an' ugly, an' de rheumatiz, an' dat I want a new wife whut's a good looker an dat will show off de fine clothes dat I hangs on her.[70]

By limiting the discussion of divorce to those whose marriages rested upon economic rather than companionate foundations and by displacing the subject into a forum tantamount to a minstrel show, *Good Housekeeping* effectively put divorce out of the purview of those whose concerns lay with the "*higher* interests of the household."

However, Dix's "Mirandy" column often provided an alternative perspective on the relationship between marriage, divorce and work, and thus subtly undermined the magazine's philosophical interests. Whereas *Good Housekeeping* generally restricted its focus in order to insist that a woman's work after marriage led inevitably to marital discord and perhaps divorce, "Mirandy" introduced the fact that divorced women, no matter how they had spent their time as wives, might very well need to work to combat their dire economic position:

> So many women dat land in divorsch co't . . . has to take in washin' ever after to suppo't demselves and deir chillun, which is 'bout what one of dese heah decrees gives a woman de privilege of doin' after she done gone and got hit.[71]

Indeed, although there are no separate employment figures for divorced women, they were roughly three times as likely to be in the work force as were married women during the decade 1910–1919. In 1900, 32.5 per cent of all widowed and divorced women in the United States were employed outside the home, a figure that remained stable until the 1930s when the percentage rose slightly to 34.4 per cent.[72] Despite the fact that by 1920 divorced, separated or widowed women comprised as much as 16.3 per cent of the female workforce in some areas of the country, *Good Housekeeping* virtually ignored the plight of those women for whom work was an economic necessity rather than a staging ground for marriage.[73] Certainly, the specter of the divorced woman undermined the magazine's notion of the ideal family structure, but an equally likely explanation for the total absence of representations of divorced women workers was the anxiety that, once shown the way, more women would be empowered to leave the home. Such representations, especially if they bore out statistics that showed these divorcées often supported children, parents and even siblings, could legitimize alternative domestic arrangements that made women the heads of households. Finally, having constructed the job market as a fruitful extension of the marriage market, it is possible that *Good Housekeeping* was in no hurry to place "used goods" on display, for divorced women had, by middle-class standards, forfeited their chance to be wives and thus would occupy space that could be better utilized by legitimate matrimonial material.

III

If *Good Housekeeping* cautiously negotiated the issue of a working woman's independence, Edna Ferber's immensely popular novels *Roast Beef Medium* (1913) and *Emma McChesney and Co.* (1915) celebrated it, detailing the rise of a woman who, "divorced, penniless, refusing support from the man she had married,"[74] finds success as a businesswoman, a mother and, later, as a working wife. Certainly, one of the novels' aims is to counter the stock images of the divorcée as the heartless opportunist or the abandoned and helpless victim. Emma McChesney clearly is neither. Rather, she represents that clear-eyed woman who paradoxically ends her marriage *because* she is a devoted family woman:

> When a girl of eighteen she married a man of the sort that must put whiskey into his stomach before the machinery of his day would take up its creaking round. Out of the degradation of that marriage she had emerged triumphantly, sweet and unsullied, and she had succeeded in

bringing her son, Jock McChesney, out into the clear sunlight with her. (*EM* 89)

Emma's emergence "sweet and unsullied" from the degrading experience of her marriage has the effect of revirginalizing her, thus making her an appropriate candidate for future marriage as an ingenue. Divorce, the process by which she effects this triumphant re-emergence (*and* purifies her family to boot), is left out of the passage, no doubt because it throws a rather quotidian weight on an otherwise miraculous rebirth.

Ferber eagerly seeks to redefine the parameters of "womanly" conduct both inside and outside the workplace, combining in Emma tough-minded competitiveness and feminine charm in her job as a "drummer" for Featherloom Petticoats—work generally considered inappropriate for women because of its inherent publicity and rootlessness. As Emma herself protests when told her job isn't properly feminine, "Any work is women's work that a woman can do well" (*RBM* 258). Extra-domestic labor, although taken up out of necessity, proves doubly rewarding in Emma's case for it not only provides the economic means to keep mother and son together, it also allows her to discover a latent talent for business management and to exercise that power on the job. Yet Emma's business success in no way compromises her desire or her capacity for domesticity and mothering. Indeed, Ferber seems to argue that women need not be forced to choose between marriage/family and career, but that they may take on both with success. In a 1915 New York *Times Magazine* interview, she said of Emma McChesney, "She is a type, and she is a very young type . . . . She is so new that she is worth talking about. But ten years from now a talk like this will be an anachronism. The idea that anyone ever questioned the propriety of a woman's going into business, or thought that such an act on her part was inconsistent with domesticity, will be obsolete as milestones."[75]

As a blend of traditionally masculine and feminine characteristics, Emma is constructed to prove that a woman belongs equally in the business world and the domestic sphere. Youthfully trim, attractive and charming, her eyes are likely to become "suddenly misty" when sentiment overcomes her; those same eyes convey her "maddeningly half-cocked manner" or seem to possess vision beyond the ken of the normally sighted individual:

> But something in Emma McChesney's eyes, and something in her set, unsmiling face, told him she was not seeing seashores. She was staring straight at him, straight through him, miles beyond him. There was about her that tense, electric, breathless air of complete detachment, which always enveloped her when her lightning mind was leaping ahead to a goal unguessed by the slower thinking. (*EM* 5)

As T. A. Buck, the titular head of the Featherloom Company, observes of his star employee, she has "imagination, and foresight, and nerve, and daring, and that's the stuff that admirals are made of" (*EM* 12). Because she possess this range of character traits and capabilities, Emma has not surprisingly achieved remarkable integration between her business and domestic selves. Upon realizing that she must get the jump on a business competitor and peddle the Featherloom line in South America, Emma takes care of last minute office details "with the thoroughness and dispatch of a housewife who, before going to the seashore, forgets not instructions to the iceman, the milkman, the janitor, and the maid . . . . she foresaw factory emergencies, dictated office policies, [and] made sure of staff organization . . . ."(*EM* 13–14). On the other hand, when aboard the South America-bound ship she arranges her domestic and social affairs "like the business woman that she was" (*EM* 20). The notion that housewives make good business managers because they deal daily with countless small details and exigencies is obviously in play here, as is the familiar argument that business can serve as a training ground for domestic efficiency. In Emma these complementary ideas achieve so perfect a balance that her domestic and her business lives metaphorize each other. However, Ferber so ardently desires her heroine be the model of the well-rounded New Woman who excels in everything into which she puts heart and mind that she bypasses the goal of equality between the sexes and reinscribes the traditional active-passive power dynamics of male-female relations into Emma's dealings, particularly as they involve T. A. Buck.

Although Emma and T. A. technically are partners, Emma dominates T. A. in the domesticated work environment. He may acknowledge the domestic quality of their business relationship and refer to her as the "little woman" (*EM* 11) or assert protectively that the South American venture is no job for a woman, but Emma clearly wears the pants in the Featherloom firm:

> When trouble threatened in the workroom, it was to Mrs. McChesney that the forewoman came. When an irascible customer in Green Bay, Wisconsin, waxed impatient over the delayed shipment of a Featherloom order, it was to Emma McChesney that his typewritten protest was addressed. When the office machinery needed mental oiling, when a new hand demanded to be put on silk-work instead of mercerized, when a consignment of skirt material turned out to be more than usually metallic, it was in Mrs. Emma McChesney's little private office that the tangle was unsnarled. (*EM* 44)

Because Emma is so obviously the active element of the partnership, T. A. is frequently feminized, pouting when Emma neglects him for business or feeling "like an old maid who's staying home with her knitting" when she departs for South America (*EM* 2, 20). Indeed, T. A.'s "too feminine mouth" (*RBM* 284) and his failure to assert himself in the business had once caused Emma to reject him as a matrimonial partner. Yet when she returns from her successful sales trip, after having "cast her ordinary load of business responsibilities on the unaccustomed shoulders" of her partner (*EM* 43), she finds a marked change in him: "His very attitude as he sat there, erect, brisk, confident, was in direct contrast to his old, graceful indolence" (*EM* 46). The *Good Housekeeping* truism that ineffectual men, left to their own devices, will regain masculine competence is borne out by such changes. In her absence, not only is T. A. transformed into hard-edged and erect "maleness," but he transforms the workplace to reflect his new-found authority. Desks are rearranged, partitions erected and, most significantly, he becomes the person to whom the staff turns for decisions and with whom clients discuss their business. The "new order of things" which emerges in Emma's absence may harbor a subtle warning to women desiring careers. Since in this novel the domestic is projected onto the business world and Emma, as a traveling salesperson, leaves "home" to pursue her career, her alienation and loss of power upon her return demonstrate the fate of women who embrace extra-domestic careers.

Displaced by T. A.'s newfound authority and perhaps threatened by the sexual power it portends, Emma "bolt[s] into her own office . . . and close[s] the door behind her" (*EM* 55).[76] For some time she holds herself aloof, stung by the ease with which old business patterns have been recast and loyalties transferred. Eventually, however, she feels a "great pang" of womanly sympathy and, before long, she is swept off her feet by the new T. A. who sues for a "closer corporation" in marriage (*EM* 76). With this, the transposition of character traits is complete. T. A. as the husband-to-be is confirmed in his masculinity by his "brisk, quick-thinking, quick-speaking" manner; Emma, once the "erect," "brisk," "alert," "vibrating" "pacemaker" of the office, dwindles—as Congreve's Millamant feared to do—into a wife, "floundering, hesitating, absentminded . . . strangely starry as to eyes, strangely dreamy as to mood, decidedly deficient as to dictation" (*EM* 77–78). Even when Emma recovers her former competency, she learns that the requirements of domestic efficiency are not those of business:

> She had stood quietly by while Buck attended to their trunks. . . . Once there was some trifling mistake—Buck's fault. Emma, with her experience of the road, saw his error. She could have set it right with a word. It was on the tip of her tongue. By sheer force of will she withheld that word, fought back the almost overwhelming inclination to take things in hand, set them right. It was just an incident, almost trifling in itself. But its import was tremendous, for her conduct, that moment, shaped the happiness of their future life together. (*EM* 99)

Having invoked the domestic to figure the businesswoman's world and desiring to prove her heroine's natural fitness to flourish in that world, Ferber is confronted by conflicting mandates: since the traditional model of domesticity rests upon hierarchy and T. A. Buck has to be elevated to be deserving of so talented a woman, Emma's power must necessarily be diminished. If in business the exceptional woman may sometimes be empowered to "take things in hand," in marriage she must defer to her partner and relinquish her hold.

After marriage, Emma embarks upon a short-lived career as a "doll-wife," a Veblenesque consumer-ornament whose primary duties are to shop and to greet her husband as he departs for and returns from work each day (*EM* 114–15). Although we are assured that she "was too much a woman not to feel a certain exquisite pleasure" in her leisure, it isn't long before Emma begins to chafe at her relative inactivity and feel "something's lacking" in her life (*EM* 117, 129). She decides to return to work, arguing to T. A., "if I had been a homebody, we wouldn't be married." Perhaps in part to dispel the familiar notion that the workplace was akin to the marriage market, Ferber uses an entire chapter and a variety of working women's voices to tout the value of work, from its benefit as a "self-oiler" keeping the body and mind fit and flexible to its virtue in providing productive—not simply time-consuming—activity (*EM* 121, 124).[77] Counter to the popular wisdom of the time, Ferber goes so far as to suggest that one beneficial effect of work for women is a happier marital relation; rather than arising when wives work, divorce ensues when modern wives, their household tasks speedily dispatched with the aid of labor-saving devices, are kept from filling their time productively and thus become bored and capricious.[78]

Despite her insistence on the importance of work in women's lives, Ferber betrays her essential conservatism by characterizing the domestic sphere as the norm. Although business may provide a woman's livelihood or the opportunity for recognition in useful service, it can never rival the home as the center of her true interest. While Emma enjoys her life as a traveling salesperson and revels in the excitement and energy of its competitiveness, the mention of spring house-cleaning is enough to bring a "troubled, yearning light to her eyes," and the sight of roasts in a butcher's window or produce in a grocer's display generates within her an "ache" to "turn back her sleeves and don a blue-and-white checked apron" (*RBM* 33,36–7). As she rides the train across her sales territory, through small towns and country hamlets, Emma glimpses that which constitutes "real life":

> As the train slowed down, there could be a glimpse of a matronly housewife moving deftly about in the kitchen's warm-yellow glow, a man reading a paper in slippered, short-sleeved comfort, a pig-tailed girl at the piano, a woman with a baby in her arms, or a family group, perhaps, seated about the table, deep in an after-supper conclave. It had made her as homeless as she was homesick. (*EM 110*–11)

Nor is Emma unique in this longing. In her travels she meets Blanche LeHaye, an aging vaudeville entertainer of questionable reputation who proves to be a sister under the skin when it comes to the undeniable tug of domesticity. Stopping together in a small town, Emma invites Blanche to visit a friend's home where they can "act like human being[s] for one day." Together, the women don aprons and get down to "real" work. For Blanche, "the heat and the bustle of the kitchen seemed to work some miraculous change": "her eyes brightened. Her lips smiled. Once Emma . . . heard her crooning one of those tuneless chants women hum when they wring out dishcloths in soapy water" (*RBM* 126–9). As the site of "real" life and work where "real" female beings emerge, the home stands as the locus of a woman's authentic self; business, the antithesis of the real for women, offers but an artificial, incomplete identity.

Thus unindulged domestic urges frequently surface in the workplace itself, providing assurances that "real" women remain essentially feminine even on the job. While on the road, Emma lavishes attention on her Featherloom samples, arranging them "with loving care . . . look[ing] at them as a mother's eyes rest fondly on the shining faces, the well-brushed hair, the clean pinafores of her brood" (*EM 35*). When she "conceives" of a radical idea for a hoop petticoat, pregnancy and birth figure the process—even the voluminous petticoat figures into the "pregnant" idea. She says to factory visitors, "We're just bringing a new skirt into the world. I thought you might like to be in at the birth" (*EM* 190). Similarly, fellow worker Ethel Morrisey's "shrewd, twinkling, far-sighted, reckoning eyes" mark her as a business woman, but her manner suggests that work is merely the means of displacing energy unused in the care of children or a home. Indeed, as Emma asserts, Ethel's natural role is that of mother:

> When Ethel Morrisey was planned by her Maker, she had not been meant to be wasted on the skirt and suit department of a small town store. That broad, gracious breast had been planned as a resting place for heads in need of comfort. Those plump firm arms were meant to enfold the weak and distressed. Those capable hands should have smoothed troubled heads and patted plump cheeks, instead of wasting their gifts in folding piles of petticoats and deftly twitching a plait or a tuck into place. (*EM* 62)

Although Ethel had worked her way up to become the buyer for a Chicago store, her efforts are nevertheless "wasted" when compared to the woman's work she should have been doing. Like the editors of *Good Housekeeping*, Ferber regards a business career as a secondary interest, something which serves or substitutes for legitimate domestic duties.

Both *Roast Beef Medium* and *Emma McChesney* end seeming to affirm a woman's autonomy gained through the financial independence or individual recognition that a career may afford. Announcing itself a "love story with a logical ending," *Roast Beef Medium* does indeed break with the romantic tradition which would have Emma accept T. A. Buck's marriage proposal (263). In 1913, Ferber tells a love story in terms of a mother's love for her son and a woman's regard for herself; in 1915, she would seem to strike a similar note, celebrating Emma's individuality: "it's all very well to drown your identity in the music of the orchestra, but there's nothing equal to the soul-filling satisfaction [of] solo work" (*EM* 231). However, the final chapter in the Emma McChesney trilogy runs counter to this sentiment and defines the woman of the future in terms of domestic service, the "orchestra" referred to in the quotation above. Grace Galt, Emma's young double in the novel, is "one of the most expert copy writers in the advertising world" and represents the next generation of independent women (*EM* 166). Like Emma, Grace breaks into and succeeds in business territory traditionally considered male because she possesses a "clear-headed, capable manner" and "nerve—the real kind" (*EM* 166, 175). Grace, as Jock McChesney's fiancée, also shares Emma's primary love interest; yet if Emma, as Jock's mother, "made" him into a responsible young man while she worked her way up the business ladder, Grace, as his wife, retreats from that world to carry on that process. When she gives up her career to marry Jock, focus strategically shifts from the earlier emphasis on the quality of life work affords women to its quantifiable aspect. Reduced to a matter of dollars and cents, a job is easily dismissed for the rewards of love; ironically, too, this reductive assessment of work provides the standard defining the quality of love Grace bears Emma's son: "Any girl . . . who'll give up four thousand a year and her independence to marry a man does it for love"(*EM* 211). As a homemaker and especially as a mother, Grace follows the familiar *Good Housekeeping* pattern and calls upon her years of business training to transform the household routine into a model of efficiency: she enforces schedules, supervises domestic help, and follows exacting feeding formulas in adherence to "twentieth century child raising methods." Baffled by these new practices, Emma sighs, "And I thought I was a modern woman" (*EM 225*), acknowledging domestic accomplishment wrapped in quasi-scientific language as the true measure of the up-to-date woman. Thus Ferber retreats from her initial vision of women successfully managing simultaneous business and domestic careers and turns to the familiar sequential model that Grace embraces as the embodiment of the future. Ferber ultimately undermines her assertion that women's work is any work that a woman can do well by contrasting and thereby qualifying it with the "real" work which is carried out exclusively in the home. Like the vocational advice books and the *Good Housekeeping* magazines of the decade, the would-be maverick implicitly affirms that the measure of the "real" woman is to be found in her response to the domestic.

Sinclair Lewis's *The Job* (1917) follows Una Golden, a young woman "as undramatic as a field daisy,"[79] into the world of work and romance in order to counter the rosy reports of easily won business success and instant marital bliss purveyed by the period's popular literature. Indeed, marriage and business prove equally unpalatable choices for the girl of average accomplishment and intelligence. As Una's experience demonstrates, the most frequent source of business ambition is economic need fueled by personal disappointment; the greatest stimulus to marriage among working woman is the "blood-sucking tedium" of their jobs; the main cause of divorce —and, as a result, a woman's return to the workforce—is marriage itself, founded as it is upon inequality and the misconceptions each partner brings to the union. Lewis adds to this already complex cycle of forces the fact of "feminine" biology, arguing that neither professional nor personal success can override the urge for children and the nest—desires which are only imperfectly satisfied by their displacement onto the work scene. Thus, although Una survives her dead-end jobs and unfortunate marriage to find a genuinely satisfying career and a man who offers both love and support, her story ends on a note as ambivalent as Emma's:

"I will keep my job—if I've had this world of offices wished on to me, at least I'll conquer it, and give my clerks a decent time," the business woman meditated. *"But* just the same—oh, I am a woman, and I do need love. I want Walter, and I want his child, my own baby and his." (*Job* 327; emphasis added)

Una would seem to have written herself into the conventional American success story only to discover that it is essentially a male narrative. Because there is no plot that responds to her feminine ambitions and desires, such "buts"—indicative of a mode of thought in which career, marriage and family are viewed as exclusive rather than inclusive options—arise and destabilize her sense of contentment. If Ferber set out to show that any sphere is a woman's sphere, Lewis is eager to prove that so long as the way of the world is predicated upon male desire and power, the very opposite is in fact true.

Until she is twenty-four, Una Golden lives a middle class life "too respectable to permit her to have a job, and too poor to permit her to go to college," confirmed in the "faith" that a "woman's business in life was to remain respectable and secure a man" (*Job* 5–7). If she harbors an embryonic doubt as to the "divine superiority of men," Una still honors the approved custom of passively waiting for "the fairy prince" who will secure her future. But when Mr. Golden dies suddenly, leaving Una and her mother with large debts, a small insurance settlement and no prospect for the future he was supposed to guarantee, the arrangement which insists upon female dependency comes into question. If she lacks practical training or experience, Una nevertheless is a "natural executive" possessing a common sense which enables her to "size up people and affairs" and to "secretly" control the Golden household. These native abilities prove insufficient to provide for herself and her mother, however; when she surveys the options available to a woman with a high school education in her village of Panama, Pennsylvania, she finds the "fair fields of fruitful labor" confined to teaching, selling dry-goods, or marrying if she is to maintain that middle-class idol, gentility. The bleak future promised by these possibilities fill her with "hysterical protest" and she cries, "If I were only a boy. . . I could go to work in the hardware store or on the railroad and not lose respectability. Oh I *hate* being a woman" (*Job* 12–13). Una's despair is converted into newfound faith in her chances for success when she reaches the decision to go to New York and become a stenographer. Her mind filled with the images of young business women's instant and grand achievements so often retailed in popular magazine stories,[80] Una imagines her rise will be similarly swift and sure:

> She *would* go to New York, become a stenographer, a secretary to a corporation president, a rich woman, free and independent. The fact of making this revolutionary decision so quickly gave her a feeling of power, of already being a business woman. (*Job* 14–15)

The effortless mental leap which makes the distance between stenographer and woman of independent means seem tiny indeed serves to place Una's expectations in the realm of romance no more substantial than that which previously informed her thoughts. Although she no longer waits passively for a fairy prince to resolve her future, she hardly seems the agent of her own success when the means of action are so radically effaced from the imagined plot. This vision nevertheless forms the basis of Una's new creed, shored up with the belief that by the sheer force of her desire the quest will be accomplished.

Lewis's systematic characterization of Una's ambition in terms of religious faith underscores his heroine's unthinking adherence to business catechism, driving home the notion that success has become America's god and money-making its newest form of worship. When she arrives in New York and finds it a city of "golden rewards," Una quickly dedicates herself to a life of service in order to reap the bounty that seems rightfully hers:

> "Oh I want this—its mine! . . . An apartment up there—a big, broad window seat, [to] look out on all this. Oh, dear God," she was unconsciously praying to her vague Panama Wesley Methodist Church God, who gave you things if you were good, "I will work for all of this. . . ." (*Job* 20)

She enrolls in Whiteside and Schleusner's College of Commerce, undismayed by the shabbiness of the shrine or of her fellow devotees. While the others confine their learning to the basics, Una, "her belief in the sacredness of the game . . . boundless" (*Job* 23), prepares herself by adding English grammar, spelling and letter-composition to the requisite shorthand and typing, and soon begins to feel "the theory of efficiency, the ideal of Big Business" fill her like the holy spirit (*Job* 25). Significantly, Una becomes a solitary and genderless figure when she is thus consumed with business zeal. With a "daily growing faith in her commercial future," she cuts off from her fellows and becomes a "girl grind" who "devotes all of a sexless energy" to her goal of getting ahead. Although Una does maintain and even develop several personal relationships during her working years, she tends to immerse herself in business, substituting ambition for emotion when these relationships disappoint her. When the "awkward gaieties" of a business school dance fail to satisfy a vague longing for a man, she decides "I'll stick to my work;" when her true love Walter Babson leaves her to make his fortune in the West, "she again determined to be a real business woman" (*Job* 34, 109); and when a boarding house flirtation gets frighteningly out of hand, she rededicates herself to commercial success:

> I'm through! No one can get me just because of curiosity about sex again. I'm free, I can fight my way through business and still keep clean. I can! I was hungry for—for even that rat. I—Una Golden! Yes, I was. But I don't want to go back to him. I've won! (*Job* 154)[81]

Business ambition exercises its purifying effect on Una, washing away the residue of emotional entanglements or the cares of an exhausting day so that if she were "always weary at dusk" she was also "always recreated at dawn" (*Job* 163–164). However, since this ambition operates as a compensation for something lost or denied in her personal life, it proves a troubling and unsatisfying solution. Lewis thus incorporates the familiar either-or model that governs the working woman's life to demonstrate the absurdity of its mandate.

The fervor Una often manifests for her professional life would seem to suggest a far more attractive and rewarding prospect than is actually represented in *The Job*. If *Good Housekeeping* stressed the interesting people, the congenial atmosphere and the challenge of the new to be found on the job, Lewis's emphasis on the numbing tedium inherent in most employment proves that business is, at best, Janus-faced. Rather than the popularly conceived "drama and romance of the office world," Una encounters a "loveless routine," a "grind" (*Job* 41, 47) better suited to a machine's capacity for mindless repetition:

> Lists and letters and items, over and over; sitting at her typewriter till her shoulder-blades ached and she had to shut her eyes to the blur of the keys. The racket of the office noises all day. The three o'clock hour when she felt that she simply could not endure the mill until five o'clock. No interest in anything she wrote. Then the blessed hour of release, the stretching of cramped legs, and the blind creeping into the Subway, the crush in the train . . . . Such was Una's routine in the early months of 1906. After the novelty of the first week it was all rigidly the same. . . . (*Job* 48)

Even when she moves to the responsible position as an office manager, the fixity of Una's routine, the "airless, unnatural, straining life" (*Job* 162) saps her strength and wears down her nerves. She plans to follow the self-improvement advice of the "syndicated philosophers" to study or exercise in her "free" sixteen hours away from work, but her mental and physical exhaustion undermine her best intentions. Given these conditions, it is not surprising that Lewis invokes the image of the domesticated work environment but once when he notes with savage irony that the hire of a "tall, beautiful blonde" "wrecked Una's little office home" (*Job* 219). Instead of controlling the workplace by running it along the lines of the familiar and cozy household, the working woman is herself controlled, used up and replaced by an exploitive "husband-boss."

Repeated in the impersonal corridors of Big Business, this scenario proves far more menacing. At the giant advertising agency Pemberton's, Una suffers from the same tedious office routine, but she also discovers that the "feminine influence" within a rigid office caste system engenders "factional rivalry," "jealousy of position, cattishness, and envy of social standing" among the secretaries, making survival a truly Darwinian experience. She sees girls of twenty growing tired, women of twenty-eight getting "dry and stringy" (*Job* 234), yet all desperately hold out against being replaced like worn-out machine parts. Una watches one "stratum" of survivors with particular interest, the white-haired women of fifty or sixty or seventy years "for whom life was nothing but a desk. . . . Now and then one of them would weep, cry for an hour altogether, with her white head on her desk blotter, till she forgot her homelessness and her uselessness" (*Job* 234). In this "polite version of hell," Una's faith in business falters; she feels as if "she and her fellows were doomed, unless the met by chance with marriage or death; or unless they crawled to the top of the heap" (*Job* 236).

The familiar image of the workplace as an attractive extension of the marriage market to be tapped by would-be wives crumbles in the face of this representation. While work does indeed transform its female workers into wives, it is only by dint of its life-denying demands. Counter to the idea that having a job and money meant a woman didn't have to "settle" for marriage, Lewis shows that working women choose to wed as a means of escaping business and not to satisfy any longing for domesticity. For Una, lost in the rigid daily round and the uniform sea of faces on her first job, the "distinct" personality of Walter Babson emerges to ease her "loveless routine" with his small attentions, humanizing her work experience: "their hands touched as he gave her papers to file; there was affection in his voice when he dictated, and once, outside the office door, he kissed her" (*Job* 89). Una's thoughts, previously centered upon her own discomfort, begin to focus instead upon Walter and how she might "make him value her precious little store of purity and tenderness" (*Job* 88). After Walter leaves to go west, Una tries with increasing desperation to recapture the saving grace of affection in her routine, finding temporary distraction in a motion picture love scene or a "surge of emotion" when " a man, not much of a man, but a man, had wanted contact with her hand, been eager to be with her" (*Job* 147). "Tired and office-soaked," her emotions at low-ebb, Una renews an acquaintance with a "typical American business man," Eddie Schwirtz. Although Schwirtz, with his "unexercised, coffee-soaked, tobacco-filled, whiskey-rotted, fattily degenerated city body" (*Job* 203), would hardly seem a model candidate for matrimony, Una feels only her growing exhaustion and sees through to this vital fact: "He would take care of me. He's kind" (*Job* 215). She overcomes the dissonance between her belief that marriage proceeds from romantic love and her fundamental aversion to Schwirtz's body and mind with a necessary rationalization:

... she had not been particularly fond of Mr. Schwirtz, but had anointed herself for his coming because he was representative of men, yet after months of thus dignifying his attentions, the very effort made her suppose that she must be fond of him. (*Job* 238)

Before long, Una becomes Mrs. Eddie Schwirtz, not in answer to some popularly stereotyped feminine desire for hearth and home, but to escape obliteration in the office's "million blood-sucker details" (*Job* 241). Marriage, however, does not prove the sanctuary Una craves. Indeed, rather than providing her with a respite from the worrisome demands of the workplace, Una faces a whole new set of problems in her position as a wife. The "unleashed brutality" (*Job* 246) of Schwirtz's sexual demands and the coarseness of his hygienic rituals fill Una with disgust, while his spendthrift habits make her fearful that his income will fail to meet their basic needs. Nor is the home that Schwirtz provides any freer of business's tedious and impersonal atmosphere:

> For two years Una Golden Schwirtz moved amid the blank procession of phantoms who haunt cheap family hotels, the apparitions of the corridors, to whom there is no home, nor purpose, nor permanence. . . . The women sit and rock, empty hearted and barren of hands. When they try to make individual homes out of their fixed mold of rooms—the hard walls, the brass bedsteads, the inevitable bureaus, the small rockers and the transoms that always let in too much light from the hall at night—then they are only the more pathetic. . . . For two years—two years snatched out of her life and traded for somnambulatory peace, Una lived this spectral life of one room in a family hotel on a side street near Sixth Avenue. (*Job* 251–252)

Una is frequently left alone by Schwirtz, first because of the traveling requirements of his sales job and then by his pursuit of a "fluffy blonde" who knows how to have a good time. When they are together, he heaps acrimonious insult upon her, questioning her femininity by charging that "business unfits a skirt for marriage" (*Job* 269). As a result, Una again feels the life being crushed from her: "She hadn't realized a woman can die so many times and still live. Dead as her heart had been at Pemberton's, yet it had secreted enough life to suffer horribly now, when it was again being mauled to death" *(Job* 247). Casting about for relief from this oppressive death-in-life situation, Una considers divorce as a means to revive herself. But when Schwirtz loses his job, she finds liberation of a different sort; economic necessity frees her to return to the workforce, "to the splendor of . . . something to do that seemed worthwhile" *(Job* 279). Her move back into business is figured as a chrysalis bursting, freeing the new Una "to quest and meet whatever surprises life might hold" *(Job* 275). Insofar as her return to the workforce violates the categorical prohibition Schwirtz proclaims against wives' employment, the move proves as effective as a divorce in driving them forever apart. When he does finally get a job after months of dependency upon her, Una is able to break the moral tie—if not yet the legal one—between them. She announces, "now that you can take care of yourself, I'll do the same" *(Job* 299).

As if the trials of marriage had somehow galvanized her, Una re-enters business "a keen, wide-awake woman" who takes herself and her goals seriously. She becomes a confidential secretary to a real-estate man, but it isn't long before her newfound persistence and resourcefulness propel her "above the rank of assistant to the rank of people who do things" *(Job* 304). Rather than confining her talents to homemaking on a traditional scale, Una takes up the work of "making suburban homes for men and women and children" *(Job* 281), drawing upon her feminine insight to develop properties in answer to the special concerns of families. Una continues in this vein, turning her attention to the possibilities of transforming a chain of inns from indifferent accommodations into cozy, homelike environments for professional and vacation travelers alike. As she tells the hotel's general manager, "it's women who make the homes for people at home, and why not the homes for people traveling?" *(Job* 322). Una conceives the payoff from such changes to come not only from increased profits, but also from the improved moral atmosphere for patrons and workers. [82]

With such pioneering business ideas, Una begins to fulfill the promise Lewis envisions as part of women's growing social and economic power. According to Lewis, women's influence on moribund patriarchal institutions would make them more humane, more responsive to the needs of a general population rather than only to a select and powerful few. Una herself envisioned "a complete change in the fundamental purpose of organized business from increased production of soap—or books or munitions—to the increased production of happiness" (*Job* 235). In marriage, too, radical change would be effected: "the business woman will bring about a new kind of marriage" of "love and comradeship" (*Job* 270). Not unlike Ferber, Lewis champions the interpenetration of domestic and business spheres under women's "naturally" ethical stewardship. However, as the conclusion of *The Job* reveals, no such "golden" age is yet available to Una. Although her Prince Charming returns from his exploits in the west to offer the companionate marriage Una desires, her pivotal "but" undermines the possibility of the fairy tale ending. Indeed, until women succeed in reforming the world and its institutions, no such tale may be told. Against the grain of all other *Good Housekeeping* articles on the subject, "The Homesick Woman" (November 1915) voices the dilemma of women forced to choose between home or career, declaring that "the task of our age" is to ensure that women are afforded the opportunity for manifold expression of their talents and desires:

> For it is not bread *or* water that we want, it is bread *and* water—the outer *and* the inner life, the social *and* the personal expression. And there need be no hope of our showing anything more than spasmodic, intermittent periods of contentment until we get them both.

*

Faced with the fact that women in ever increasing numbers were entering the workforce, these guardians of public thinking sanctioned a limited number of scenarios allowing for and, in some cases, idealizing women's participation in the public world of business, yet effectively containing their efforts by defining the form of their striving. Women were assured that a job could be exciting as well as financially rewarding, but were simultaneously reminded of the primacy of their domestic responsibility. Work in the interim between school and marriage became a norm enforced by a variety of voiced and unvoiced threats, with the image of the masculinized woman who divorces her husband and her duties the most potent tool to this end. The woman who extended her working years beyond that norm in effect shirked her social duty of marrying, bearing children and establishing a home of the type that would produce good citizens. Certainly, the conflicting messages the decade's women received did little to stem their increasing numbers in the general workforce, but the pervasive anxiety over what constituted "natural," "normal" and "real" womanhood undoubtedly hampered their entry into traditionally "male" occupations and delayed the recognition that the boundaries of female aspiration and desire had forever changed.

If Ferber and Lewis attempt to counter the either-or mandate in their novels by portraying divorced women and their struggles to maintain respectability, they are unable, finally, to provide plots for the single woman that do not circle back to marriage and family. Yet both Emma's and Una's movements back and forth between the private and the public spheres of home and work (movements defined by divorce or marriage) as well as their ultimate mastery of both realms suggest confusion and dissatisfaction with their culturally encoded roles. Thus by foregrounding the necessity of choice for two such competent women, both authors interrogate the traditional narrative conventions which valorize a woman's "natural" vocation over all others.

NOTES

1. William L. O'Neill, *Everyone Was Brave* (Chicago: Quadrangle Books, 1969), 147.

2. Mary A. Laselle and Katherine E. Wiley, *Vocations for Girls* (Boston: Houghton-Mifflin, 1913), 79.

3. Of the 303 occupations listed in the 1900 United States Census, over five million women earned wages in 294 of them; by 1910, 8,075,772 women—or nearly one in every four—were employed across the country, and by 1920, female workers were found in all but 35 of the 572 Census-listed occupations. See Sheila M. Rothman, *Woman's Proper Place: A History of Changing Ideals and Practices* (New York: Basic Books, 1978), 42; Anna Laylor Burdick, "The Wage Earning Girl and Home Economics," *The Journal of Home Economics* (Aug. 1919): 327; and Carl Degler, *At Odds: Women and the Family in America from the Revolution to the Present* (New York: Oxford University Press, 1980), 376.

4. Harland, *Eve's Daughters; or Common Sense for Maid, Wife and Mother* (1882); Willard, *Occupations for Women* (1897); both quoted in Rothman, *Woman's Proper Place*, 43.

5. In *Out to Work: A History of Wage Earning Women in the United States* (New York: Oxford University Press, 1982), Alice Kessler-Harris counters the rosy reading of the raw 1900 Census figures on women's employment by noting that in only 43 of the touted 294 occupations were there more than 5,000 women employed (141). While women maintained their numerical dominance in jobs traditionally open to them as teachers, seamstresses, milliners, domestic servants, and factory workers, their real gains for the period were made in retail sales and clerical occupations. In 1880 there were 7,744 women employed in sales in America's stores; in 1900 their numbers had grown to 149,230, and to 526,718 in 1920. 7,040 women were clerical workers in 1880; between 1900 and 1920, their numbers increased from 187,053 to 1,421,925. Gains in the professions, however, were considerably less dramatic: for example, legal occupations, including lawyer and judge as well as justice of the peace and notary public, employed 75 women in 1880, 1,343 in 1900, and 3,221—or 2.6 percent of the female working population—in 1920. See Margery Wynn Davies, *A Woman's Place is at the Typewriter: The Feminization of Clerical Workers and Changes in Clerical Work in the United States, 1870–1930* (New York: Oxford University Press, 1980), 233–34; and Susan Porter-Benson, *Counter-Cultures: Saleswomen, Managers and Customers in American Department Stores, 1890–1940* (Urbana: University of Illinois Press, 1986), 297.

6. For the "young woman with the new education and some old fashioned notions of propriety" [Grace Dodge, *What Women can Earn: Occupations for Women and Their Compensation* (New York, 1898), 120], such advice books included Ella Rodman Church's *Money Making For Ladies* (1882), Ruth Ashmore's *The Business Girl* (1895–8), and Helen Candee's *How Women May Earn a Living* (1900). The following passage from *The Business Girl* addresses the distinction between collegiality and familiarity in the marketplace:

> Then, when she has five minutes to herself, or in the time before she begins her work, she forgets she is born of a race of gentlewomen, and she laughs and jests with one of the clerks, or assists in playing a joke on the office boy. After this, has she any right to be offended when the clerk with whom she has been so "chummy". . . addresses her by her first name?

Quoted in Sarah Eisenstein, *Give Us Bread But Give Us Roses: Working Women's Consciousness in the United States, 1890 to the First World War* (Boston: Routledge, 1983), 72–81.

7. Eisenstein, *Give Us Bread,* 73.

8. A Boston Central Labor Union official, quoted in Kessler-Harris, *Out to Work,* 154. As a marker of class distinctions, the knife signals the world of the poor, the desperate and the unassimilated. The choice of it over a gun as the metaphorical assassin's weapon conveys the message that the forces cultivating women's employment were not only unsavory low-lifes but also personally aggressive given the intimate contact necessary when wielding a knife.

9. Robert A. Woods and Albert J. Kennedy, *Young Working Girls* (Boston, 1913), 162.

10. Quoted in Kessler-Harris, *Out to Work,* 102–3.

11. Sue Ainslie Clark and Edith Wyatt, "Working Girl's Budgets," *McLure's* 35.6 (Oct. 1910): 595–604.

12. Porter Benson, *Counter-Cultures,* 135.

13. Florence Kelley, "Married Women in Industry," *Proceedings of the Academy of Political Science* (Oct. 1910): 90.

14. Degler, *At Odds,* 175; Riley, *Divorce: An American Tradition,* 145.

15. Kelley, "Married Women," 90–92.

16. Volume 15 of the *Report on the Condition of Women and Child Wage Earners in the United States,* Senate Document 645, 61st Congress, 2nd Session, 9.

17. Sarah Louise Arnold, "Vocational Training for Women," *Proceedings of the Academy of Political Science* (Oct. 1910):130–34.

18. Woods and Kennedy, *Working Girls,* 156.

19. Laselle and Wiley, *Vocations for Girls,* 13; emphasis added.

20. Helen Waite Papashvily, *All the Happy Endings: A study in the domestic novel in America, the women who wrote it, and the women who read it, in the nineteenth century* (New York: Harper, 1956), 203–4. Notably, these heroines are rewarded for their sacrifices, returned to the domestic sphere as "great ladies," either through adoption by a doting "father" or through marriage, where they remain the "staunch and true friend of the noble working girls" (205).

21. Eisenstein, *Give Us Bread,* 73.

22. Elizabeth Kemper Adams, *Women Professional Workers* (New York: Macmillan, 1921), 32.

23. See Catherine Filene, *Careers for Women: New Ideas, New Methods, New Opportunities* (Boston: Houghton-Mifflin, 1920). Of the 175 occupations described in Filene, for example, opportunities in law, medicine, science and government numbered 29 (the same number which appeared under the single heading of "Business"). Besides the paucity of descriptions of the professions, the ones that are listed seem tokens of curiosity rather than genuine paths the average woman of intelligence and ambition might choose: explorer, taxidermist and deep-sea diver come to mind.

24. Elizabeth Ammons, "The New Woman as Cultural Symbol and Social Reality," in *1915: The Cultural Moment,* ed. Adele Heller and Lois Rudnick (New York: Rutgers University Press, 1991), 83. *Good Housekeeping's* blend of non-fiction articles on domestic management, fashion and readers' views and its fiction by "name authors" gave the magazine a solid circulation of 300,000 at the beginning of the decade; by 1920, with its larger format, 250 page issues and increased fiction offerings, the magazine neared the million mark in circulation. See Frank Luther Mott, *A History of American Magazines*, vol. 5, 125–43.

25. Abby Merchant and Annette Austin, "College Girls Preferred," *Good Housekeeping* (June 1910): 727–31. In the following notes 26–73, the source is *Good Housekeeping* unless otherwise noted.

26. See "Taverns and Tea Rooms as a Business for Women" (June 1911): 691–97 and A. W. Rolker, "The Family Woman in Business" (July 1911): 147–53.

27. Kathleen Norris, "The Wooing of Julia Earle," (Nov. 1915): 555–67.

28. See Martha Bensly Brère, "The Business of Being a Bride" (May 1914): 645–50; "Efficiency Methods in the Home" (Aug. 1913): 253–58; "The Housewife's Vacation" (Aug. 1914): 192–98; and "The New Profession of Matrimony" (Feb.–May 1913).

29. Ellis Parker Butler, "The Head of the Department" (Oct. 1910): 381–86.

30. See Harvey W. Wiley, "Mobilize the Women" (April 1918): 51+; and H. Addington Bruce, "Finding Health in War Work" (July 1918): 53+.

31. See "Women's Work is Never Done" (May 1918): 36–7; "Women's Work for You and Me to *Carry On*" (June 1918): 38–9; and "Holding the Real First Line" (Sept. 1918): 42.

32. The domestic focus of the women's "duties" is obvious; only the scale of the labors have truly changed: "They have knitted millions of warm sweaters and stockings and mufflers for both army and navy. They are supplying every

transport with magazines, tobacco, cigarettes and chewing-gum. Over four-hundred New York women are enrolled in the New York City motor service. Six hundred and twenty women are teaching and demonstrating food conservation. Many others are teaching home gardening and all branches of farming." *Life,* 70, no. 1828 (Nov. 8, 1917): 769.

33. An equally effective means of evacuating women from "men's" jobs as the army came home was to reverse the roles they had been playing. As aggressors eager to show man that they "can beat him at nearly every line of work" ("Women's Work is Never Done"), women workers were figured as an army that had "invaded every field of labor" [W. L. George, "Women and Labor" (Feb. 1919):15–16)]. But because they were merely a "labor reserve," it was a force to be disbanded at will; see Anna Lalor Burdick, "The Wage Earning Girl and Home Economics," *The Journal of Home Economics* (Aug. 1919): 327–36; and N. A. Smythe, "Why Women Must Work" (Nov. 1918): 124.

34. See Claudia Cranston, "How the Pantry Shelf Came to Fifth Avenue" (Nov. 1919) for a profile of Mrs. Florence Reynolds explaining how she became "one of the most successful women in America" by putting up jams even though she "had never made a dollar in her life"(49).

35. Anne Shannon Monroe, "Old Fields for New Women" (July 1919): 72; this article offers views of the women who have retrieved "their own lost fields" of weaving and textile deign and returned them to the home.

36. "Women in the Business World" by "A Business Woman," *The Outlook* (11 May 1895) 778. Other negative portrayals from the turn of century abound, and include Marion Harland's "The Incapacity of Business Women," *North American Review* (Dec. 1889): 707–712; and "The Return of the Business Woman," *Ladies Home Journal* (March 1900).

37. Examples include Alice Stebbins Wells, Los Angeles' first female police officer, who is described as discharging official duties "no less varied than her brother officers, and often identical with them" in "The Police Woman" (Feb. 1911); and Frances Kessler, who occupies "a unique position in American business" as its "highest salaried woman traveling on the road." See "On the Road" (Oct. 1919).

38. Rose Young, "Your Daughter's Career" (July 1915): 66; "Young Matrons and Marriage" (Feb. 1911): 197–202.

39. Maude Radford Warren, "Sing as You Go" (Feb. 1916): 202.

40. "Your Daughter's Career," 62. That women's careers outside the home generated great anxiety is evident beyond the either/or constructions. As

"amazing" as the twentieth century changes for women might have been, one has the sense of the troubled parent facing the dragon career-question for a daughter (while the son's options "excite") that will be "problematic" and fraught with "uncertainty" no matter the answer.

41. "College Girls Preferred," 741.

42. *Life* 65, no. 1697 (May 6, 1915).

43. "Your Daughter's Career," 66.

44. See "The Clothes of the Business Woman" (Oct. 1915): 527–29; and Carolyn Trowbridge Radnor-Lewis, "Her Wardrobe: The Business Woman's Outfit" (Nov. 1911): 633–6.

45. Jenette Lee, "The College Woman in the Community" (Sept. 1914): 365–7. The idea that men had usurped women's domestic jobs and placed them outside the home in factories appeared frequently at mid-decade as the justification for a woman going into the workforce and following their "traditional pursuits." See also Rose Young, "Men, Women and Sex Antagonism" (April 1914): 487–90; and Anna Lalor Burdick, "The Wage Earning Girl and Home Economics" in *The Journal of Home Economics* (Aug. 1919): 333.

46. See Lois Scharf, *To Work and to Wed: Female Employment, Feminism, and the Great Depression* (Westport, Conn.: Greenwood Press, 1980), 13; Porter-Benson, *Counter-Cultures,* 130.

47. Martha Keeler, "Fifteen Minutes Plus" (Nov. 1913): 678–80. In a competing journal, one business man stated that the skills he looked for in a good stenographer were comprised of technical skills (20%), general knowledge of business (30%) and personality (50%). The worker was expected to exude harmony and optimism, be agreeable, adaptable and courteous, and "take an interest in the things I am trying to do." See Harry C. Spillman, "The Stenographer Plus," *Ladies Home Journal* (Feb. 1916): 33. In "How I Became a Confidential Secretary" [*Ladies Home Journal* (Sept. 1916)], Helen Gladwyn explains how she learned "the value of a smile and an agreeable accommodating manner." The subtle equation of secretarial and wifely duties is made clearly in this exchange between boss and employee:

> "I want to turn over to you all my personal accounts and give you my power of attorney. . . . Hereafter you will be my confidential secretary in every sense of the word."

Nothing else ever thrilled me quite so much as did that conversation, not even my first proposal, and I doubt if anything else ever will.

48. Warren, "Sing as You Go," 192–94.

49. Monroe, "On the Road," 52. Similarly, Mrs. Wells, "The Policewoman," carries out her duties in a distinctly feminine way, transferring her capacity to mother from the home to the street. Perceiving that "a woman's sympathy may be more effective than a man's power," she creates an environment in which women may, "with greater freedom and confidence . . . appeal to the department for advice and protection" (297).

50. See "Bachelors—Why? The Views of Five Hundred of them on the Income Needed for Matrimony and the Fitness of Girls for Household Management" (March 1910): 335–40; and "A Plain Statement" (Jan. 1910): 133.

51. "How Can The Unasked Girl Marry?" (Sept. 1913): 353.

52. Carolyn Wells, "The Tale of Melissa Clarissa DeLisle" (Jan.–May 1910). See also Kathleen Norris, "Saturday's Child" (Nov. 1913–Sept. 1914) in which another office girl heroine hopes to parlay her position into a domestic career. Susan Brown sets her sights on the boss's son to deliver her from the "groove":

Now, tonight for the first time, the tiny spark of definite ambition was added to her natural endowment: She would study the work of the office systematically, she would be promoted, she would be head girl someday, some day very soon, and obliged, as head girl, to come in and out of Peter Coleman's office constantly.

However, she finds the rich too careless a class and, properly chastened by her desires, rediscovers love in her own circle of friends.

53. Martha Keeler, "Speaking of Promotion" (Jan. 1915): 81–83. The text of a *Life* cartoon of Jan. 26, 1899 demonstrates the savvy of an office worker who parlays a disagreeable boss into a husband, and a mere job into a career:

First Typist: How did you come to marry your employer?
Second Typist: He became so disagreeable I couldn't get along with him—as an employer.

54. Sarah Comstock, "The Spindle and the Distaff" (July 1916): 35–44.

55. Norris, "The Wooing of Julia Earle" (Nov. 1915).

56. See in particular Elizabeth Jordan's serialized novel "May Iverson's Career" (Dec. 1913–Nov. 1914) in which a young woman embarks upon an adventurous career in journalism and discovers the contours of "real life" along the way. She emerges from her working days "a perfectly rounded woman" who, as she "approaches the triumph of her career," discovers her work had been merely a rehearsal for life as a wife:

> My professional life . . . lay behind me. Little it seemed to count in the new world I was entering. Until tonight, I had merely been a player in the wings. Now, out in front, I heard the orchestra playing. The curtain of life was going up and I had my cue in Godfrey's voice.

Nor did the Great War do much to alter this model: a June 1919 story argues that work—in this case as a front line nurse on the Somme—is the necessary catalyst which transforms a girl into a potential wife. Sheila O'Leary's vague idealism is distilled into real and effective service without regard for herself as she struggles with life and death decisions, but its is not until she marries a war correspondent that she "come[s] into her own at last." See Ruth Sawyer, "Into Her Own" (June 1919): 36+.

57. "A Woman's Honor" (May 1919).

58. "What Do You Say? A Wife's Duty to Her Husband" (May 1912): 727.

59. "Women Wage Earners" (Oct. 1910): 443.

60. Frances Gale, "Honest Partnership" (Jan. 1910): 51.

61. *Good Housekeeping* articles sounded alarm at the shift in women's position from producers to consumers: "a wife was a helpmate . . . and made wealth. Now they [sic] take it" [Jesse Lynch Williams, "The Luxury of Marriage" (Aug. 1913): 187]. A wife's unrestrained buying to keep up with her "financial superiors" ruins her husband and her marriage and, judging by the title, unsexes her in "The Woman I Failed to Be" (Feb. 1914): 199–204. See also Jesse Lynch Williams, "The New Marriage" (Feb. 1914): 181–185; Brère, "The Business of Being a Bride" (May 1914) and Clara Savage, "Buying That isn't Buying" (July 1916): 29–33.

62. "Why I Won't Let My Daughter Go Into Business, by a Successful Business Woman," *Ladies Home Journal* (Sept. 1909): 16.

63. "Fiancées—Why Not? Five Hundred Young Women Have Their Say Concerning Bachelors, Salaries and Sundry Problems Involved in Matrimony" (May 1910): 588–594.

64. Mary Fisher, "The Homemaker" (Feb. 1910): 188–191.

65. Maud O. Bartlett, "The Home Maker" (April 1910): 431–434.

66. *Life* 70, no. 1819 (Sept. 6, 1917).

67. "Les Miserables," *Life* 63, no. 1645 (May 7, 1914). The theme of the self-sufficient "New Woman" who causes her husband's demoralization was prevalent during the decade. In "Why I Will Not Let My Daughter Go Into Business," a wife's sufficiency leads not only to her husband's dependency, but also does her sons, "fine, straight-limbed lads, a grievous wrong in showing them the example of a man who 'lives off' his wife's—a woman's—earnings." The mention of her sons' physique suggests that hers is such a terrible moral error that it might blight their bodies as well as their souls. To remove the sight of the demoralized father from their view, the successful business woman divorces him. Years later, she discovers her ex is a successful man, "the shock of divorce had steadied him" (16). See also Louise Dutton, "When Lila Turned Wage-Earner," *Ladies Home Journal* (June 1916) and Clarence Budington Kelland, "His Wife's Place," *Everybody's Magazine* (Nov. 1919).

68. The story "The Odd One" (Oct. 1917) illustrates the danger inherent in the very word "divorce" by portraying the emotional anxiety a child experiences at the prospect of her family breaking up. The youngest of three children, Maida finds out from her older sister that her parents are divorcing and, as a consequence, the children will be divided between the parents. Maida, because she is the youngest, is told that she is "the odd one that's left over." Likening herself to the odd piece of candy divided up after all other pieces have been equally distributed, the youngster remembers the story of King Solomon dividing the baby in half when its parents fail to resolve their differences. Maida repeatedly envisions herself being cut in two to satisfy the "rules" of divorce, and ultimately lays the blame for the situation on her father. Although it turns out that her parents had threatened divorce in the heat of an argument and reconcile, in the best *Good Housekeeping* style, quickly and completely, Maida is left with invisible but permanent scars:

> In a week . . . Maida forgot all about the necessity of hating fathers and all that remained was a feeling that her father was not as nice as mother. Long after she forgot the reason for that feeling, it remained. Possibly it did not matter. Possibly it did.

69. "Mirandy on Matrimony and Money" (Sept. 1915). See also "Mirandy on Losing a Husband" (Dec. 1911); "Mirandy on the Love Test" (Oct. 1912); "Mirandy on Thanksgiving" (Nov. 1912); "Mirandy on Marrying for a Living" (July 1913); "Mirandy on the Amenities of Matrimony" (March 1915); "Mirandy on the Matrimonial Brand" (May 1916); and "Mirandy on First Aid to Matrimony" (Dec. 1916).

70. *Good Housekeeping* (April 1914).

71. "Mirandy on the Love Test" (Oct. 1912).

72. For instance, in Kansas in 1920, 15 per cent of women employed in retail positions were divorced, separated or widowed, as were 16.3 per cent of women working in all other occupations surveyed. In Rhode Island for the same year, 10.4 per cent of women retail workers and 7.9 per cent of women in other occupations fell into this category. See Porter-Benson, Appendix F: "Marital Status of Women in the Labor Force," *Out to Work*.

73. The *Good Housekeeping* articles "The Policewoman" (Feb. 1911), "Happy at Half-Past Forty" (Nov. 1914) and "On the Road" (Oct. 1919) all deal with widows in the workplace, although very little is made of their marital status. Except as the pathetically abandoned wife, the divorced woman made no appearance in the magazine's pages.

74. Edna Ferber, *Roast Beef Medium* (New York: Frederick A. Stokes, 1913), 198; quotations from this text shall be cited as *RBM* and appear parenthetically in the text. *Emma McChesney & Co* (New York: Frederick A. Stokes, 1915) shall be cited as *EM*.

75. Julie Goldsmith Gilbert, *Ferber: A Biography* (New York: Doubleday, 1978), 410.

76. In *Roast Beef Medium*, when Emma is still the far-seeing, self-reliant business woman, she easily brushes off T. A. Buck's awkward advances. When he tentatively calls her "girlie" and offers her a ride in his new car, she flusters him into retreat by precisely articulating his invitation's implicit demand: "Let's get down to cases. If I let you make love to me, I keep my job. Is that it?" (*RBM* 160). Later, when T. A. has become appropriately aware of Emma's virtues as a business person and a woman, he asks her to marry him. Again, she easily controls the situation: "I can imagine nothing more beautiful on earth for a woman than being married to a man she cares for and who cares for her. But, T. A., you're not that man" (288). Earlier, too, Emma easily repulsed the young traveling salesman's advances. See *RBM* 13–17.

Theodore Roosevelt, desiring a more traditional sense of closure to Emma McChesney's career to date, wrote to Ferber: "I wonder if you feel that I am hopelessly sentimental because my only objection to the last twelve pages is that I would have liked somehow to see not only the boy marry, but poor Emma McChesney at last have the chance herself to marry somebody decent with whom she is in love." Quoted in Gilbert, *Ferber,* 409.

77. Although her plot—and Emma's comment about her work-related marriage—finally work against her, Ferber clearly tries to counter the popular idea that business provided women with a happy hunting ground for husbands. When T. A. goes out on the road as a salesman, *he* becomes the object of the female gaze and, in a workforce increasingly composed of women, is valued for his "sex-appeal" (an appeal akin to his potential as a husband-provider) in the way women had been. Piqued, Emma reminds the would-be Mrs. Bucks that Featherlooms "is a business house, not a matrimonial parlor" *(EM* 60). She similarly rebuffs advances made to her on the job (see above note).

78. In *The Worth of a Girl* (New York: Thomas Crowell, 1916), Bertha Pratt King concurs with Ferber that work enriches a woman in more than financial respects:

> The woman who is economically independent is free,—not in the sense of license; but free in the fine sense of being able to develop her own powers and capabilities to her own delight; and who can tell, in cases of high talent, perhaps to the delight of mankind! Self-supporting wives will go far towards solving the divorce evil. Fancy a man full grown in mind and character bound for life to a wife with the undeveloped brains of seventeen! Divorce is a godsend to such a man unless he can use his wife as a housekeeper. (27)

79. Sinclair Lewis, *The Job: An American Novel* (New York: Harcourt, Brace, and Company, 1917), 13. Subsequent quotations are from this edition and will be cited parenthetically in the text as *Job.*

80. Una's general references to "women's magazines" occur throughout the novel. Upon arriving in New York, she dreams she will have "such an apartment of white enamel and glass doors and mahogany as she saw described" in a *Good Housekeeping*-like periodical. Her opinions on fashion and her taste in the arts are similarly formed by what she reads in those magazines. See *The Job,* 38, 115, 162, 195, 198.

81. Although Lewis focuses his attention on the plight of women in the workforce, he is quick to note that it is an inimical environment for "little" men like Schwirtz as well. He, too, looks at passion as a drug that will allow him to

escape the frustrations of the job. He says unhappily to Una, "you can't understand that there are wives who've got so much passion in 'em that if their husbands came home clean-licked, like I am, they'd—oh, their husbands would just naturally completely forget their troubles in love—real love, with fire in it" (*Job* 266–267).

82. For a discussion of the domesticated workspace in *The Job* and Una's desire to "mother" her office workers, see Martha Banta, *Taylored Lives: Narrative Productions in the Age of Taylor, Veblen and Ford* (Chicago: University of Chicago Press, 1993), 189–193.

Afterword

Edith Wharton's 1911 story "Autres Temps" chronicles a Mrs.
Lidcote's return to America from Europe after an "exile" of some
eighteen years.[1] Having fled family, society and country in disgrace as a
divorcée, she braves this journey back in order to be with her daughter
Leila as she confronts her own divorce crisis. However, while yet on
board the New York-bound ship, Mrs. Lidcote gets the first inkling that
the society which judged her so mercilessly has radically changed its
ideas about marriage and divorce; indeed, now everyone "seem[s] to be
divorced" (AT 189) without adverse effect to their social standing or
respectability. Thus, after nearly two decades of "behaving as if her life
were over" (AT 193), Mrs. Lidcote begins to hope there might be a
change in attitude about her own "case":

> If the old processes were changed, her case changed with them; she,
> too, was a part of the general readjustment, a tiny fragment of the
> new pattern worked out in bolder freer harmonies. Since her daughter
> had no penalty to pay, was not she herself released by the same
> stroke? The rich arrears of youth and joy were gone; but was there
> not time enough to accumulate new stores of happiness? (AT 195)

Although Leila's case excited nary a raised brow, Mrs. Lidcote
discovers that neither time nor the new tolerance serve to vindicate her;
she "sinned," not simply against the institution of marriage, but against
what were implacable social sanctions of her own day. Mrs. Lidcote
remains outside the boundaries of acceptable society, an embarrassment
even to her own daughter.

229

In a potent sense, "Autres Temps" recapitulates the attitudes toward divorce expressed in the narratives examined in this project. For Isabel Archer, divorce was indeed a social and moral anathema; despite the accessibility of such legal remedy, women were expected to endure rather than escape their marital plights and plots. Divorce exists at the margins not only of society, but also of the narrative itself: only Henrietta Stackpole, that "vanguard" of social change, mentions it by name, linking it specifically with the West and the future—entities yet on the horizon. With Undine Spragg's marital career, however, divorce assumes center stage, fully acknowledged as a means of multiplying a woman's "business" opportunities and capitalizing upon social success. By the time Emma McChesney and Una Golden's stories are told, divorce has become such an American trademark (particularly for women) that it has been in a sense remarginalized in these texts as something so familiar one need hardly mention it.[2]

The generational division in socio-cultural values represented in "Autres Temps" itself metaphorizes divorce—a seemingly unbridgable gap in attitude which divides Mrs. Lidcote from her daughter and her "set." But if attitudes had shifted, one essential fact linking the generations remains: women, whether married or divorced, are still defined according to their marital status. Divorce, rather than setting women outside the inevitable trajectories of the marriage plot, anchors them ever more firmly within it. Leila's immediate remarriage after her divorce openly proclaims the centrality of matrimony in describing a woman's occupation, or "business." That Mrs. Lidcote had lived in exile "as if her life were over" after her divorce restates essentially the same fact. As Nancy Bentley has observed, divorcées were society's "unmarried married" women, doubly defined by the matrimonial institution rather than liberated from it.[3] Indeed, the rise in American divorce represented not a decline in the ideal, but its validation.

The Progressive age novels by James, Wharton, Ferber and Lewis examined in this study seem to ask whether a woman—if *defined* by matrimonial status—need be *contained* by it. The strategies employed by the female characters, from renegotiating the traditional hierarchical marital relation to the exploration of simultaneous domestic and extra-domestic roles, do indeed destabilize the marriage plot and interrogate the ideal. Finally, however, it is not until the 1930s with characters such as Zora Neale Hurston's Janie (*Their Eyes Were Watching God*, 1937) and Faulkner's Charlotte Rittenmeyer (*Wild Palms*, 1939) that the plot truly begins to unravel. Bypassing the law for either sanctioning or dissolving marital partnerships, these women resist the institution that would have them contain their love within the bounds defined by money, contract and "business." Although Charlotte is most appallingly punished for her defiant transgression, Janie survives to articulate the significance of her own narrative: it is the unmediated self—its "feeling and thinking," its sovereign memory—and not the law nor its institutions which determines one's status within or without the plot.

NOTES

1. "Autres Temps," *The Selected Short Stories of Edith Wharton*, ed. R. W. B. Lewis (New York: Scribners, 1991), 185. Subsequent quotations are from this edition and will be cited parenthetically in the text as AT.

2. As Nancy Bentley observes, "American divorce was formalized as a feminine institution" by the early twentieth century so that when a Wharton character in *The Custom of the Country* announces "She's American—she's divorced," it was as if "she were merely stating the same fact in two different ways." "Edith Wharton and the alienation of divorce," *The Ethnography of Manners: Hawthorne, James, and Wharton* (New York: Cambridge University Press, 1995), 161.

3. Bentley, *Ethnography*, 160.

Bibliography

Adams, Elizabeth Kemper. *Women Professional Workers.* New York: Macmillan, 1921.

American Code of Manners: A Study of Usages, Laws and Observances which Govern Intercourse in the Best Social Circles, and the Principles which Underlie Them. New York: W. R. Andrews, 1880.

Ammons, Elizabeth. *Edith Wharton's Argument with America.* Athens: University of Georgia Press, 1980.

————. "The New Woman as Cultural Symbol and Social Reality." In *1915: The Cultural Moment,* edited by Adele Heller and Loise Rudnick. New York: Rutgers, 1991.

Anold, Sarah Louise. "Vocational Training for Women." *Proceedings of the Academy of Political Science* (Oct. 1910): 130–134.

Arthur, T. S. *The Hand But Not the Heart: or, the Life Trials of Jessie Loring.* New York: Derby & Jackson, 1858.

————. "Marrying a Beauty." In *Orange Blossoms Fresh and Faded.* Philadelphia: J.M. Stoddart & Co., 1871.

————. *Out in the World.* New York: Carlton, 1864.

Ashmore, Ruth [Mrs. Isabel Allerdice Mallon]. *The Business Girl in every phase of her life.* Philadelphia: Doubleday & McClure Co., 1898.

"A Study of Sioux Falls, South Dakota." [unidentified newspaper, Old Courthouse Museum Archive, SF, SD.] 16 Dec. 1894.

Banta, Martha. "From Harry Jim to St. James in *Life Magazine,* (1883–1916): Twitting the Author, Prompting the Public." *Henry James Review* 14 (1993): 237–56.

————. *Imaging American Women: Idea and Ideals in Cutural History.* New York: Columbia University Press, 1987.

————. "Introduction." In *New Essays on The American,* edited by Martha Banta. New York: Cambridge University Press, 1987: 1–42.

———— *Taylored Lives: Narrative Productions in the Age of Taylor, Veblen and Ford.* Chicago: University of Chicago Press, 1993.

Barnett, James Harwood. *Divorce and the American Divorce Novel, 1858–1937: A Study in Literary Reflections of Social Influences.* Philadelphia: University of Pennsylvania, 1939.

Basch, Norma. *Framing American Divorce: From the Revolutionary Generation to the Victorians.* Berkeley and Los Angeles: University of California, 1999.

Bates, Lindell. "The Divorce of Americans in France." *Law and Contemporary Problems* 2 (June 1935): 322–328.

Bell, Millicent. *Meaning in Henry James.* Cambridge, Mass.: Harvard University Press, 1991.

Benjamin, Walter. "The Work of Art in the Age of Mechanical Reproduction." *Illuminations.* Edited and with an introduction by Hannah Arendt. New York: Schoken Books, 1968.

Benstock, Shari. *No Gifts From Chance: A Biography of Edith Wharton.* New York: Scribner's, 1994.

Bentley, Nancy. *The Ethnography of Manners: Hawthorne, James and Wharton.* New York: Cambridge University Press, 1995.

Berger, John. *Ways of Seeing.* New York: Viking-Penguin, 1977.

Bergman, Frank. *Robert Grant.* Boston: Twayne, 1982.

Blake, Nelson Manfred. *The Road to Reno: A History of Divorce in the United States.* New York: Macmillan, 1962.

Boone, Joseph Allen. "Modernist Maneuverings in the Marriage Plot: Breaking Ideologies of Gender and Genre in James's *The Golden Bowl." PMLA* 101 (May 1986): 374–388.

————. *Tradition Counter Tradition: Love and the Form of Fiction.* Chicago: University of Chicago Press, 1987.

————. "Wedlock as Deadlock and Beyond: Closure and the Victorian Marriage Ideal." *Mosaic* 17 (1984): 65–81.

"Bounty on Marriage." *American Phrenological Journal* (February 1866): 56–57.

Boydston, Jeanne. "Grave Endearing Traditions: Edith Wharton and the Domestic Novel." In *Faith of a (Woman)Writer, edited by* Alice Kessler Harris and William McBrien. New York: Greenwood Press, 1988.

Brown, Gillian. *Domestic Individualism: Imagining the Self in Nineteenth-Century America.* Berkeley and Los Angeles: University of California Press, 1990.

Burdick, Anna Laylor. "The Wage Earning Girl and Home Economics." *The Journal of Home Economics* (August 1919).

Burr, Jane. *Letters of a Dakota Divorcee.* Boston: Roxbourgh Publishing, 1909.

Burrows, Edwin G. and Michael Wallace. "The American Revolution: The Ideology and Psychology of National Liberation." In *Perspectives in American History,* edited by Donald Flemming and Bernard Bailyn. Cambridge, Mass.: Harvard University Press, 1972.

Cable, Mary. *American Manners and Morals.* New York: American Heritage Publications, 1969.

Cahen, Alfred. *Statistical Analysis of American Divorce.* New York: Columbia University Press, 1932.

Candee, Helen. *How Women May Earn a Living.* New York: Macmillan, 1900.

Carson, William E. *The Marriage Revolt: A Study in Marriage and Divorce.* New York: Hearst International, 1915.

Censer, Jane Turner. "'Smiling Through Her Tears': Ante-Bellum Southern Women and Divorce." *American Journal of Legal History* 25 (1981): 24–47.

Church, Ella Rodman. *Money Making for Ladies.* New York: Harper and Bros., 1882.

Clark, Sue Ainslie. "Working Girl's Budgets." *McClure's* 35.6 (Oct. 1910): 595–604.

Correct Social Usage: A Course in Good Form, Style and Deportment. New York: The New York Society of Self Culture, 1903.

Cott, Nancy F. "Divorce and the Changing Status of Women in Eighteenth Century Massachusetts." *William and Mary Quarterly* 3, ser. xxxiii (1976): 586–614.

Crowninshield, Francis W. *Manners for the Metropolis: An Entrance Key to the Fantastic Life of The 400.* New York: D. Appleton and Co., 1908.

Curtis, Leslie. *Reno Reveries: Impressions of Local Life.* Reno: Charles E. Week, 1912.

Davies, Margery Wynn. *A Woman's Place is at the Typewriter: The Feminization of Clerical Workers and Changes in Clerical Work in the United States, 1870–1930.* New York: Oxford University Press, 1980.

Degler, Carl. *At Odds: Women and the Family in America from the Revolution to the Present.* New York: Oxford University Press, 1980.

"Divorce." *Putnam's Monthly* 8 (Dec. 1856): 630–634.

"Divorce as a State Industry." *The Nation*, May 1892.

"Divorce in South Dakota." *The Nation*, 26 January 1896.

Dodge, Grace. *What Women Can Earn: Occupations for Women and Their Compensation.* New York: Frederick A. Stokes, 1898.

Dupree, Ellen. "Jamming the Machinery: Mimesis in *The Custom of the Country.*" *American Literary Realism* 22.2 (winter 1990): 5–16.

Dewey, Frank. "Thomas Jefferson's Notes on Divorce." *William and Mary Quarterly* 39 (1982): 206–219.

Eisenstein, Sarah. *Give Us Bread But Give Us Roses: Working Women's Consciousness in the United States, 1890 to the First World War.* Boston: Routledge, 1983.

Embury, Emma. "The Mistaken Choice; or, Three Years of Married Life." *Graham's Magazine* 19 (July 1841): 13–17.

Ewen, Stuart and Elizabeth Ewen. "The Americanization of Consumption." *Telos* 37 (fall 1978): 42–51.

———. *Channels of Desire: Mass Images and the Shaping of American Consciousness.* New York: McGraw-Hill, 1982.

Ferber, Edna. *Emma McChesney and Co.* New York: Frederick A. Stokes, 1915.

———. *Roast Beef Medium.* New York: Frederick A. Stokes, 1917.

Fern, Fanny [Mrs. Sara Payson Parton]. *Rose Clark.* New York: Mason Brothers, 1856.

Filene, Catherine. *Careers For Women: New Ideas, New Methods, New Opportunities.* Boston: Houghton-Mifflin, 1920.

Fitch, George. "Shuffling Families in Sioux Falls." *The American Magazine* 66 (September 1908): 442–551.

Fliegelman, Jay. *Prodigals and Pilgrims: The American Revolution Against Patriarchal Authority, 1750–1800.* New York: Cambridge University Press, 1982.

Foner, Eric. *Tom Paine and Revolutionary America.* New York: Oxford University Press, 1976.

Fryer, Judith. *Felicitous Space: The Imaginative Structures of Edith Wharton and Willa Cather.* Chapel Hill: University of North Carolina Press, 1986.

Gilbert, Julie Goldsmith. *Ferber: A Biography.* New York: Doubleday, 1978.

Gillespie, Mrs. E. D. *A Book of Remembrance.* Philadelphia: J. B. Lippincott, 1901.

Gilman, Charlotte Perkins. *Women and Economics: A Study of the Economic Relation Between Men and Women as a Factor in Social Evolution.* Edited by Carl N. Degler. New York: Harper and Row, 1966.

Gorton, D.A. "The Ethics of Marriage and Divorce." *The National Quarterly Review* 37 (July 1878): 27–49.

Griswold, Robert. "The Evolution of the Doctrine of Mental Cruelty in Victorian American Divorce, 1790–1900." *Journal of Social History* 19 (1986): 127–148.

Grossberg, Michael. *Governing the Hearth.: Law and the Family in Nineteenth-Century America.* Chapel Hill: University of North Carolina Press, 1980.

Groves, Ernest. "Migratory Divorce." *Law and Contemporary Problems* 2.3 (June 1935): 293–301.

Habegger, Alfred. *The Father: A Life of Henry James,Sr.* New York: Farrar, Straus and Giroux, 1994.

———. *Henry James and the Woman Business.* New York: Cambridge University Press, 1989.

Hale, Sarah Josepha. *Manners; or, Happy Homes and Good Society All the Year Round.* Boston: J. E. Tilton and Company, 1868.

Hamilton, Gail [Mary Abagail Dodge]. *Woman's Wrongs: A Counter-Irritant.* Boston: Ticknor and Fields, 1868.

Harland, Marion. *Eve's Daughters; or Common Sense for Maid, Wife and Mother.* New York: J. R. Anderson and H. S. Allen, 1882.

Hazel, Harry and S. L. Lewis. *The Divorce Mill: Realistic Sketches of the South Dakota Divorce Colony.* New York: Mascot Publishing Co., 1895.

Hinz, Evelyn J. "Hierogamy vs. Wedlock: Types of Marriage Plots and Their Relationship to Genres of Prose Fiction." *PMLA* 91 (1976): 900–913.

Holland, Laurence B. *The Expense of Vision.* Baltimore: The Johns Hopkins University Press, 1964. Reprint, 1982.

Horowitz, Daniel. *The Morality of Spending: Attitudes Toward the Consumer Society in America, 1875–1940.* Baltimore: Johns Hopkins University Press, 1985.

Howard, George Elliot. "Divorce and Public Welfare." *McClure's Magazine* 34 (December 1909): 232–242.

Howe, M. A. deWolfe. *The Life and Labors of Bishop Hare, Apostle to the Sioux.* New York: Sturgis & Walton, 1911.

Howells, William Dean. *A Modern Instance.* Introduction by William H. Cady. New York: Penguin, 1988.

———. "A Sennight of the Centennial." *Atlantic Monthly* 38 (1876): 97–107.

"In and About the Fair." *Scribner's Monthly* 12 (1876): 742–749.

Ingraham, Frank and G. A. Ballard. "The Business of Migratory Divorce in Nevada." *Law and Contemporary Problems* 2.3 (June 1935): 302–309.

Ingram, V.S. *The Centennial Exposition.* Philadelphia: Hubbard Bros., 1876.

James, Henry. *The American Scene.* New York: St. Martins, 1987.

———. *The Art of the Novel: Critical Prefaces by Henry James.* Forward by R. W. B. Lewis, with an introduction by R. P. Blackmur. Boston: Northeastern University Press, 1984.

———. *The Complete Notebooks of Henry James.* Edited by Leon Edel and Lyall H. Powers. New York: Oxford University Press, 1987.

———. *The Golden Bowl.* Edited with an introduction by Virginia Llewellyn Smith. New York: Oxford University Press, 1983.

———. "An International Episode." Vol 14, *The New York Henry James.* Fairfield, New Jersey: Augustus Kelley, 1976.

———. *Letters, vol. 2 (1875–1903).* Edited by Leon Edel. Cambridge, Mass.: Harvard University Press, 1975.

———. *The Portrait of a Lady.* Edited by Leon Edel. Boston: Riverside Editions, 1963.

———. "The Special Type." Vol. 10, *The Complete Tales of Henry James.* Edited by Leon Edel. Philadelphia: Lippincott, 1964.

Jones, Mary Sommerville. *An Historical Geography of Changing Divorce Laws in the United States.* Ann Arbor: University Microfilms, 1980.

Kelley, Florence. "Married Women in Industry." *Proceedings of the Academy of Political Science* (Oct. 1910).

Kerber, Linda K. *Women of the Republic: Intellect and Ideology in Revolutionary America.* Chapel Hill: University of North Carolina Press, 1980.

Kessler-Harris, Alice. *Out to Work: A History of Wage Earning Women in the United States.* New York: Oxford University Press, 1982

Kiely, Robert. *Beyond Egoism: Fiction of James Joyce, Virginia Woolf and D. H. Lawrence.* Cambridge, Mass.: Harvard University Press, 1980.

King, Bertha Pratt. *The Worth of a Girl.* New York: Thomas Crowell, 1916.

Kraditor, Aileen S. *The Ideas of the Woman Suffrage Movement, 1890–1920.* New York: Columbia University Press, 1965.

Krook, Dorothea. *The Ordeal of Consciousness in Henry James.* Cambridge, Mass.: Cambridge University Press, 1963.

Laselle, Mary A. and Katharine E. Wiley. *Vocations for Girls.* Boston: Houghton-Mifflin, 1913.

Lears, T. Jackson. "From Salvation to Self-Realization: Advertising and the Therapeutic Roots of Consumer Culture, 1880–1930." In *The Culture of Consumption: Critical Essays in American History, 1880–1980,* edited by Richard Wightman Fox and T. Jackson Lears. New York: Pantheon Books, 1983.

Leach, William. *Land of Desire: Merchants, Power and the Rise of a New American Culture.* New York: Pantheon Books, 1993.

———. *True Love and Perfect Union: The Femnist Reform of Sex and Society.* 2nd ed. Middletown, Conn: Wesleyan University Press, 1989.

Lee, Alfred McClung. *The Daily Newspaper in America: The Evolution of a Social Instrument.* New York: MacMillan, 1947.

Lee, Margaret. *Divorce; or, Faithful and Unfaithful.* 1883. Reprint New York: Frank E. Lovell, 1889.

Lewis, R. W. B. *Edith Wharton: A Biography.* New York: Fromm International, 1985.

Lewis, Sinclair. *The Job: An American Novel.* New York: Harcourt, Brace and Co., 1917.

Lichtenberger, James P. *Divorce: A Social Interpretation.* New York: McGraw, 1931.

Lindberg, Gary H. *Edith Wharton and the Novel of Manners.* Charlottesville: University Press of Virgina, 1975.

Love, Marriage and Divorce, and the Sovereignty of the Individual: A Discussion Between Henry James Sr., Horace Greeley, and Stephen Pearl Andrews. Edited by Charles Shively. Weston, Ma.: M & S Press, 1975.

Lynd, Robert S. and Helen Merrell Lynd. *Middletown: A Study in American Culture.* New York: Harcourt, Brace, Jovanovich, 1957.

Marchand, Roland. *Advertising and the American Dream: Making Way for Modernity, 1920–1940.* Berkeley and Los Angeles: University of California Press, 1985.

Margolin, Victor, Ira Brichta and Vivian Brichta. *The Promise and the Product: Two Hundred Years of American Advertising Posters.* New York: Macmillian, 1979.

Margolis, Maxine L. *Mothers and Such: Views of American Women and Why They Changed.* Berkeley and Los Angeles: University of California Press, 1984.

Matsuda, Mari J. "The West and the Status of Women: Explanation of Frontier Feminism." *Journal of the West* 24 (January 1985): 47–56.

May, Elaine Tyler. *Great Expectations: Marriage and Divorce in Post Victorian America*. Chicago: University of Chicago Press, 1980.

————. "The Pressure to Provide: Class, Consumerism, and Divorce in Urban America, 1880–1920." *Journal of Social History* 12 (1978): 180–193.

McAllister, Ward. *Society as I Have Found It*. New York: Cassell Publishing, 1890.

McCabe, James D. *The Illustrated History of the Centennial Exhibition*. Philadelphia: National Publishing Co., 1876.

McColl, Gail and Carol McD. Wallace, *To Marry an English Lord*. New York: Workman, 1989.

Meehan, Thomas R. "Not Made Out of Levity: Evolution of Divorce in Early Pennsylvania." *Pennsylvania Magazine of History and Biography*. 92 (1968): 441–464.

Miller, Elise. "The Marriages of Henry James and Henrietta Stackpole." *Henry James Review* (winter 1989): 15–31.

Mitchell, Langdon. *The New York Idea*. Boston: Walter H. Baker & Co., 1907.

Mott, Frank Luther. *A History of American Magazines*. 5 Vols. Cambridge, Mass.: Harvard University Press, 1938–1968.

"Must We Wait a Year for Divorce? The Question that Threatens to Reduce South Dakota's Popularity." *The Minneapolis Journal* 5 (July 1908).

Nevius, Blake. *Edith Wharton: A Study of Her Fiction*. Berkeley and Los Angeles: University of California Press, 1953.

Nichols, Charles Wilbur de Lyon. *The 469 Ultra-Fashionables of America: a social guide book and register to date*. New York: Broadway Publishing, 1912.

————. *The Ultra-Fashionable Peerage of America*. New York: George Harjes, 1904. Reprint, New York: Arno Press, 1975.

Nichols, Mary Sargeant. *Mary Lyndon; or, Revelations of a Life*. New York: Stringer and Townsend, 1855.

Niemtzow, Annette. "Marriage and the New Woman in *The Portrait of a Lady*." *American Literature* 47 (1975): 377–95.

Nolan, Val. "Indiana: Birthplace of Migratory Divorce." *Indiana Law Journal* 26 (summer 1951): 515–527.

Norris, James D. *Advertising and the transformation of American Society, 1865–1920*. New York: Greenwood Press, 1990.

O'Neill, William. "Divorce as a Moral Issue: A Hundred Years of Controversy." In *Remember the Ladies: New Perspectives on Women in*

American History, edited by Carol V. R. George. New York: Viking Press, 1975.

———. *Divorce in the Progressive Era.* New Haven: Yale University Press, 1967.

———. *Everyone was Brave.* Chicago: Quadrangle Books, 1969.

Orvel, Miles. *The Real Thing: Imitation and Authenticity in American Culture, 1880–1940.* Chapel Hill: University of North Carolina Press, 1989.

Papashvily, Helen Waite. *All the Happy Endings: A study in the domestic novel in America, the women who wrote it, and the women who read it, in the nineteenth century.* New York: Harper, 1956.

Pateman, Carole. *The Sexual Contract.* Stanford: Stanford University Press, 1988.

Patten, Simon N. *The Consumption of Wealth.* Philadelphia: University of Pennsylvania, 1901.

———. *The New Basis of Civilization.* New York: Macmillan, 1907.

———. *The Theory of Dynamic Economics.* Philadelphia: University of Pennsylvania, 1892.

Phillips, Roderick. *Putting Asunder: A History of Divorce in Western Society.* Cambridge: Cambridge University Press, 1988.

Porter, Carolyn. *Seeing and Being: The Plight of Participant Observers in Emerson, James, Adams and Faulkner.* Middletown, Conn.: Wesleyan University Press, 1981.

Porter-Benson, Susan. *Counter-Cultures: Saleswomen, Managers and Customers in American Department Stores, 1890–1940.* Urbana: University of Illinois Press, 1986.

Powers, Lyall H., ed. *Henry James and Edith Wharton: Letters 1900–1915.* New York: Scribners, 1990.

Rahi, G. S. *Edith Wharton: A Study of Her Ethos and Her Art.* Amritsar: Guru Nanak Dev University Press, 1983.

Realf, James. "The Sioux Falls Divorce Colony and Some Noted Colonists." *The Arena* 4 (November 1891): 696–703.

Richardson, Bertha June. *The Woman Who Spends: A Study of Her Economic Function.* Boston: Whitcomb & Burrows, 1904.

Riley, Glenda. *Divorce: An American Tradition.* New York: Oxford University Press, 1991.

Roberts, Helen L. *Putnam's Handbook of Etiquette: A Cyclopaedia of Social Usage, Giving the Manners and Customs of the Twentieth Century.* New York: G. P. Putnam's Sons, 1913.

Robinson, Doane. "Divorce in Dakota." *South Dakota Historical Collection* 12 (1924): 268–280.

Robinson, Lelia Josphina. *The Law of Husband and Wife: Compiled for Popular Use.* Boston: Lee and Shepard, 1889.

Rothman, Sheila M. *Woman's Proper Place: A History of Changing Ideals and Practices.* New York: Basic Books, 1978.

Schaffer, Connie De Velder. "Money versus Morality: The Divorce Industry of Sioux Falls." *South Dakota History* 20.3 (fall 1990): 207–227.

Scharf, Lois. *To Work and to Wed: Female Employment, Feminism, and the Great Depression.* Westport, Conn.: Greenwood Press, 1980.

Shanley, Mary L. "The Marriage Contract in Seventeenth-Century English Political Thought." *Western Political Quarterly* 32.1 (1979): 79–91.

Shudson, Michael. *Advertising The Uneasy Persuasion: Its Dubious Impact on American Society.* New York: Basic Books, 1984.

Smith, Adam. *An Introduction into the Nature and Causes of the Wealth of Nations.* Edited by Edwin Cannan. New York: Modern Library, 1937.

Stanton, Elizabeth Cady, Susan B. Anthony and Mathilda Joslyn, eds. *A History of Woman Suffrage,* Vol. 3. Salem, New Hampshire: Ayer, 1969.

Stanton, Theodore and Harriet Stanton Blatch, eds. *Elizabeth Cady Stanton, as Revealed in her Letters, Diaries and Reminiscences.* New York: Harper's, 1922.

Stein, Allen F. *After the Vows Were Spoken: Marriage in American Literary Realism.* Columbus: Ohio State University Press, 1984.

Stevens, John D. "Social Utility of Sensational News: Murder and Divorce in the 1920's." *Journalism Quarterly* (1985): 53–58.

Stowe, Harriet Beecher. *My Wife and I.* Boston: Houghton-Miflin, 1896.

———. *Pink and White Tyranny.* New York: New American Library, 1988.

———. "The Ravages of a Carpet." *Household Papers and Stories.* Boston: Houghton-Mifflin, 1896.

Tanner, Tony. *Adultery in the Novel: Contract and Transgression.* Baltimore: Johns Hopkins University Press, 1979.

Thomas, Brook. "The Construction of Privacy in and around *The Bostonians.*" *American Literature* 64 (December 1992): 719–747.

Tintner, Adeline. "The Centennial of 1876 and *The Portrait of a Lady.*" *Markham Review* 10 (1980–81): 27–29.

Traill, David A. "Schliemann's American Citizenship and Divorce." *The Classical Journal* 77 (May 1982): 336–340.

Uba, George R. "Status and Contract: The Divorce Dispute of the 'Eighties and Howells' *A Modern Instance.*" *Colby Library Quarterly* 19 (June 1983): 78–89.

Vanderbilt, Arthur T. *The Fall of the House of Vanderbilt.* New York: William Morrow, 1989.

Veblen, Thorstein. *The Theory of the Leisure Class.* Introduction by Robert Lekachman. New York: Penguin, 1979.

Vienne, Veronique. "In a Class by Themselves." *Town and Country* (Nov. 1994): 175+

Voloshin, Beverly R. "Exchange in Edith Wharton's *The Custom of the Country.*" *Pacific Coast Philology* 22 (1987): 98–104.

Waid, Candace. *Edith Wharton's Letters from the Underworld: Fictions of Women and Writing.* Chapel Hill: University of North Carolina Press, 1991.

Walker, Mary E. *H.I.T.* New York: American News Co., 1871.

Walton, Geoffrey. *Edith Wharton: A Critical Interpretation.* Rutherford, N.J.: Farleigh-Dickinson University Press, 1970.

Warren, Joyce W. *Fanny Fern: An Independent Woman.* New Brunswick: Rutgers University Press, 1992.

———. "Fanny Fern's *Rose Clark.*" *Legacy* 8.2 (fall 1991): 92–103.

Wecter, Dixon. *The Saga of American Society: A Record of Social Aspiration, 1607–1937.* New York: Scribner's, 1937.

Wells, Kate Gannett. "The Transitional American Woman." *Atlantic Monthly* (December 1880): 817–823.

Wershoven, Carol. *The Female Intruder in the Novels of Edith Wharton.* Rutherford, N J: Farleigh Dickinson University Press, 1982.

Wharton, Edith. *The Age of Innocence.* Introduction by R. W. B. Lewis. New York: Collier Books, 1968.

———. *The Custom of the Country.* New York: Scribner's, 1913.

———. *The House of Mirth.* Introduction by Mary Gordon. New York: Library of America, 1985.

———. "The Other Two." *The Selected Short Stories of Edith Wharton.* Edited by R. W. B. Lewis. New York: Scribner's, 1991.

White, Robert. "Love, Marriage and Divorce: The Matter of Sexuality in *The Portrait of a Lady.*" *The Henry James Review* 7.2–3 (1986): 59–71.

Willard, Frances. *Occupations for Women.* New York: The Success Co., 1897.

Wires, Richard. *The Divorce Issue and Reform in Nineteenth Century Indiana.* Ball State Monograph No 8. Publications in History, No 2. Muncie, Indiana: Ball State University, 1967.

Wolff, Cynthia Griffin. *A Feast of Words: The Triumph of Edith Wharton.* New York: Oxford University Press, 1977.

Wood, Gordon. *The Creation of the American Republic, 1776–1787.* Chapel Hill: University of North Carolina Press, 1969.

Woods, Robert A. and Albert J. Kennedy. *Young Working Girls.* Boston: 1913.

Yeazell, Ruth Barnard. *Language and Knowledge in the Late Novels of Henry James.* Chicago: Chicago University Press, 1976.

Index

ADZ-7432